Advance Praise for

The Success Healthcheck for IT Projects

An Insider's Guide to Managing IT Investment and Business Change

J. A. Flinn speaks with a wisdom gained from many years of wishing for the best but preparing for the worst on complex IT and business change initiatives. Results risk management is critical. Anything that can be done to improve the probability of success of your IT projects is worthwhile doing, so start with reading this book!

Mark Bryant
Partner, Infosys

Flinn created a mix of very practical, realistic and performance-driven solutions by combining her IT experience with the wisdom of timeless principles. Her lively, probing, authentic style is consistent with her view of seeing these complex systems as ecological living organisms where people and systems integrate in a natural way.

Professor Peter Robertson
Author of Always Change a Winning Team
Founder, Human Insight

Flinn distills a complex topic into a clear usable approach for leaders to achieve real success by significantly improving project portfolio returns, and shows leaders how to avoid the staggering project failure rates which is common today. Flinn's latest publication is a real winner.

Susan Breniman
Associate Director, Proctor and Gamble

Once again we sat round a table scratching our heads wondering why all the things we had spent so much time planning completely failed to materialize! J. A. Flinn explains with great clarity why project implementation and benefits realization is an art and needs the right combination of people, processes and planning to succeed.

Arvind Mathur
Partner, Hiedricks and Struggles

I have met J. A. Flinn in exotic locations and have been impressed by her skills, knowledge, love for life, love for travel and the book that she has produced. I have been a business coach for most of my business life and it this capacity I have worked with many, many business. *The Success Healthcheck for IT Projects* gives amazing business tools. Well done! I make it an important step in the education of my clients to read and master J. A. Flinn's book!

Martin Jimmink
Master Coach, Action International Business Coaches

THE SUCCESS HEALTHCHECK FOR IT PROJECTS

AN INSIDER'S GUIDE TO MANAGING IT INVESTMENT AND BUSINESS CHANGE

100 percent of IT projects intend to succeed,
but 93 percent fail.
Just 7 percent are star performers.
Which is yours?

THE SUCCESS HEALTHCHECK FOR IT PROJECTS

AN INSIDER'S GUIDE TO MANAGING IT INVESTMENT AND BUSINESS CHANGE

J. A. FLINN

John Wiley & Sons (Asia) Pte. Ltd.

Published in 2010 by John Wiley & Sons (Asia) Pte. Ltd.
2 Clementi Loop, #02–01, Singapore 129809

Other Wiley Editorial Offices
John Wiley & Sons, 111 River Street, Hoboken, NJ 07030, USA
John Wiley & Sons, The Atrium, Southern Gate, Chichester, West Sussex, P019 8SQ, United Kingdom
John Wiley & Sons (Canada) Ltd., 5353 Dundas Street West, Suite 400, Toronto, Ontario, M9B 6HB, Canada
John Wiley & Sons Australia Ltd., 42 McDougall Street, Milton, Queensland 4064, Australia
Wiley-VCH, Boschstrasse 12, D-69469 Weinheim, Germany

Library of Congress Cataloging-in-Publication Data
ISBN 978–0–470–82572–3

Typeset in 9.5/12pt Palatino Linotype by Thomson Digital, India
Printed in Singapore by Toppan Security Printing Pte. Ltd.
10 9 8 7 6 5 4 3 2 1

Contents

Foreword

In 1982, I was the director of the MSc in Engineering Construction Project Management at the Cranfield School of Management. I went to a seminar in London on project management in IT that was attended by more than 100 IT project managers and specialists. At the end of the day, the chairman summarized the findings of the day. The first was that so many IT projects would have been more successful . . . if there were no clients! Wow! With no clients no one in the seminar would have been employed.

Recently there has been a recognition that projects are a means to an end and not an end in themselves. In the early days of project management in the construction industry many thought that the project was the only goal and often asked clients to step back while the specialists delivered the project—not that anyone in IT would ever think of doing that! This, of course, missed the point of projects and project management entirely. As J. A. Flinn so correctly points out in this new book, it takes two to make a project a success:

- A project manager to deliver a successful output from the project.
- A project sponsor to utilize the output to achieve the desired outcome for the organization.

The desired outcome should have been used to justify the project investment in the first place.

The organization owning the project could be in any of the three work sectors:

1. Business seeking a project outcome to increase competitiveness performance;
2. Public sector seeking a project outcome that delivers effective policies;
3. Not-for-profit sector seeking to deliver outcomes that maximize help to the maximum number of beneficiaries.

Too many projects continue to an unsuccessful outcome, often because the participants are blind to the intended outcome, or fail to gauge the likely outcome during the delivery process. Flinn suggests a number of refreshing ways in which owners and sponsors can diagnose the heath of a project at a stage where decisions can still be made to bring it back on track or stop it before wasting further sunk costs.

This book will be of great benefit to those who sponsor, own, or deliver IT projects. It contains many practical suggestions and numerous helpful case studies, which focus on the success of the final outcome to the investing organization. Many IT projects are really business projects with the IT being, like the project management, merely a means to an end. This book helpfully makes this clear throughout.

I commend the book and its contents to you.

As one Austrian friend would say—''Happy Projects!''

Alan Harpham
Chairman of the Association for Project Managers, UK

Alan Harpham BSc MBA (1975) CMC FAPM FIBC

Alan is the Chairman of the APM Group (www.apmgroup.co.uk). He is a former director of P^5—the Power of Projects, managing director of Nichols Associates (now The Nichols Group), and Director of the MSc in Project Management at Cranfield University. His early career was spent in construction with John Laing. He also focuses on pro-bono work with charities involved with spirituality at work and the Church.

Acknowledgments

No man is an island entire of himself.

—*John Donne*

All creative efforts come as a result of ideas, people, support, and inspiration. So do mine.

Many thanks to all who have helped me on my way.

May this help you on your way to success.

—J. A.

Many people have contributed to the book in a myriad of ways.

The IITA and IRRI scientists who lead the Green Revolution were my earliest demonstration that amazing results come from the application of science, economics, and dynamic systems to productivity and business results.

My colleagues in the companies I've worked for and with, as well as my clients who provided the real world in which projects deliver results with the business.

Many individuals have made this possible. Particular thanks for their support, ideas, suggestions, reviews, and encouragement including Sue Breniman, Mark Bryant, Darryl Dickens, Peter Robinson, Karen Kang, Philip Idenburg, Hema Prakesh, Alan Heug, Laurie Young, and Tim Harford.

My colleagues at the Change Leaders (tCL): Nick Herpers, John Freeman, Nadine Theimann, and Patricia Shafer—the reflective practitioner is alive and well. Thanks also to Saïd

Business School, Oxford University and HEC for the support they have given tCL and for running the Master of Science degree and research programs that started this book.

The team at John Wiley & Sons (Asia): C. J. Hwu, Nick Melchior, Joel Balbin, Cynthia Mak, Cindy Chu, and Camy Boey.

My family and friends, who've given me all that I've needed to make this possible.

Introduction
In The Beginning There Was . . .

. . . a project that succeeded

Project reality differs for most business executives. Expectations are unmet. Other projects are begun, and they too disappoint. Transformations grind to a halt. Strategies are diverted.

Information technology (IT) is a profession that measures project success and even has the guts to publish it. They report:

- Productivity growth from IT has dropped in the 2000s.[1]
- 93 percent of IT projects fall short[2] of expectations: 60 percent just a little, and up to 33 percent by a lot.
- 50 percent spend double their budget, and 20 percent are written off.[3]

To put this in hard numbers, over 20 years ago, the estimated cost of IT failure in the United States alone was $55 billion per annum. These days, global IT spending is greater; the cost of failure is $333 billion.[4]

This is a major capital cost, which is unpalatable in good financial times, and unacceptable in tight times.

Do some of your projects disappoint or fail?

How can you lift your success rates?

Would you like to turn a "little off" to "right on!?"

How would it benefit your business if you can identify those projects that are likely to fail early?

Would you like to be ahead of the curve when your project delivers what *you* want?

Are you curious why projects so rarely succeed, even with all the hard work?

Would you like to be more successful?

If you've answered yes to any of these questions, then this book is for you.

> **Take action now:** Diagnose the health of a current project now at www.successhealthcheck.com. Use the code "shelton-methods" to receive a valuable bonus offer as a purchaser of this book.

In this life, death and taxes are 100 percent guaranteed. Projects are not. However, like improving your health, when you know what to look for, and take action on that information, then your health can be great. If you keep up the same old habits, your prognosis will not change.

Success

War stories, data, and experience suggest that success from projects is rarer than most executives would like. Every project intends to succeed, but intent is not the same as results. Results are key. Results are the reality. Are benefits realized?

This book shows you how to:

1. Identify projects that are likely to succeed or to fail. Up front. Before substantial investment of financial or political capital. It also tells you what to do about what you find.
2. Benchmark and baseline your current project results. If projects in your organization are underperforming, then your business has a competitive disadvantage. Businesses that can deliver projects with predictable, accountable results can change more rapidly than those that can't deliver and are more successful in turbulent times.

3. Look past size as a factor for failure. Yes, size matters. Large projects are more likely to fail than small projects.[5] Since big projects are often required for big change, this book also helps you identify where large projects are likely to succeed or fail so that you can proactively address the risks to your results.
4. Deliver transformation and strategy. If your IT projects are more likely to succeed, so will your intended business transformation or strategies. Few strategies these days will succeed where component projects that deliver that strategy fail.

Sidebar: On Superpowers

This book is about real life. Yours. Your business and your projects.

This book contains research, some theory, lots of other people's experiences, and many real-life stories.

This book goes further. It includes diagnostics.

The diagnostics are your superpower that allows you to X-ray into success or failure on Day One instead of on Delivery Day.

Entrepreneurial executives strive for success. They want higher ROI on their projects. They want to avoid the expense and embarrassment of a capital write-off from project failure. They want risk mitigation. They want their projects to succeed.

Proactive project managers want their projects to succeed. They do what it takes to get there. They want to know the potential risks early so they can do something about them before it's too late.

Both want to know if a project is set up to fail or succeed.

So what is success in the context of projects? Simply, a successful project is one that delivers the value the business intended. This means that:

- The project delivers what was wanted, when it was wanted for the amount agreed.
  And

- The business uses the capacities delivered by the project to generate business results.

If either fails, there is no success. Something else is created: cost of the project on the bottom line and frustration for people in the business.

Entrepreneurial executives and proactive project managers are aware that successfully introducing a project or a change in the business is also about leadership.

This book is about:

- Results, Risk, and Leadership.
- Why smart, successful executives set up projects that are likely to fail.
- Data. Your data and experience. Other people's data is interesting. Your own data is important.
- Improving the results from projects.

The book uses IT projects as the basis for assessing projects. Why?

Most businesses use IT to improve their productivity and business performance. IT is a key component of transformation projects and is critical to the success of many merger integration programs.

Successful IT projects are precursors to successful business projects. Business executives will see that success practices for IT projects apply equally to other types of projects.

Founded on Robust Research

Given the billions of dollars invested in IT each year this topic is well researched. Key research groups[6] include:

- Standish Group's Chaos Report covers nearly 20 years of tracking IT project performance from the executive perspective.
- The Economist Intelligence Unit's research published in 2008 shows reported project performance results across the globe.

- Research from the IT project manager perspective from Chris Sauer, Belinda Tesch, and Mark Keil and colleagues.
- My own research on the risk factors affecting project success from the perspective of business executives completed at Saïd Business School, Oxford University and HEC in Paris (École des Hautes Études Commerciales de Paris).

This research is used to identify what makes a project succeed or fail with a simple-to-use diagnostic process for executives and project managers.

Prestory

My curiosity was caught in late 1998. I'd just delivered the final country in a regional transformational IT project in a global bank during the Asian Financial Crisis. The IT project replaced the entire business system across each country in Asia. The final country had 22 integrated IT systems ranging from the ATM systems, through the products systems to the finance, tax, and management reporting applications, the complete Front-to-Back Office suite of applications.

I was brought in when the project was running 18 months late and was in jeopardy of not delivering at all. After the review, I was asked to stay on as project manager.

Six months later, we implemented over a regular weekend. We made the "go" decision early Sunday afternoon. Zero operational issues. Zero.[7] The CIO said, "This became our dream project. What we did here stood out shoulders above the other countries."

I reflected—*what had we done differently*? This was followed by extensive research and road testing on *"what does it take to get these results reliably?"*

In the real world of IT and business projects I found that in most businesses:

- Actual project success rates and their impact on business results were rarely measured in terms of benefits realized after the project.

- Risks to benefits, results, and success were rarely recognized or addressed before or during the project.
- Projects were usually considered independent of the business. The business context was usually overlooked.
- Both the project and the business were usually simplified into terms like ''the project'' or ''the business''—yet in real life, each involves multiple parties, interests, and agendas that all need to work coherently to a common goal if benefits are to be achieved and sustained.

Success came when projects activity managed for results. When they proactively managed the risks to results. This is called Results Risk Management (RRM for those that like acronyms) in Figure 0.1.

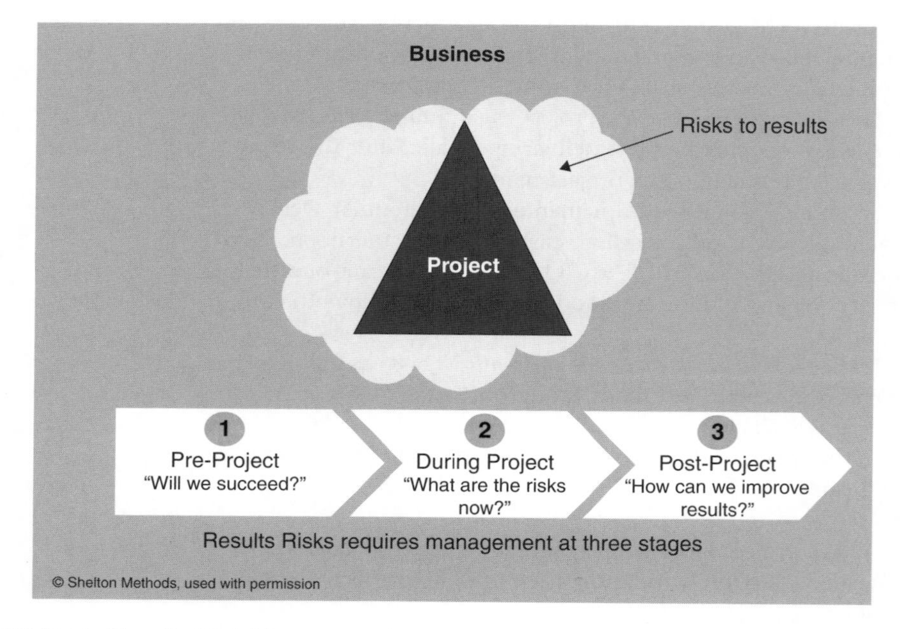

FIGURE 0.1 Results Risk Management

Successful projects managed results at three stages of the project:

1. Before and during project set-up;
2. During the IT requirements, design, configuration, testing and deployment phases;
3. Post implementation.

They considered risks to results irrespective of where they arose: in the project, in IT, or in the business. All were considered necessary for results and success.

This book is written for both audiences: the project (the CIO and project manager) *and* the business (line executives, CEOs, CFOs, and CHROs).

Results risk management focus shifts as the project progresses (Table 0.1).

An analogy—a project is like a golfer playing a round. A golfer aims to get around in PAR. If the golfer is experienced, practiced and disciplined, he will follow good practices, pay attention to the lay of the course, and keep his mind on the game. He might do well on a couple of holes, and later get tired or distracted and his game drop off in the back 9. How well he actually does will also depend on the complexity of the golf course. Projects that get results pay attention to their own game

TABLE 0.1
Focus of Results Risk Management by Phase

Phase	Focus	Project Deliverable
Pre-Project	Will this project succeed? What do we need to do to lift its success rate?	Project and Portfolio Track Record Key Risks to Results Results Risk Management Plan
During Project	What are the risks now? Which are priorities to address?	Updated Results Risk Management Plan Additional actions to preserve or improve results
Post-Project	What results are achieved? Where can we improve? Are issues repeated across projects?	Post-implementation results review Results action items Systemic issues that affect project results

(risks that arise from the project) as well as the course layout and conditions (risks that arise from the business context).

Sidebar: On Benefits Realization and Better Practice

Benefits are what we want. Better practice program management has a process called "Benefits Realization." This focuses on defining benefits and then monitoring their delivery. It may include formal organizational change management programs.

Results are what we get. Some will be positive (benefit), some will be negative. This is real life. A project that restructures the organization may be good for the sustainability of the corporate business but negative for the individuals who lose their jobs. Both are results from the project. Both need to be considered and managed.

This book is about results risk management—what risks are likely to get in the way of the results desired? Is enough being done to deal with the negative results, so that the positive results will flow?

Results risk management™ is better practice than benefits realization. It takes a systemic view of the business and of results—and it takes good practice investment management practices to heart: Don't invest in something that will lose capital. That's rule #1 for investment. Invest where there is a probability of a positive return.

For projects, rule #1 is don't do projects doomed to fail. Reformulate them to succeed.

My research also found that 80 percent of the risks to results can be indentified up front. This is good news. The fastest and easiest way to improve the success rates of projects is to address projects that are likely to fail up front before substantial funds are sunk into the project.

Risks to results can be reassessed periodically to fine-tune and even improve the business results from the project.

This book is a healthcheck. It is structured so that you can assess where you are at and identify the key risks that affect results from your project. It is personal. Your health is important. Other people's is interesting. Your organization's track record reflects the situation that projects commonly face when delivering business results. Your project faces specific risks to results.

Part 1: **Productivity** is the place to start, particularly if you are CIO, CFO, or a business executive funding projects. **Productivity** looks at the benchmark for project results. It shows you the components for measuring results from projects in the form of a yield. It also shows you how to measure results from the portfolio and assess the track record or PAR for projects in your business. It covers four areas critical to achieving results from projects.

The key questions for any project are always the same:

- Is my return worth the investment?
- Is my capital investment likely to be repaid?
- Is this project likely to succeed?
- Where do I need to focus my attention to improve my success?

If you are the project manager or project sponsor responsible for a project, you may like to move directly to Part 2: **Probability** to begin spotting the risks to your results. This section provides the foundation for effective management of risks to results. It introduces results risk management as a process. It also introduces a results risk management diagnostic method called the 8-Fold Path to Success.

My research, applied and tested in major projects at well known multi-national organizations found eights sets of risk factors. Four of these primarily focus on the **Project** (Part 3) while the other four sets of risks are more associated with the **Presence** (Part 4) of particular risks to results that arise from the business context. Part 4 concludes with a risk diagnostic that you can use to assess your project and to prioritize the risks to your results.

Together, Project and Presence cover the eight factors that are critical to successful results risk management.

Each chapter ends with a short set of warning signs to allow you to diagnose the health of your project like a healthcheck.

Note: Some projects, due to their size, complexity, or criticality, need a full executive healthcheck and consultation with a doctor. If your project involves large sums of money, board approval, or is mission critical, a full healthcheck is recommended. You can begin with the one in this book and consider consulting a professional.

The final chapter found in Part 5: **Performance** looks at where to next.

Some of the risks and challenges raised in this book will be well known to one profession yet not to another. Sections that cover familiar territory serve as a useful reminder and checklist of the good practices and disciplines that lead to successful results. Other sections will shed new light on issues that need attention.

Endnotes

1 Non-Farm U.S. Productivity Growth, Bureau of Labor Statistics, U.S. Department. of Commerce.
2 Sauer, C., Gemino, A., and Reich, B. H. (Nov. 2007), ''The Impact of Size and Volatility on IT Project Performance,'' *Communications of the ACM* 50, No. 11: 80.
3 Standish (1994, 2007). Rubinstein, David, ''Standish Group Report: There is Less Development Chaos Today.'' SD Times on the Web, March 1, 2007. http://www.sdtimes.com/content/article.aspx?ArticleID=30247.
4 Forester IT global expenditure of US$ 1.66 trillion for 2008.
5 Sauer, Chris (Summer 2008), ''Unreasonable Expectations, Greek Choruses and the Games Institutions Play,'' *Templeton Views*: 22–23; Standish Group Report (1995), *Chaos*, http://net.educause.edu/ir/library/pdf/NCP08083B.pdf; and Jones, Capers (2009), ''Return on Investment in Software Project Management Tools and Software Quality Controls,'' *Software Productivity Research*. http://www.itmpi.org/assets/base/images/itmpi/privaterooms/capersjones/Capers_PrMgtROI2009.pdf. Capers focuses on the metrics of very large software projects. In his words ''the construction of large software systems is one of the most hazardous activities of the business world. The failure or cancellation rate of large software systems is over 50 percent. Of those that are completed, about two thirds experience schedule delays and cost over-runs,'' pages 3–4. He points out that these very large software projects can cost more than a domed football stadium, a 50-story skyscraper, or a 90,000 ton cruise ship.
6 Gartner and Forrester are two leading IT industry research groups who focus on the companies and tools provided in the software space. Project and Portfolio Management (PPM) is also a software category.

This book is about the business issues that create risks to successful projects, not which PPM software to select.

7 In the interests of full disclosure, one printer in the telling hall was not connected. It took five minutes to fix. Other countries had had six months of data clean up, spent hundreds of thousands of dollars in fixes, and needed to make apologies to customers.

Part 1

Productivity

What productivity do we get from our projects and the investment we make?

How can a business or CIO measure the functional yield of projects and the project portfolio?

What is the cost of failure?

What are the four actions we need to take to lift productivity and project success?

Is it good enough for the business when it "just survives" delivery of a project? No.

What are the three things we need to do predictably and reliably to get results from projects?

How project investments need to consider risk as well as investment.

What is the risk profile of projects?

How can a project manager or sponsor benchmark project track records to determine the risk or probable success of projects?

Chapter 1
IT Projects Are Investments

It was the best of times, it was the worst of times.

—Charles Dickens

Chinese symbol for crisis: opportunity + danger.

—Traditional interpretation

IT is the source of much of the productivity growth in business over the last 20 years.[1] That's the good news. The bad news for businesses and other organizations is that productivity is not growing as fast as it did.

As competition increases through globalization, innovation, outsourcing, and even changes in the global financial system, the competitive edge goes to organizations that manage projects effectively.

Why? Because projects are the means to introduce change.

Success in a moving world is founded on the ability to change effectively even when the environment is turbulent.

Projects are a way of:

- Consciously identifying and introducing change;
- Defining a start and end, an intended result, and a set of assigned resources;
- Tracking investments in change and holding people accountable for those results.

A project is an investment to achieve a return, a result, such as keeping the business operating, meeting regulatory needs and deadlines, or building a strategic capacity for a business unit.

CIOs are aware of the problem—many track projects closely. They introduce software delivery performance improvement processes like CMMI, ITIL, or Six Sigma–inspired processes. They hire experienced project managers. They invest in PPM systems.

Experienced PMs report that a "good" project is one that is on time, with slight budget overrun and functional shortfall.

This is not enough for sustained business results.

In the investment world, returns are associated with risks. These risks require management for capital preservation and positive returns. Managing the risks to returns is as critical in projects as it is the investment world.

Effective projects generate results—a capacity needs to be used, an idea or innovation adopted and acted upon, or people aligned and acting in a new direction. If this fails, results fail.

Those who actually measure their success rates are surprised with what they find internally even when they are familiar with well-known IT project statistics mentioned in the Introduction. When 93 percent of projects underperform or are outright written off, any project that truly succeeds deserves celebration.

The real cost of failure is not talked about. The real rate of return is rarely calculated. The purpose of **Productivity** (Part 1) is to set a benchmark for the real productivity or ROI from our investments in technology and business change.

Chapter 2 benchmarks the real returns of three well-known IT project portfolios. Four actions to take to lift success rates and results are covered in Chapter 3. A pragmatic approach to calculating your own benchmark based on your project track record is covered in Chapter 4. The last chapter in this Part is a diagnostic for those wanting to see the track record of projects in their own organization—like a golfer's PAR.

This chapter looks at productivity, failure, and opportunity. The big picture business issues.

Avoiding the failure rate simply means it is not dealt with. Few wish to raise such information to the executive committee or board. On the other hand, recognizing what the failure rate in the current track record costs the company (Part 1) and then being able to identify where to proactively act to address and improve the track record (Parts 2–5) has real business value.

Executives know it takes courage to call the issue. They may use a consultant or their own staff to evaluate the probable performance results of 10 of their top projects. They *will* get the data. They will address the projects that affect their lines of business. They don't want failures or write-offs. They don't want failure. They want Predictable, Accountable Results (PAR).

Successful projects help their business grow. Unsuccessful ones hinder growth.

Failure or success is predictable. IT project performance can be diagnosed from leading indicators in the same way that high blood pressure can predict a possible heart attack.

The Back Story on Productivity

Taking a very macro picture of productivity growth in business, in the last 30 years, technology and other corporate practices have transformed productivity in many countries.

To take just one country, the United States:[2]

- 1973–1995: 1.4 percent productivity improvement;
- 1995–2003: 3.2 percent productivity improvement;
- 2004–: productivity has dropped.

This 3.2 percent annual productivity growth fueled the last business cycle.

Others[3] demonstrate that the greatest gains in productivity have been in East Asia where it has doubled in a decade, which is interesting in these days of global competition and supply chains.

The U.S. Department of Commerce attributes North American improvements primarily to **technology**. Others also give credit to rising levels of M&A, to labor arbitrage via outsourcing[4] and offshoring. The International Labor Organization[5] finds that increases in productivity in the last 10 years are primarily the result of firms **better** combining capital, labor, and technology.

It's technology, but it is not just technology that gets better results.[6]

The Productivity Challenge and IT

In practice, productivity improves when there are more successful changes than unsuccessful.

The reality is that the net sum is just barely positive.

The 3.2 percent annual growth in productivity attributed to technology in Figure 1.1 below sounds good until you recall the failure rate statistics of up to 93 percent[7] of projects failing at some level.

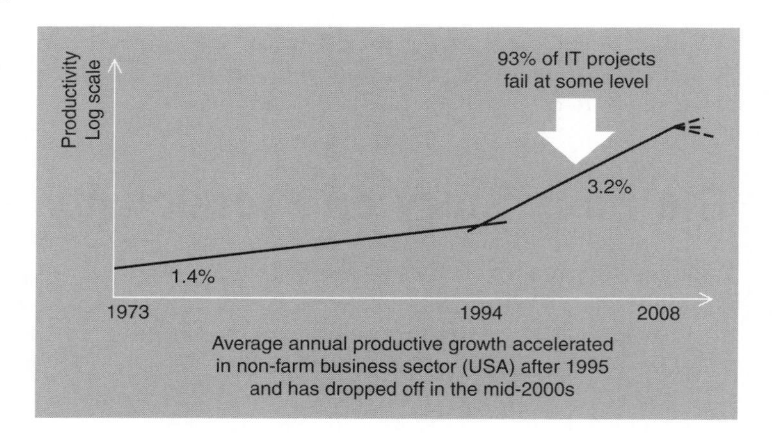

FIGURE 1.1 The Productivity Challenge

This productivity growth is underperforming. Improving the results from projects is a real source of competitive advantage. Executives in companies large and small, domestic and international, talk of their frustrations when introducing change to improve productivity and results.

CEOs Say They Cannot Continue to Introduce Change in the Same Way

CEOs see significant change ahead, but the gap between expected change and the ability to manage it has almost tripled.[8]

Globally, IT executives know this[9] as they report that initiatives frequently fail to make a positive impact on the business as Table 1.1 shows.

This is a sizable business problem.

TABLE 1.1 *IT Executives Belief in the Impact of Projects on Business*

Region	% Believing that 25% or More of Projects Failed to Make a Positive Impact on the Business
Europe	40%
Americas	30%
Asia	Over 50%

- CIOs and IT get credit for honesty. These figures are not palatable to the business. They do make it clear that good results are rarer than is publicly acknowledged. The need for a broader approach to managing the risks to achieving business results is clear.[10]

Productivity growth requires IT and business to deliver results together.

Sidebar: Success Depends on Your Perspective

Many providers of IT services—software houses or independent developers—say, "We don't fail like that. I don't understand where they get their statistics from." IT service providers are looking at project results from a different point of view.

Success as a service provider means:

- Functional changes and associated budget variations are agreed.
- The customer accepted the work and paid for it promptly.
- The customer recommends or uses the service provider again.

However, the business person or organization who paid for the IT project will have a different definition of success.

- Did it meet early expectations (scope, cost, time, quality)?
- Was the process of working with the supplier pleasant?
- Did the project output work with the other components of their business to produce the business result anticipated?

What Is Success?

Some say success is a "positive contribution." That's a lukewarm description of success.

A pragmatic definition of success is delivering what was expected, when it is expected, for the price expected. Better

Projects fail if they are:
- Late, which results in lost time to market.
- Over budget, which means additional resources need to be allocated to the project.
- Shortfall in scope—capacities are not delivered.
- Terminated—capital invested is written off.

yet, success is delivering more than expected—as any customer will happily say.

A more exciting definition of success would be projects receiving accolades like "dream result," "wow," "fantastic," and "what a brilliant experience." The magic of a da Vinci experience of grace, precision, creativity and beauty.

Research[11] finds success using any of the above definitions rare. Success is often considered delivery within 10 percent of agreed parameters. Good is within 7 percent. Excellent is meeting expectations.

This is not good enough. The cost of accepting this practice is a heavy burden on the business results from projects. This cost is benchmarked in the next chapter.

As results depend on capacities delivered and used by the business, this book considers success when a project delivers what was wanted, when it was agreed, for the price agreed. It also considers the service experience.

A Non-IT Project Example

A few years ago I renovated my kitchen and replaced all the cupboards, bench tops, and utilities. I agreed to a granite bench top at price $x. I was disappointed when a Formica bench top was delivered. I'd paid my money, but I'd not gotten what I'd expected. Yes, it is still a bench top, and it allows kitchen functions to be performed, but it wasn't what was agreed. From the business perspective, this was underdelivery in quality terms.

When they were also two shelves short, a 7 percent shortfall, I was definitely not impressed.

Without those two shelves, I had boxes of tin cans sitting on the kitchen floor. I couldn't put all of my cooking equipment away. After about a week of frustration, I called a handyman who came and fitted two shelves for me. I'd found my workaround at extra cost and inconvenience.[12]

Project Failure Is the Untapped Source of Productivity Growth

IT project failure rates have a direct bottom line cost. Non-delivery also affects productivity growth.

Today productivity grows an average of 3.2 percent per annum with a project failure rate[13] that includes up to

20 percent project write-offs and 73 percent of projects underperforming. What could productivity be if projects were successful more often?

Why This Failure Rate Continues to Exist

Executives and project managers assume they are doing fine, that these results are normal and acceptable. Everyone assumes their project will succeed. Or if not, they will keep quiet.

Project sponsors know that failure is likely. They also know it is better to try and fail than not to try at all.

IT people are realistic. They know the results are not good enough, but they don't want to be shot for making the real results public.

Few want to accept failure as the default option, yet experience and data say it is. It will stay this way until investing for success is seen as having greater value (financially for the business and motivationally for people and performance) than underinvesting in projects and failure.

Sidebar: Rational Response . . . Who Wants to Be the Messenger?

Few people want to put their reputation at risk (messengers are often shot) or lose their job (if the project is terminated). At the individual level, it makes sense to just keep going.

Some of the contributors to project failure are outside the project team. The team is focused on their work, and everything else is "someone else's problem." Even if the team has the experience to know these external factors may affect project results, they have little incentive to raise a warning. Not only may the messenger be shot, they might be perceived as commenting on an area outside their remit—a behavior that is rarely politically smart.

(*continued*)

(continued)

To keep silent is rational for the individual or the team. It is not functional for the business. This combination of a behavior's being rational from the perspective of one group but dysfunctional elsewhere in the business is a **rational dysfunction**.

Rational dysfunctions underlie several of the factors that hinder the long-term health of IT projects since IT projects often reach across boundaries within the organization. More on these in Part 2: Probability.

Sidebar: Irrational Response—Paying Attention to Sunk Costs

The old-fashioned expression for this is "don't throw good money after bad." Businesses (executives and projects) often justify continuing to invest in a project on the basis of "we've decided we are going to do this" or "we've invested so much." Financially and economically, this is irrational. If a project is discovered to be highly likely to fail, there are only two rational responses:

1. Identify what it will take to address the potential points of failure and address them
   OR
2. Close down the project.

In many organizations, it is easier to act as if all problems are surmountable. They continue spending and still fail.

Rationally, the funds and capital already spent are "sunk." They're gone. They're not recoverable. Future funds, in contrast, can be used for some other need that has a strong probability of success.

Data suggests that the assumption of success needs to be challenged by leaders.

Get data on your projects. Verify. Until you have data, the only valid assumption is that your project results will be just like everyone else's. A high probability of failure.

CASE STUDY

FROM REAL LIFE[14]

David saw that his IT department was supporting many business changes projects, but he realized that executives had no idea about the resources required for these projects or the outcomes that were expected.

David organized an inventory of all 300 projects. Most lacked a business case evaluating expected results against the investment. Some projects were in conflict with others. A project portfolio management process was introduced so that leadership had visibility and governance of the changes underway.

Improving Productivity Is a Process

By definition, productivity improvements are a result of continuously improving. Continuous change is a process not a transaction. The process of change needs to be sustainable so that productivity can continue into the next period.

Ninety-three percent failure suggests significant room for improvement.

What would a 10 percent transformation to your project effectiveness achieve? To your line of business? To your organization? Competitively? In terms of all of your bottom lines: financial, social, environmental?

In these terms, IT project success becomes more than a successful project; it becomes a foundation of how the organization grows strategically.

Survival of the Fittest

Back in the 1860s, Darwin saw competition as a means of survival for the species best able to adapt to change. Modern-day executives should relate to the way he put it:

> *The race goes not to the most fleet of foot, nor to the strongest, but to the species that is the most responsive to change.*
>
> —Charles Darwin

Productivity as a single step forward is one thing. Productivity gains that *help* the next step forward are even better.

The business challenge for IT projects is to create positive changes that re-enforce the strategic direction while minimizing negative implications.

A negative change affects the pace of future changes, which are then forced to invest more effort to create a positive impact.

CASE STUDY

FROM REAL LIFE

Winston presented two IT options to amend existing systems to support the design of a new process and function for the business.

- One was rough, patching three systems together: fast, cheap, not robust in terms of IT architecture or capacity to support future growth.
- One considered and addressed longer-term business needs and potential growth. Slightly longer delivery time, more effort, more cost. More robust.

The business chose the cheap short-term option, which was more expensive in the long term as the business grew. The costs of future changes were ignored.

Ignoring the broader implications of a project can also occur for changes that mix business processes and technology.

CASE STUDY

FROM REAL LIFE

CEO Rick felt an economic downcycle approaching and directed the company to be more cost conscious. He kicked off a shared services project that included several IT solutions: one system to support managing work in the new shared services structure, another system to provide direct web-based customer support and services.

The systems were delivered: on time, to specification and budget.

Staff heard of the secret project via the internal grapevine. Key staff began taking sick leave or left. Local productivity and customer services plummeted. Customers didn't like using the web-based system.

Extensive actions and additional investment was required to neutralize these foreseeable consequences. Additional investment was required to neutralize the impact.

A direct impact was the need to redo the externally facing web-based system to make it acceptable to customers.

Another impact was more effort required for the next changes (dealing with doubt, uncertainty, and cynicism depending on the group), a reduced commitment to the company and higher staff turnover in a company already challenged by staff turnover levels.

At the end of the day, for the business, responsibility for business results is shared. All play a role in leading successful change. In this case, the predictable responses outside the technical process weren't considered.

These additional flow-on effects are legitimate costs of the original change and are often overlooked.

Takeaways

- Productivity growth has dropped significantly. This is a long-term strategic issue for CEOs, CIOs, and business leaders.
- Productivity growth is a result of the cumulative effect of projects on business results.
- The 93 percent project failure rate provides untapped opportunities for competitive positioning and productivity growth.
- A substantial number of IT professionals recognize that IT projects fail to make a positive impact on their businesses.

- At a practical level:
  - Each project counts, each needs to succeed.
  - Productivity growth from projects requires IT and business to deliver results.
  - It takes courage and commitment to deliver success—as any champion golfer would say.

The next chapter measures productivity thorough benchmarks assessing the ROI delivered by project portfolios.

Endnotes

1 U.S. Department of Commerce.

2 Ibid.

3 International Labor Organization (2007), *Key Indicators of the Labor Market*, ILO/07/47.

4 Khan, Habibullah and Islam, M. Shahidul (2006), *Outsourcing, Migration and Brain Drain in the Global Economy.*

5 International Labor Organization (2007), *Key Indicators of the Labor Markets*, 5th ed.

6 What contributed to ''better?'' The last few decades have seen major improvements in technology, in corporate management, practices, in capital markets and financial risk management and in the disciplines for delivering projects and change. To mention a few that are relevant to business transformation:

On the technology front:

- *Hardware and Infrastructure:* Processing chips, telecommunications, routers, server farms, satellites, robotics, optical fiber, Internet, Web 2.0, cloud, and a myriad of other components of technology have provided the backbone of productivity transformation.
- *Software and services management:* Software ranging from custom-developed applications to open source, MS Office, and ERP programs like SAP or databases. IT governance, including portfolio management, CMMI, ITIL, SaaS, and so on, have improved IT services delivery.

Corporate management practices:

- Efficiency methods including Six Sigma, LEAN, MPRII, Just-In-Time (JIT), activity-based costing (ABC), outsourcing, and offshoring have improved cost efficiency.
- Alignment and motivational methods including Vision/ Mission, Balanced Scorecard (BSC), leadership programs, coaching and mentoring, Key Performance Indicators (KPIs) and bonuses, learning organization and systems thinking have improved the productivity of the human side of business.

Capital markets and risk management:

- Risk sharing and hedging, more sophisticated global financial systems and products, including an increased access to finance, have affected the ability of companies to fund growth.
- Regulatory frameworks including SOX have added to internal risk management practices.

Methods for managing and introducing change:

- Project management methodologies became widespread in the 1990s and are widely applied to technology projects, thanks to PM-BOK, PMI, and PRINCE II.
- Organizational change management: PW-MORI research was released as Kotter published in the *Harvard Business Review* in 1994. Change management becomes part of the executive and M&A tool kit.

7 Sauer, C., Gemino, A., and Reich, B. H. (Nov. 2007), ''The Impact of Size and Volatility on IT Project Performance.'' *Communications of the ACM* 50, No. 11: 80. doi: http://Doi.Acm.Org/10.1145/1297797.1297801.

8 IBM 7 survey of CEOs.

9 Bourne, Vanson (July 2008), ''Getting Smarter about IT Risks.'' http://mitsloan.mit.edu/cisr/pdf/EIU_GettingSmarterAboutITRisks.pdf.

Interestingly, IT executives have different perspectives of their primary role depending on where they are in the world, reflecting the different issues they face, as shown in the following table.

	Total	Americas	EMEA	Asia-Pacific
Improve competitiveness/agility	36 %	37 %	32 %	43 %
Reduce costs	30 %	29 %	33 %	26 %
Increase revenue	12 %	17 %	8 %	12 %
Mitigate risk	12 %	8 %	14 %	10 %
Ensure regulatory compliance	10 %	7 %	12 %	7 %
Other	1 %	1 %	0 %	2 %

10 The majority of IT executives feel that the ''complexity of business process, the speed of operations and the continued emergence of new technology paradigms will require increasing cooperation between IT and the business if business risks are to be reduced.'' (EIU ''Getting Smarter about IT Risks, 2008''). This highlights the need for a broader approach to managing the risks to project results than ''IT risk alone.''

11 Standish Data, http://www.infoq.com/articles/Interview-Johnson-Standish-CHAOS and http://www.infoq.com/articles/chaos-1998-failure-stats, provide an interesting comparison over the period from 1994 to 2006. The variability in the success rates suggests that, while project management has helped, it's not the solution to the results problem. Standish still reports that less than one-third of projects succeed.

Chris Sauer's research uses data provided by experienced PMs. (Other research shows that the failure to have a skilled PM is a leading indicator of failure—more on leading indicators of potential IT project failure in Part 3: Project.) Even with this expert group, 33 percent of IT underperform substantially, and 60 percent underperform slightly.

Petouhoff, Natalie L., Chandler, Tamra, and Montag-Schultz, Beth (2006), ''The Business Impact of Change Management, What is the Common Denominator for High Project ROI's?'' *Graziiado Business Report*, Pepperdine University, http://gbr.pepperdine.edu/063/change.html shows the negative impact of underinvestment in the non-technology components of change on ROI.

12 In a numbers-focused business world, we often focus on the facts over the experience or emotions that occur as we deliver a product or a service. More on this in Chapter 4.

13 Standish Group: 20 to 30 percent are written off in the viewpoint of business executives. Sauer reported from the Project Manager's perspective that 10 percent of projects are cancelled.

14 Each of the stories from real life is true. Names are changed to protect both the innocent and the guilty.

The stories reflect decisions made as a result of the actual situation at hand in those organizations. The real-life examples are to the point at hand. They are not recommendations, as each of these occurred in the context of the business change in that organization. Do consult your CM/PM/transformation advisor. This is a normal health and responsibility reminder and warning for mature, informed, accountable decision making. In every case, a diagnosis of what is real and what is needed occurred.

Chapter 2
Measure Success

Benchmark current practices and results like a yield on an investment.

Measuring the Cost of Project Failure

Some prefer not to focus on this. It feels negative. Yet like checking blood pressure, it provides useful data on just how healthy a person may be. A reading outside the expected healthy range suggests that attention may be required.

Failure is to not succeed. A project is successful when it delivers the value the business intended. This means that:

- The project delivers what was wanted, when it was wanted, for the amount agreed.
  And
- The business uses the capacities delivered by the project to generate business results.

A project is an investment. Many investments are part of a portfolio—the business wants an overall gain on the portfolio and to minimize losses. This is productivity in financial terms.

In financial terms, it is comparatively easy to assess return on investment (ROI). Professional accountants tell me that they can usually create a good business case; experienced ones ask what benefits a project will bring and why there should be confidence in achieving those benefits.

Sidebar: the Dangers of NINJAs

One of the causes of the recent financial crisis is particularly useful for project managers and project sponsors.

Unlike the Japanese heroes of story books, these NINJAs were loans supplied to customers who had "No Income, No Job, or Assets" (NINJA). Just how the banks expected these to be repaid is a demonstration of hope over reality. In the rosy days of constant growth, the growth engine hid the reality—that as soon as growth was not guaranteed, or a hiccup occurred, then the NINJAs had no capacity to repay their loans. They had no job or income. They also had no assets of value to cover their debts.

For businesses, NINJA products made their business portfolios look bigger. For some, bigger is seen as better.

In project terms, a NINJA project is a project that has no prospect of generating benefits. It may be worthy from the view of social or political views. If you have such projects, ensure the budget is clearly allocated as a policy decision to support a worthy cause.

The Functional Yield Measures of IT Project Productivity

Functional yield allows you to compare the results of projects. It helps an apples-to-apples comparison of projects. It also allows you to benchmark and compare the results your projects deliver to those of other businesses.

Ultimately, projects are investments, so we'll begin here, focusing on the return. In later Parts, we will look at the probability of that project investment generating a real return.

Simple Return on Investment

An investment generates a return if it generates more value than was put in. A $100 investment that generates $110 in a year is a gain. If it only generates $90, that's a loss.

When calculation a basic return on investment, a time period is set, often a year, and then the dollar value of the investment is compared between the beginning and the end. I had $100 on January 1 of this year. Will this investment give me at least $100 back on January 1 of next year?[1]

IT projects give returns that are not simply financial. An IT system provides functions that are used to then generate products and services that customers pay for. Only at this stage can project results be seen as financial.

This is why it is more appropriate to look at IT projects in terms of their functional yield: Did we get the functions we expected, for the amount we expected, when we expected it?

In the case of my kitchen, did I get the kitchen I'd expected? No. The change in the bench top and the lack of shelves meant that it didn't have the functionality I wanted. It cost me extra because I had to hire a handyman to make and fit the shelves that were missing. The functional yield on my kitchen was less than expected.

The Functional Yield

The productivity of an IT project can be measured by the functional yield (FY).

The functional yield is the business value achieved as a result of the investment. For example, if I expect to pay $100 for a piece of software and it is received on time, at that price, and with the agreed features, which perform as I expected, the functional yield is 100 percent. I got what I expected.

Consider the three sets of IT projects in Figure 2.1 representing three different IT portfolios.

The functional yield depends on

- *Dollars:* The original budget and what was really spent.
- *Time:* The intended delivery date and the actual date that the functionality is really available. What is the impact of time to the yield? Delays affect capital costs as well as market opportunity.
- *Functions:* The original scope and what is really delivered.
- *Perceived Value:* What does the business think of the project? Is it great? Were they disappointed? Do they say it was a waste? Are the capabilities shelfware or actually used?

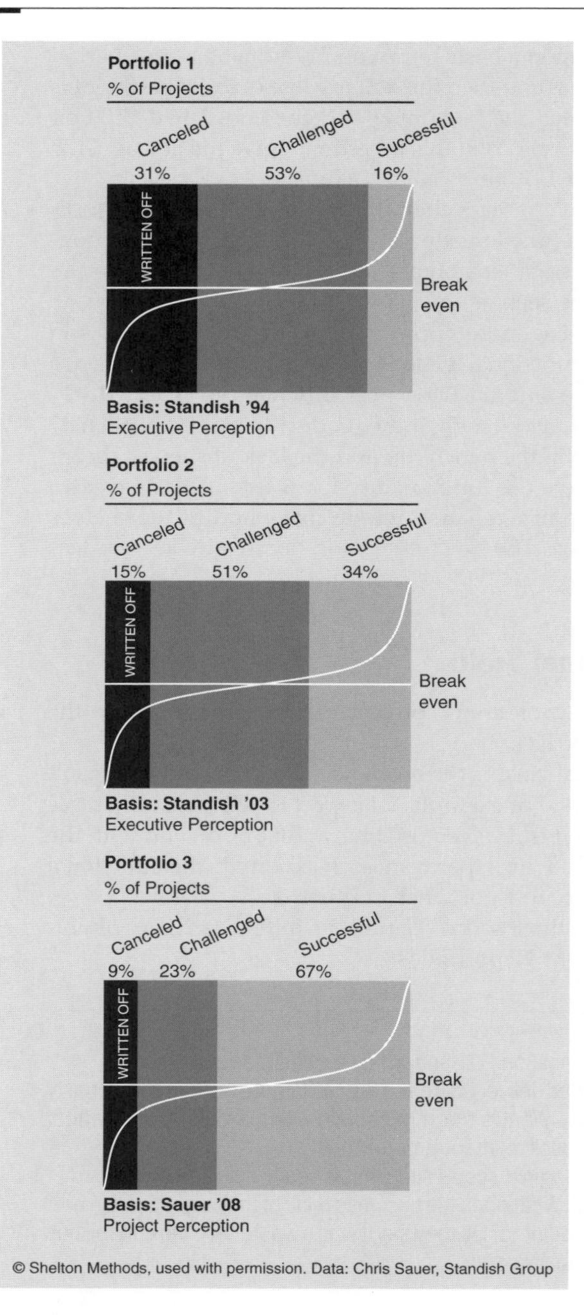

FIGURE 2.1 Benchmark IT Project Portfolios

Success here was measured as being on time and on budget. The results are:

- Black = project write-offs;
- Dark Grey = projects significantly over budget or schedule;
- Light Grey = projects on time and on budget (within a 10 percent variation).

This looks good. Black write-offs are falling and light grey successful projects are increasing. But this data does not show if functional results actually delivered.

Portfolio 3 looks pretty good. Portfolio 2 is less good, while Portfolio 1 is frankly ugly.

This diagram fails to show the real results: given actual funds and time invested, what expected proportion was delivered?

The yellow circles in Figure 2.2 show the real results. Yellow is the functional yield—what the business actually got as a result of changes in functional scope, in schedule, and in budget.

The functional yield is lower if it reflects undelivered functionality—like the kitchen renovation.

When a project is evaluated in terms of its functional yield, most people are surprised at the results.

Compared to the benchmark, all three IT project portfolios generated negative yields. The benchmark result ranged from –23 percent to –70 percent.

Let's put this in investment terms using that $100 investment example. To break even I need to get at least $100 of value. A 30 percent return means that I got $30 of the original investment back but I *lost* $70 on the investment.

The functional yield evaluates the percent of the "functions" delivered, not dollars. Project investments generate value in tangible returns like cash, *and* they generate returns in intangibles like more effective data for decision making.

From a business perspective, even a project portfolio as good as Portfolio 3 has at least 27 percent room for improvement.

The Cost of a Little Under to the Business

The value of reliable delivery is often underappreciated.

In the mid-1990s, IT projects were notorious for their failure rates. Portfolio 1 shows that Standish Group reported a 31 percent cancellation rate, over 53 percent running a 190 percent budget overrun and 222 percent over schedule.[2]

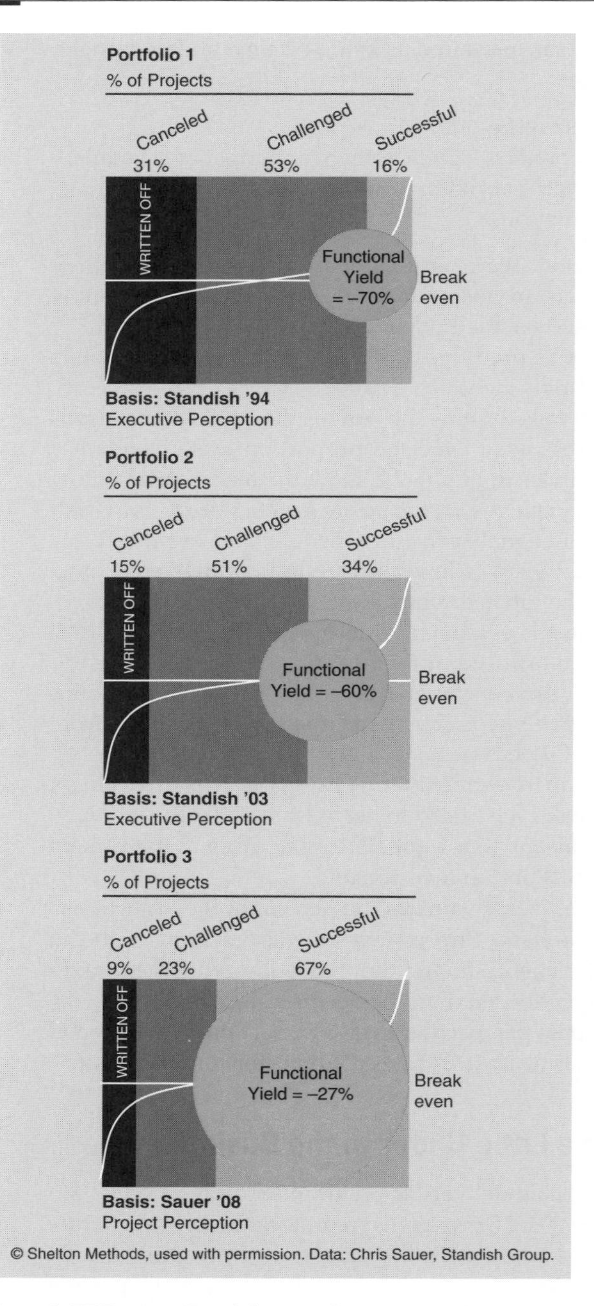

FIGURE 2.2 Benchmark IT Project Portfolios with Functional Yield

IT projects improved dramatically over the last 20 years. This is worth celebrating.

Portfolio 2 shows reported projects results in 2003 by the Standish Group with only 15 percent of projects canceled and written off.

Better still, a 7 percent variation in project budget and schedule was reported by Sauer in 2007. A few percent off was perfectly acceptable. Portfolio 3 shows that today, a project is considered successful if it delivers a little *less* than expected for a little *more* than expected, a little *later* than expected.[3]

Put on your business hat for a moment.

A customer is **not ok** with a project that is a little late, a little over budget and a little less functional than expected. Each little disappointment has a negative impact on business results.

- *Time:* Late has a market cost and a business cost for rescheduling and delaying deployment.
- *Functionality:* Less functionality means manual work. A "manual workaround" does not delight a business manager as she reworks a process and reassigns staff.
- *Budget:* Over budget means funds need to be reallocated from the business budget. The business (i.e., customer) will have fewer funds and resources to do other important things.

Not a recipe for a happy customer. The difference between Portfolios 2 and 3 shows why business executives report a lower level of project success than project managers.

The experience of attaining the expected results matters as much as the result itself. If "the project was a nightmare" like something from Hieronymus Bosch, then the business outcome is jeopardized. This is part of the Perceived Value component the Functional Yield. Far preferable for the team and the business is a project akin to Monet's Garden.[4]

Back to the kitchen renovation. Quotation changed, dates changed. Calls weren't returned, and I couldn't understand his kitchen design—it didn't make sense. Once it installed, frustrations arose.

Another home renovation was a dream. I received samples. I saw full illustrations that made sense. I even could see what it would be like to cook a meal in it (we did it as a mock up). I was relaxed. Psychological value is value.

Improving Project Productivity

The mind remembers stories better than lists or statistics. Stories are an effective means of communicating, allowing people to compare their own experiences to what's happening in the story.

Table 2.1 shows what needs to be evaluated to benchmark project results and lift productivity. There are three sets of data needed to assess productivity from projects.

1. What we expect as a result of the project
2. Probability of achieving those results
3. The results that actually turn out.

TABLE 2.1 *Project Productivity Data*

Data Set	Measured By
Expectations	Expected Functional Yield When the project was budgeted, the business and IT agree on a project charter and business case, stating what is expected, when it is expected, and what it will cost.
Probability	Risk Adjusted or Effective Functional Yield (EFY) A means of foresight and risk reduction. Probability of success should be assessed at the beginning of the project or when major funds are committed. What business results are achieved from the investment is important. When capital is scarce or project results are paramount, the question "How likely will this project deliver successfully?" becomes critical. Risks to business results must be assessed. EFY asks, "How probable is this result?" EFY enables foresight, a **pre-project** review. EFY is reviewed in a robust gated funding approach to project investment. If the project's risk assessment shows a high risk of failure, an entrepreneurial executive can reformulate the project to improve success, or terminate it early to avoid the capital write-offs of a failed project. Part 2—**Probability** looks at assessing the risks to results.
Results	Realized Functional Yield (RFY) What was realized from the project when complete—the realized functional yield (RFY). RFY is pragmatic. RFY asks, "What did we actually get for what we spent?" This is the **post-project review**. The buck stops here. Accountability for results delivered sits here.

Sidebar: Raffy and Effie as Characters[5]

If this book was a parable, like *Who Moved My Cheese?*, RFY would be called Raffy. He is active—visualize Raffy at the gym, toning his muscles and calculating nutritional value. Not quite "my body is a temple" but getting there. He loves problems involving fairness and equity, as well as numbers, money, and sustainable results for the business and community. The triple bottom line counts. He watched *An Inconvenient Truth*. While Raffy is results focused, his frame of reference is broader than "show me the numbers" alone.

EFY would be called Effie. Effie is quieter, more reflective, and considers "What if?" She'd prefer to think about what may happen and to do something to prevent it. Effie assesses health by looking at actions that help her be healthy physically and mentally—an apple a day, Pilates, and mediation. Effie looks at what really is. If Effy saw a situation that is okay now, but would cause a problem later, she has the courage to say, "Let's recognize it and plan for it."[6]

Both Raffy and Effy care about long-term consequences. They plan on long healthy lives. They may not always take action, but they do make conscious choices about convenience now vs. cost later. Their story reflects practices that lead to healthy project results.

Ultimately, the productivity of the IT project portfolio is built from individual project successes. RFY provides a measure of what was actually achieved and a basis for accountability of results. A single project can have a significant impact on the portfolio's RFY.

Takeaway

The happy words of an executive: ''Our projects are fine. Yes, an occasional project may not do so well, but that's the exception.'' He thinks his projects and IT portfolio are well-in-hand.

The benchmark data suggests otherwise.

- Success is:
  - Delivering what was expected, when it was expected at the expected price.
  - The experience of reaching the expected results.

CASE STUDY

FROM REAL LIFE

Situation: A major bank undertook a large Core Banking project to replace the IT engine supporting all products and services.

Strategic: Yes. IT can be up to 60 percent of a bank's running costs. Without this program, any other bank in their geography that successfully "cored" would have faster time to market for new products and services with a lower average running cost for IT. The project was two years into a four-year delivery schedule. The loss-in-market cost was assessed at $5 million per month.

Capital/Cost: The initial budget approved by the board was $400 million. $400 million was already spent. Expected additional overrun was another $400 million. The external running cost per annum of the program was over $250 million.

Externally observable decision: A financial crisis affects the region. The project was suspended when only partially delivered. All pending services were terminated (people retrenched, contracts closed . . .).

Consider: A collapsed share price (common across banks during that crisis) and $400 million already spent. There was value in the strategic capacity already created, even if it was not fully delivered. By suspending the project, significant investment was written off. The fundamental business issues were still unresolved.

The real functional yield on this project is negative. If the project restarts, most of the investment-to-date was lost. Re-investment will be required.

The effective functional yield was doubtful at the beginning. The project was strategically necessary, but the way it was formulated did not address key risks to business results. The EFY assessment was completed informally. It identified key risks and issues to achieving the project's ambitious targets. These were not addressed. One organizational issue alone contributed $75 million dollars to the overrun.

- **Only 7 percent of IT projects succeed: 93 percent fail at some level**. Projects are late, overrun budgets, deliver below expectations, or are cancelled or written off.
- Expected results are measurable with the effective functional yield (EFY).
- Achieved results are measurable with the realized functional yield (RFY).

- **IT portfolios deliver a benchmark functional yield result ranging from –23 percent to –70 percent.**
- Perceptions of results vary. An IT project could be viewed by some as Monet's Garden and by others as Hieronymus Bosch's Hell.

There is substantial opportunity for improve:

- The functional yield from IT project investments.
- Project results and their bottom line impact.

Next, we turn to four actions that highly successful projects take to lift success rates and real functional yields.

Endnotes

1 With inflation and deflation, this is a real question. Those well-versed in finance will want what is called a real return. One that covers:
  1. Capital invested.
  2. Depreciation (this is to make up for any reduction in purchasing power of the capital. $100 now often buys more than $100 will in a year's time).
  3. Interest: something for the use of the money. The company could have put the capital in a bank and received a few percent return. This usually includes a factor for the risk of the investment. Investments that are risky are expected to pay higher interest than those that are certain. A business may choose to do the same for projects.

2 Standish Group Report (1995), *Chaos*. http://net.educause.edu/ir/library/pdf/NCP08083B.pdf.

3 Sauer, C., Gemino, A., and Reich, B. H. (Nov. 2007), ''The Impact of Size and Volatility on IT Project Performance,'' *Communications of the ACM* 50, No. 11: 79–84. doi: http://Doi.Acm.Org/10.1145/1297797.1297801.

4 By now you will have noticed occasional reference and imagery to great painters and creators. This is deliberate. IT systems design and delivery is a creative process. A vision is seen of what is wanted. Then the teams work out how to

achieve it and what materials (or systems components) will work. They put it together (and it may take more than one go); they then test to see if it achieves what was intended.

Artists call this process the process of resolving. If you look at artists like Leonardo da Vinci, they paid intense attention to what was there through precise observation. They created things that had not previously existed. They saw what could be and expressed it in the pre-IT mediums of words, paint, and art.

It is one of those strange things, that a great design for an IT system is usually aesthetically beautiful. The principle of elegance is a quality used by systems and project architects and designers to test the overall "rightness" of the design. They sit back and say, "That's an elegant solution."

Pictures and imagery are also powerful communicators of ideas, complexity, and even feeling.

5 Stories and characters may seem out of place in a book about ROI and project risks; however, here is an interesting statistic:

When Kotter published his seminal book on change in 1994, he sold around 150,000 copies over a couple of years. A few years later, Spencer Johnson wrote a very short book called *Who Moved My Cheese?* on essentially the same topic—dealing with change. It was a story of two mice who went looking for cheese when their cheese supply changed and two humans, Hem and Haw, who hemmed and hawed around until they nearly starved before they started to look for cheese elsewhere. It sold 15,000,000 copies over an equivalent period.

More people could relate to the mice, cheese, and Hem and Haw than to Kotter's book. The mice and the parables are remembered and discussed. They are effective.

6 An investment is only sensible if the probable results exceed the investment.

Chapter 3
Take Action to Lift Success

Success is more than simply not failing. Not failing is neutral. For many business executives, it is good enough that an IT project that does not disrupt their business. It is not. Neutral is just not good enough.

Projects should aim for success.

My research shows there are four specific steps that lead to project success.

1. Admit success is not guaranteed. Calculate the real probability of project success.
2. Measure the non-performing project (NPP) ratio. Recognize that it is not enough to accept the cost of a project that is a little under, a little late, a little over budget.
3. Value the reduced risk of failure (to achieve business results). Invest in reducing the risks to results.
4. Explicitly use results-based risk management to fund changes in the plan.

This is where the Entrepreneurial Executive, the CIO, and the Proactive Project Manager step forward. Success is a team sport.

There are benefits to set up for success.

1. Success is more likely.
2. Repeated points of project failure can be proactively addressed.
3. Results are more predictable.

Overall, PAR lifts.

Publicly Acknowledge That Success Is Not Guaranteed

The first step to success is to explicitly recognize that **the assumption** of "100 percent success" is unrealistic. As long as 100 percent success is assumed, it is difficult for the project to publicly admit risks, to escalate them, or to find the resources to address them.

IT project results are not certain even if we wish they were.

Acting as if success is assured is one way executives set up projects to fail.

Many organizations simply allocate project funds based on the ROI. They ask, "Does it meet our hurdle criteria?" and allocate funds until the available budget runs out.

With the assumption of certainty relaxed, it makes sense to consider projects in light of three dimensions:

1. The expected return on investment (horizontal axis).
2. The probability of achieving that return (vertical axis).
3. The investment required (represented by the bubbles in Figure 3.1).

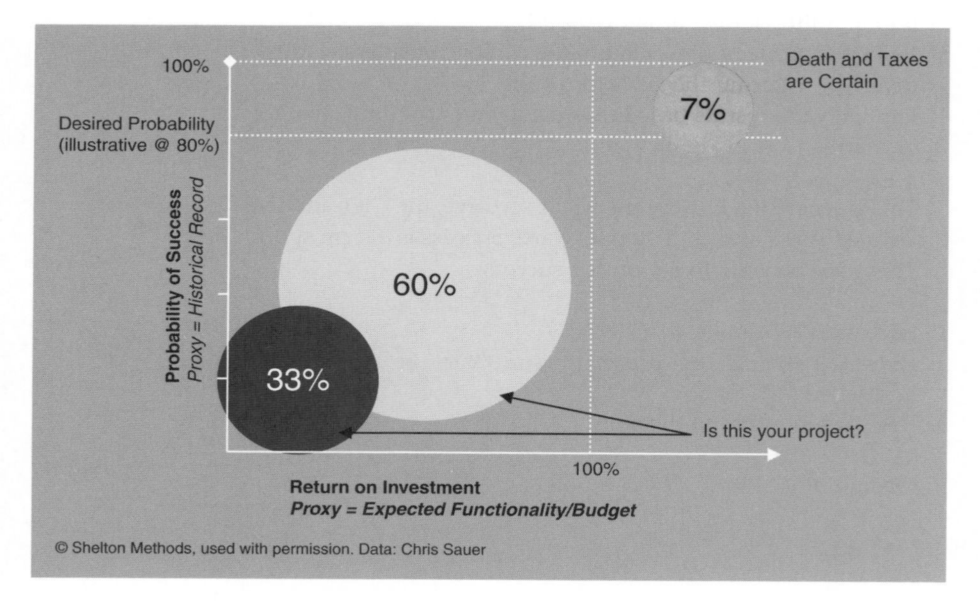

FIGURE 3.1 IT Performance Project Overall

This generates a useful project profile.

Consistently projects are in the lower left quadrant: low success and well over budget. Not good.

Bottom Line: What Is the Likely Success Rate of Your Project?

Assessment and diagnosis of a project or IT portfolio's health is valuable. Without consistent, commonly understood project data and a predictable, accountable, reliable process to track project success, research statistics are the best indicator of results. Data allows you to have confidence in the projects you support. Data and processes allow you to manage and improve both success rates and ROI.

A private equity executive once said that he planned his IT projects on the basis of: "Double the budget then hope for the best."

It is possible to do more than hope.

Probability (Part 2) contains diagnostics you can use to evaluate the likely success of your project.

Own Up to the NPP Ratio

Yield and NPP Ratios

In banking, there is a critical metric that is monitored with the fervor of a diabetic watching his insulin levels: the non-performing loan (NPL) ratio.

Banks know that if the NPL level rises above a certain level their business is in jeopardy.

If they approve 100 loans for $10,000, they have a portfolio of $1,000,000. If they earn 10 percent interest per annum, they get a simple return of $100,000. With everything going well, at the end of the year they have $1,100,000. Pretty good for not much work, you may say.

However, the business has risk—some loans are not repaid. Or repaid late. Say 10 of the loans don't repay, there is "only" a 10 percent failure rate—that is $100,000 in loans written off.

Look at the impact to the business: the balance sheet is now $900,000 and if loans are not repaid, then the income is lower too, $90,000. Net result at the end of the year with a 90 percent success rate is a portfolio of $990,000. That is a real loss.

When banks talk about managing their portfolio, this is what they mean.

Let's take it one step further to make it more realistic. The funds used in the portfolio are not free—banks pay deposit interest for the use of the funds. Let's reflect the cost of money as well. Banks do this by looking at their margin. The margin is how much they are going to make over how much it costs them. So if they make 10 percent interest and it costs them 5 percent, they make a margin of 5 percent. The margin is important. It is what allows a bank to stay in business. If they can't make more than they put in, the bank goes bankrupt.

This bank has worked hard and reduced the NPL ratio to just 3 percent while ensuring the margin stayed at 5 percent. The project sponsor, CFO, and CEO sat down and reviewed the portfolio. They found they made just under 2 percent yield.

They wrote off $30,000. They made $48,500 on the loans that delivered (97 percent × 1,000,000 × 5 percent). They are now up $18,500. The bank has now made something on their portfolio.

Reducing the write-off has a big effect on the overall results.

Write-offs and Functional Shortfalls

For an IT portfolio, a project that doesn't deliver what was expected has the *same effect as NPLs* on the real value of the IT Portfolio.

- A project that is cancelled and written off is like a loan that is not repaid.
- A project that underdelivers on functionality (or is a little late or over budget) is like a loan that has a lower margin.

This is where functional yield (FY) evaluation comes to the fore. It can be calculated for a specific project or program or across a portfolio, depending on your preferred frame of reference.

If many organizations were a bank, the NPL ratio implied by the functional yield (the yellow circles in the previous chapter) would bankrupt the business. The results don't cover the investment.

At the returns shown on the three IT portfolios in the previous chapter, the business is funding projects as a speculative investment—it is hoping that one or two projects pay off massively.

To justify this sort of investment practice, any nonfinancial returns need to be explicitly stated and delivered.

A bank manager looking at lending money on these projects should say, "Loan not approved." She should ask, "How will you lift the probability of getting a return so you can repay the loan?"

Recently, banks have received a well-deserved beating for their past performance. Much of it was due to ignoring good lending and investment practices:

- Assessing creditworthiness and lending to those who can pay back.
- Pricing the expected return based on the risks.
- Monitoring implications of changes in risk while knowing where the risks lie (complex products made this like mud).
- Moderating greed with good sense in the use of KPIs and performance measures.
- These good practices are equally applicable to project investments.

CASE STUDY

FROM REAL LIFE

An executive asked James if a major CRM (customer relationship management) program was successful. James said yes. The executive looked surprised. James explained, "The project had two objectives, one of which was to demonstrate that IT could deliver a large complex project rapidly (1800 seats across 16 business units in nine months). The project achieved this."

Certainly, he admitted, in terms of the second objective, business results had been poor.

The project highlighted the need to address issues around how the business could get value from IT rather than solely focus on IT's capacity to deliver.

The track record of IT projects as a portfolio will generally show a negative functional yield when functional shortfalls and project write-offs are recognized. An investment review would expect these projects to deliver significant nonfinancial results to be considered sensible investments.

Ignoring the potential of a project to be nonperforming is one way executives set up projects for failure. A "credit check" process is as needed as a quality assurance process for success. It focuses on "How will we get paid back for our investment (the principal) and our interest (our return)?"

Chapter 5 is a diagnostic for those interested in evaluating the productivity of their IT project results.

Value the Reduced Risk of Failure (to Achieve Business Results)

A bank manager knows that not all loans will be repaid. He wants to reduce the likelihood of nonpayment and increase the returns on the loans that can repay.

TABLE 3.1 *Use of Organizational Change Management*

	Little Use or Poor of OCM	Effective Use of OCM
Results achieved	– 64 percent	+ 46 percent

To do this, he assesses each loan for its creditworthiness. A key component of creditworthiness is the degree to which the borrower can reduce the risk of failure and the degree to which he is investing to create success.

A bank manager knows that it's a better investment to invest a little more if it improves the probability of success. Being too tight can guarantee failure.

For example, a business wants a loan to improve its performance by updating its technology to serve customers better. The bank manager would also want to see the associated marketing plans and staffing plans, since both of these contribute to getting the business result. A bank manager asks: ''*How will business results improve if there is new technology but customers and staff still do things the old way?*'' He knows that changing customers and staff behavior also require investment.

For IT projects, the associated investment is called ''organizational change management'' (OCM).

Independent research by McKinsey[1] finds that the degree to which projects invest in organizational change management affects their results significantly (Table 3.1).

Health Check: Is the necessary organizational change management part of the project definition and project plan?
[ ] Yes
[ ] No

The use of good organizational change management makes the difference between achieving business results from the project investment or not.

Investing in success has greater value both financially and in people's motivation and performance than underinvesting and failure.

Sidebar: Doing the Ostrich with Change Management

Organizational change management takes additional investment. It requires resources, skills, tasks, coordination, monitoring. Many projects overlook the need for organizational change management, but Entrepreneurial Executives won't. They want reliable results.

To assess the value of organizational change management, consider the following investments:

Investment A—without OCM	**Investment B—with OCM**
Investment amount: $100,000	Investment amount: $150,000
Probability of success: 0.35	Probability of success: 0.80
Return on investment: 10%	Return on investment: 15%

Many project managers and sponsors will happily pick Investment A. Yet, from a financial perspective, Investment B is the better investment.

This may seem strange. It is another **rational dysfunction**. Investment A means the Sponsor and Project Manager are asking for a lower investment. Many do so because they are more likely to get the funds and thus the chance to have a go at success. Since few organizations formally consider the probability of success, they are being quite rational.

A bird in the hand is worth two in the bush.

—*Traditional saying*

Finance funds allocations policies have a significant impact on this behavior.

A CFO would call this a dysfunctional investment decision. Like the bank manager—the CFO is more likely to be concerned about the probability of the project delivering real results. He wants to keep the write-offs (the NPP ratio) low.

As a rule of thumb, organizational change management is often 50 percent of IT project expenditure and can be higher if significant changes are required in the business.

Executives set projects up to fail when they underinvest in success factors such as organizational change management. A project will fail if management acts as if project delivery equals project results. The additional effort required to get results takes time, energy, attention, and resources.

Investing in success has greater value both financially and in people's motivation and performance than underinvesting in projects and failure.

Rule of Thumb: Organizational Change Management investment is often 50 percent of the IT project investment.

Results Risk Management™

Another assumption that reduces business results is the assumption that "the project plan will never change." It is not true. Project and business reality is that events occur which may or may not be anticipated.

The business situation changes. Competitive action may change the need for functionality or the priority of delivery. Other events may affect potential business results. A feature could be found in an underlying application that reduces the effectiveness of the IT solution proposed.

To modify the Duke of Wellington's comments on battle plans: *No plan survives engagement with reality.*

Acting as if the plan will not change will set up a project to fail.

When things happen, the implications for the capacity and likelihood of the project delivering results need to be considered and assessed in order to achieve predictable, accountable results.

In its most Zen form, results risk management includes:

- A contingency assessment is a means of monitoring for events that could jeopardize results. Organizations can develop event lists to help identify events. More sophisticated monitoring is open to the possibility of unpredicted or left field events.
- A results risk management plan is a process for assessing implications to the capacity of the business and the project to deliver results from continued investment.
- A results risk escalation process is required to review and act on high impact events so that the project maintains its relevancy.

Each of these risks is strongly linked to projects running over schedule or running over budget or failing outright.

Most projects can survive one or two of these risks. Few projects have the resilience to manage several risks.

The effects add up. A couple of changes in scope and a shortage of a key skill can have as much impact on the overall success of a project as a change in project manager (Sauer).

Contingency Planning for Results Risks

Contingency planning is the technical term for planning for the unexpected. When we plan, we tend to work on the basis of "if this goes right" and develop a best-case plan. A contingency plan looks at "what if this goes wrong . . . ?" and thinks what it could do about it.

Table 3.2 shows some of the most common risks to the business results on projects.

Risks will appear during the course of the project. It helps project success if a plan is made to address these risks before the project begins.[2] In **Probability**, the focus is on the upfront risks to business results from the project.

TABLE 3.2
Results Risk and Contingency Plans

Results Risk	Possible Contingency Plan
Sponsor changes, new sponsor changes business priorities.	Sponsor commits to seeing the project through. Formal review of the project when sponsor changes to adjust to business priorities.
Project manager changes.	Project manager commits to seeing the project through. Project manager has a formal "2IC" to understudy for a pre-agreed handover period.
Skills not available.	Key skills identified and resourced. Agreed escalation process with sponsor. Be specific about the skills required and the impact if not available at the right time—the impact will vary depending on the project phase.
New technology more complex than anticipated.	Pilot technology. Contract expertise to support initial builds.
Business climate changes from growth to slowdown. Functions *x*, *y* will be lower priority while others will be higher priority. Staff likely to be concerned for jobs and distracted.	Agreed process for changing functional priorities and releases. Agreed policy for project staff and business staff to address concerns.
Staff reject the solution.	Identify why staff might reject the solution and address specifics. Each group will have its own reasons.

(*continued*)

TABLE 3.2 *(Continued)*

Results Risk	Possible Contingency Plan
	This is often the remit of organizational change management.
Funds inadequate to acquire required resources.	Evaluate if the project is likely to deliver results given current formulation.
	Identify ways of more cost effectively delivering results.
	Reconsider the project and funding priorities.

Accountability for Results Risk Management

Accountability for managing results risk lies with the project sponsor and is supported by the escalations of the project manager.

If there is no process for assessing ''What is the implication of this risk to results?'', if no one is accountable for the assessment, or if there is no process for escalating the *high impact* findings, then projects will continue on their merry way and subsequently fail.

CASE STUDY

FROM REAL LIFE

Joanne was project managing the delivery of a large program. In the last week of testing, one of the testers described a problem he'd found. "Joanne, we can't track this one down. Occasionally we just lose a session and can't restore the data that the user has entered." On investigation, it appeared to occur about once every thousand transactions.

Some would have said that was a small problem.

Joanne recommended that the CIO and business sponsor cease the project and consider other IT options for the business. At that stage, some

$20 million had been invested in the project. This was a big project to recommend writing off.

The business sponsor and CIO agreed. They had focused their discussion on three points:

- The business users would not have confidence in the data if they found that the occasional transaction was lost. In a bank, losing a transaction is unacceptable. They didn't want the staff to doubt any of the other IT applications because this one had "a small loss." The risk to business results was high if they deployed the solution as it was.
- The fault found was an undocumented feature in an underlying application. The customer application would have to change its architecture and fully rebuild to work around this problem. Expected delay on the vendor side was up to a year to deliver a new, tested, stable product.
- The cost of deployment had yet to be made. The back of the envelope assessment was when fully costed in business terms, deployment and long-term investment commitments (staff time in training and learning, back filling, software licenses, operational hardware, etc.) was on the order of a further $30 million investment.

To sink further funds into a project that was now carrying a high risk of failure was considered inappropriate.

When they reconfigured the project—which required starting the technical build from scratch with new software—they explicitly used a results risk management process. The process helped identify the implication of events that occurred outside the direct remit of the project on the project ROI.

New information often comes to light as the project proceeds. It may be technical in nature. It may be related to the business. Assessing the implications of these events to the likely achievement of business results is the fourth and final step to lifting the real functional yield of a project.

Executives set projects up to fail when they overlook results risk management and fail to fund adequate contingency funds in the project to manage these (fairly obvious) risks.

The Benefits of Setting Up for Success

Setting up for success has benefits:

- Reduced project write-offs;
- More effective allocation of project investment funds;
- Higher probability of achieving a return;
- Higher returns and productivity.

It does take investment. These four steps take resources and attention. It is tempting to simply get a project started and then deal with the issues later. These steps require owning up to realities that might not be palatable in the business or IT.

Behind these steps, IT and Business need operate on the principles that:

1. Success is not guaranteed. Risks need to be addressed.
2. Repeated project failure and underdelivery is a governance issue.
3. Focusing on delivery of predictable accountable results (PAR) improves the political acceptability of mentioning risks to results.

It is better to invest for a higher probability of return than to underinvest in a project and have failure.

Address Risks to Success

If you want success, it takes courage. Clearly you do; you are reading this book. Here's how to take action—and preserve your head.

Address the risks to results, the risks to success directly. Pretending they will go away or are in a ''someone else's problem'' field is not effective.

CASE STUDY

FROM REAL LIFE

This case is one of my own, the IT transformation project that I spoke of at the beginning of this book.

Once we had the project management structures properly in place and the project was humming along again, I took the afternoon off and went to a nearby café. I needed to think. My colleagues in other countries had mentioned some scary stories about things going wrong after implementation. Problems with data files that led to 50 people doing data clean-up for six months. Customer exits had exploded in another country as service standards dropped. Technically, this was not my problem. I was there to get the project cut-over to live production.

However, I'd run businesses. I knew that if the business heads were aware of the risk, they'd be concerned. I also knew that no matter how perfect our cut-over was, if business operations failed, the project had failed.

I could say, "We assessed the risks and presented them to the CEO with an action plan"—which doesn't really say much. So I'll share the process, as part of the challenge with these risks is the art of introducing the consequences without getting shot for bringing bad news.

So what did I do? I suggested to the Business Sponsor that two of her staff visit the other locations to learn from them. We realized that while no one would admit to big problems publicly, they might talk in a more private setting. Staff members visited two countries and spoke to colleagues in two others. They were shocked by what they found. They did not want the problems they heard about to happen to their business. They asked me, "What can we do?"

I made two suggestions. They said, "Okay, but we can't say this to the Country Manager, can we?" I said that I would.

The Business Sponsor decided that, since she owned the business that had the problem, she'd step up.

We prepared some more. The discussion with the Country Manager went something like this (it's been a few years so the words are not exact).

CM: "Good to see you, what is it that you'd like to talk to me about?"

Me: "I had some concerns based on what I've heard from my colleagues in other countries. I brought these to the attention of the Biz Sponsor. I'd like her to share some data with you."

Biz Sponsor tells him the risk and the impacts found elsewhere (researched data). She wraps up with the potential impact on the business here based on the data her team gathered.

CM: "Okay, we don't need that. What do we do?"

Me: "Are you willing to invest to avoid these costs?"

CM: "Yes."

Me, nodding: "Then my suggestions are, firstly that we officially add 'Zero operational problems on Day One' to our project goals—so that we are clear what our business goal is."

All agree.

This may seem an obvious goal however it is rare to be explicit about it. We did. It helped. It legitimized the next step—investing additional resources.

Me: "Next we look at how we can test this before we go live. We want to know we have mitigated this risk as the cost if it goes wrong is so great."

CM: "Okay, what do we need to do, and what will this cost me?"

We outlined the plan—after we had a clean data conversion and the user acceptance test results were okay, we had all front line staff come in on Saturday to do a day's operations on the testing system. We'd run the overnight batches; then the back office would come in on Sunday and do their operations. We'd compare results from the business and see where there were problems. Then we'd fix them.

The bottom line cost was that we'd need to pay two days, plus the preparation time, for the business to come in for the weekend, and we'd need to fund the IT team for this additional testing.

CM: "Done. This is a good investment."

The day after the project went live, the Business Sponsor said, "This is the lowest reconciliation adjustment I've ever had in my 15 years of managing operations. Amazing! We've had no problems. Thank you."

On target: Zero operational problems. Very happy project team. Very happy business.

Sidebar: Why It Is Hard to Admit That a Project May Fail

If a project is doomed, it's good to put it out of its misery.

One of the reasons people don't admit that projects are likely to fail is that they don't want to people to lose their jobs, "if the project goes, you go."

Fair enough. Deal with the job question another way. Does your employment or contracting approach encourages people to keep failing projects going? Or to avoid being on the project team? Either action may be rational for the individuals!

The business must recognize the risks that may doom a project. Deal with the human issue.

A second reason may be that the project manager or sponsor may not want to admit that it's going wrong, because in personal terms of reputation and political fallout admitting problems is unattractive. No one likes to fail. It is often better to try and pretend all is fine—and hope that no one will notice. In most organizations, others won't notice much. Someone may gripe that a project has not been good, but in most cases it doesn't matter.

This is not a recommendation to sweep it all under the carpet. This is a business issue that requires executive ownership at the C level.

CASE STUDY

FROM REAL LIFE

Frank guaranteed continuity of employment for project members. They would be treated by the same principles as staff attached to the business should business changes occur, that is, they had no additional risk to their jobs if problems were found in the project.

Repeated Project Failure Is a Governance Issue

If there is a regular pattern of projects failing, being written off, underdelivering, disappointing, or being frustrating, consider addressing this as a business and IT portfolio governance issue.

Given the issues described, IT Project Portfolio Governance is critical.

Armed with information on the likelihood of project success (or failure), you can make an informed results-risk-based decision about the project.

Given the risks to results, should the project be kept, killed, or reconsidered?

Keep | Kill | Reconsider

The fastest way to lift success rates and results is to identify the projects that are likely to fail. The action choices are simple:

1. *Keep* projects that will succeed.
2. *Kill* projects that are doomed. Do not wait until further capital is invested.
3. *Reconsider* projects if success is in doubt. Deal with the doubts: address the risks to failure, set the project up for success with the additional resources it needs, and then re-evaluate the business case.

CIO Moment: Portfolio Governance and the 7 Keys to Success

To lose one parent, Mr. Worthing, may be regarded as a misfortune; to lose both looks like carelessness.
—Oscar Wilde, *The Importance of Being Earnest*

CIOs by their nature are not careless. However, projects do fail, and portfolios underperform. Seven elements appeared in my research, which provide extra depth to portfolio robustness, results, and strategic delivery, and form the basis for the Shelton Method to portfolio governance. The **7 Keys to Portfolio Success**™ are:

1. Project success is evaluated.
2. Risks to results are addressed.
3. Capital-at-risk is reduced.
4. Results are optimized.
5. Cross-functional project risks are reduced.
6. Portfolio risk allocation is explicit.
7. Portfolio is aligned to strategy.

The benefits of applying these include:

1. Overall portfolio performance improves. Refining the +/− variations of project cost/schedule from 10 to 5 percent is valuable. Improving benefits realization by 10 or 20 percent adds value. Incremental value is achieved by more reliable delivery of nonfinancial benefits.
2. Projects with a high probability of success will attract investment and support. Decisions are informed by risks and data rather than by optimism.

3. Returns on investment are apparent and accountable.
4. Capital is more easily preserved because early failure is reduced.
5. Systemic or recurring problems are readily identified that reduce project results or cause additional investment. The business and IT can address problems to reduce the costs of introducing successful change.
6. More projects succeed.

My research also revealed pertinent points about portfolio governance practices for very successful projects:

- A governance process exists and is followed.
- Funds are allocated based on business case or a neutral evaluated basis.
- Executives on the governance board are competent, reflect a mix of business and technology interests, and have a clear understanding and commitment to the broader business strategy.
- Governance meetings are conducted with good meeting practices.
  - Agenda circulated with preparatory information.
  - Key issues are discussed, and time is effectively managed
  - Minutes and action items are recorded and followed up.
  - Respect and mutual trust operate so that difficult issues can be put on the table and discussed meaningfully rather than ignored.

Predictable Accountable Results (PAR)

For the CEO, CIO, and Proactive Project Manager, the question is what does it take to get predictable accountable results? Project results are the track record showing how likely it is for the next project to succeed—if old practices continue. It's like a golfer expecting his PAR to change without changing his game.

Part of the challenge is acknowledging the reality of where projects actually stand. Are results predictable? Are the right people accountable for results delivery? Are the processes that deliver results reliable? Are the results positive? After all, who is really looking for a sustained series of negative results?

- **Predictable.** Change must predictably deliver. Confidence in outcomes is based on fact. On track record. Not on wishful thinking.
- It's about doing projects in a way that delivers anticipated results predictably. The track record of current practices don't. Current practices generate predictable, unaccountable failure.
- How much waste, frustration, and cynicism do people feel as a result of these ongoing failures? A lot.
- How much capital is wasted and written off as a consequence of projects and programs failing to deliver? Significant sums.
- **Accountable**. What's expected occurs. This is about ownership and delivery of results.
- No ownership. No monitoring for delivery. No results.
- **Repeatable Results**. What's expected occurs, time and time again.

This is PAR for projects.

Sidebar: PAR at Golf

A golfer must play 10 games to get his handicap. This handicap says how well the golfer performs. If he takes 82 strokes on a PAR 46 golf course, his handicap is 36, or 82 (his score) minus 46 (PAR). His 36 handicap reflects the extra strokes he needs given his level of skill. It is a transparent system that allows golfers to be compared across golf courses. It acknowledges that not all golfers are at the same level of competence. It encourages personal improvement.

In golf, complexity, sand pits, sloping putting greens, and water traps add to the excitement of the game. For a business, the equivalents add to the cost of doing business. A company can take action to reduce cost and excitement. The risk factors covered in **Presence** focus on many of the organizational equivalents of sand pits, sloping greens, and water traps. As a business executive, you can choose to keep your golf course complex, exciting, and expensive, or to simplify the cost of the game.

PAR is a useful acronym that focuses on what we want to achieve here. Actual PAR is the real functional yield. When you are about to play a round, you may mentally evaluate the probability of successfully achieving PAR on this course—that is, the probability of success × the expected results.

Begin with a project. Courageously ask questions such as ''Will my project fail?''; ''How do I identify the risks that jeopardize the project?''; and ''What can be done to prevent a write off?'' Many of the risks to results can be identified on Day One. Results risk spotting is the focus in the later parts of this book.

This allows you to assess the project and see if it falls in the sweet spot.

The Results Probability Map clearly shows what the IT project portfolio looks like. It incorporates four critical pieces of information (see Figure 3.2.):

1. The expected benefits or results.
2. The probability of success.
3. The investment required.
4. If these three elements have been verified—preferably by an independent QA process.

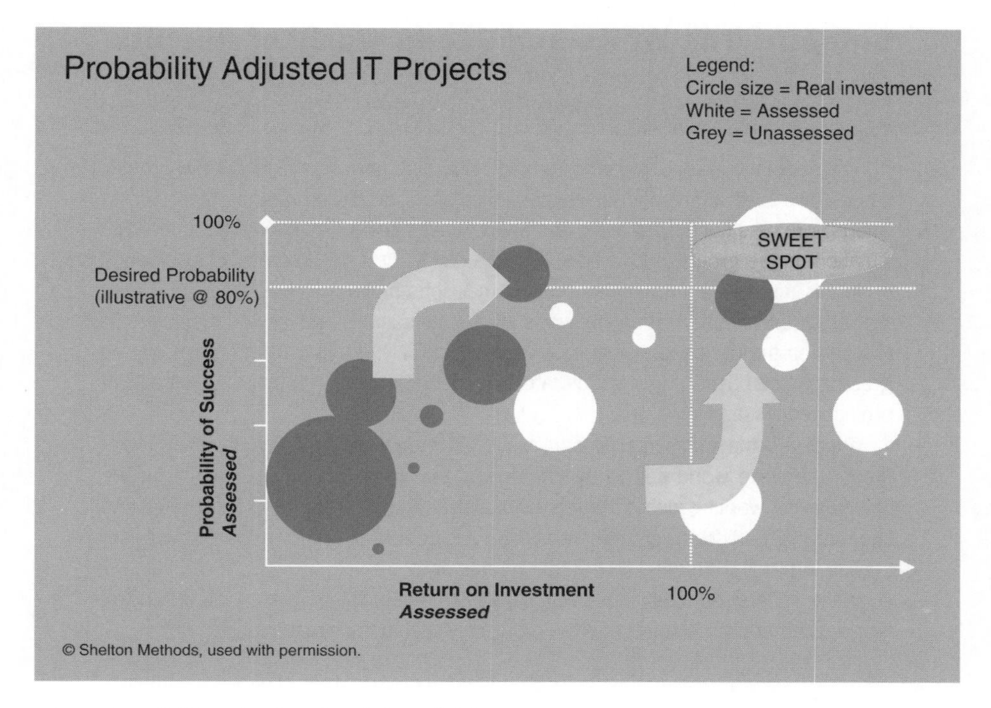

FIGURE 3.2 Lifting the Productivity of IT Investments

Begin by assessing the probable success of a project in terms of the risks to results using Parts 2–4. In investment terms, this is the likelihood of getting a return from the investment.

Based on the information uncovered, actions can be taken to improve the likely success, or the business can choose to invest the funds elsewhere. This is the Keep, Kill, or Reconsider Decision. Projects that are below the desired threshold for likely success are either improved or removed.

From the perspective of the portfolio of projects, the best place to be is large projects. This is where the benchmarks and research find the greatest risks to results. It is also where investment is greatest.

The Results Probability Map is enlightening. Consider Figure 3.1 at the beginning of this chapter—it is the benchmark revealed by independent research.[3]

Sidebar: The White and Green World of Results

There are two worlds out there that need to say "success." There is a green world and a white world.[4]

The green world of grass and hills (and cliffs) that most people work in day to day has its own frustrations and challenges. Things are dealt with step by step. This is where work gets done. Ultimately, it is where results are achieved on the ground. The situation on the ground is practical. It works easily, or it doesn't. At this level, an IT project is a success if it helps people do their jobs better.

Above the clouds, the white world of the executives and senior managers is focused on the big picture. It is easy to move quickly. Its view of the reality on the ground can be obscured by clouds. A project needs to deal with this issue as part of project processes.

Success in the white world is about results, strategy, and capacity. However, to get these, the white world has to be effective in the green world. That means understanding and working with it. As it is now. Not as it was or will be. The green world knows if it is "bad down here right now." Or if it is good. The white world needs ways of staying in touch with the reality in the green world.

In the white world, cost cutting is a number to reach. In the green world, it is being let go. Both are stressful. It is often more personal in the green world.

> White world/green world differences create complexity. The IT project may deliver a capacity that allows other business changes to occur—like work being moved to a new location or roles changing. It may be strategically important to the white world. This destabilizes the green world.
>
> If the green world does not accept the new system, many of the benefits are lost and costs increase. IT is often considered part of "what the white world did." Memory will affect how the green world reacts to the next change introduced by the white world. Or by IT.

The project results risk assessment evaluates both white and green world issues.

Addressing these issues takes leadership. Issues identified should be evaluated and assigned for resolution based on the level that holds accountability.

Some issues can be dealt with by the team and the project. Others require accountability at the level of the Sponsor or some other C-level executive.

Project teams should not be held accountable for failures caused by white world policies. The project team is accountable to identify and escalate risks caused by white world policies. The white world must address issues and align white world policies so that the green world can operate effectively and productively.

Issues identified should be evaluated and assigned for resolution based on the level that holds accountability.

If you have already identified factors that affect your ability to deliver results, you should have the courage to:

1. Accept it for what it is and acknowledge that getting results is going to be tough.
2. Raise it to the accountable parties—the Project, the Sponsor, or the Business, focusing on the impact of the factor to achieving business results.

The best way to reduce risk of failure is to spot projects that are likely to fail as soon as possible. Best of all, before they start.

For projects, the best way to reduce your own risk of failure is to assess the risks to your results upfront and get the resources you need to succeed.

For those that would like to move on to assess the risks associated with their own project move on to **Probability** (Parts 2–5), where we assess: What is the probability of this project delivering business results? What are the key risks to those business results?

For those that wish to benchmark their own productivity based on their current portfolio of project results, continue to Chapter 4.

Takeaway

Executives can inadvertently set projects up to fail when they:

- Act as if success is assured.
- Ignore the project "credit rating" and approve projects that are likely to be nonperforming.
- Underinvest in project activities that contribute to successful business results like organizational change management.
- Overlook risks to business results and fail to include resources to deal with these risks in the project plan.
- Act as if the project plan is certain.

Four ways to improve the business results from IT projects are:

1. Publicly acknowledge success is not guaranteed.
2. Assess the likely success rate of the project.
3. Addressing risks to results by investing in organizational change management.
4. Use results-based risk management to fund responses to the unexpected.

IT portfolio governance plays a key role in the delivery of results from projects.

Many of the risks to results are predictable from Day One. They can be reduced.

Endnotes

1 Lowell, Bryan and Claudia, Joyce (2005), ''The 21st Century Organization,'' *McKinsey Quarterly,* No. 3.
2 This planning process need not be complex or time consuming. Back in 1999, I ran the program office for a global contingency planning program that covered over 40 countries. We had to keep it simple and pragmatic for it to work.
3 Gemino, A., Reich, B., and Sauer, C. (Dec. 2), ''A Temporal Model of Information Technology Project Performance.'' *J. Manage. Inf. Syst.* 24, No. 3: 9–44. DOI= http://dx.doi.org/10.2753/MIS0742-1222240301.
4 Analogy thanks to Nick Herpers, a colleague from the Change Leaders and principal of OTV, Netherlands.

Chapter 4
Benchmark Productivity from IT Projects
Evaluating the Cost of Failure

What does failure cost? What is the effect of a write-off, delays, or delivering a little less? How is the real yield of the project investment calculated?

To return to my kitchen project, the functional yield is determined by four factors.

Budget: The initial budget was based on what I could afford to spend and the quotations received. The final budget was what I actually spent including the unexpected extras like the handyman's costs and unplanned dinners out when the contractor delayed installing the kitchen by two days.

Time: Kitchen Builders Pte. Ltd. originally scheduled the kitchen to be ready for delivery in four weeks with a day to remove the old kitchen and replace it with the new kitchen. The implementation schedule slipped by two weeks and took two additional days.

Functions: The original design was largely respected. The quality of the bench top was reduced from granite to Formica. They also reduced the scope by failing to deliver two shelves.

Perceived value: As the customer, my expected experience was one thing and the actual experience another. I was frustrated, inconvenienced, and felt overcharged. However, I got value from the new kitchen. The new layout is better. I enjoy cooking in it more so I cook more often.

Overall, actual functional yield from the kitchen was less than expected.

Projects can be evaluated in a similar way by considering these four elements.

A positive functional yield means a project is contributing more than it cost. A negative yield means the project cost more than the value it is generating.

Let's look at these in more detail.

Elements: Collecting Your Own Data

Funds Budgeted and Spent

Funds budgeted and spent are the financial resources committed to the project and can include:

- Staff salaries and benefits including any up-skilling required;
- External contracts and partners;
- Space;
- Hardware, software.

Your Data:

Average budget overrun: ______________

What is the *average budget overrun* for projects in your organization?

For a full list of project costs see **Fold 2—Case** where the investment side of the business case is assessed.

Time

There are several ways in which time has value for projects:

1. Average delays to the duration of projects;
2. Cost of delay to business opportunities;
3. Cost of funds.

Delays in Duration

Time in the context of projects has three components, each of which affects the final value achieved in the business:

1. How long it takes to start the project—once the need is recognized.
2. How long it takes to complete and implement the project—the schedule.
3. How long it takes to the project to achieve business results.

Your Data:

Average schedule overrun: ____________
This impacts duration.

What is the *average project schedule overrun* in your organization?

Most projects count schedule overruns based on the project duration that the business and the project team agreed as part of the project plan.

If a project delivers early, the business has more time to get value from it. If a project delivers late, then time to get value is lost.

Cost of Delay—The Value of Time to the Business

Time is money, yet few projects or project decisions consider the cost of time as part of the return. Time has value that contributes to projects:

- A function that has high demand in the marketplace has a higher value than one that does not. The sooner the function is available, the more competitive the business can be.
- A function may save business costs as it replaces manual work, and reduces errors and rework. The longer the business has to wait for the function, the longer these (higher) costs are borne by the business.
- A function may improve business information and quality of decision making. For example, if you are a business and you don't know how many customers are paying you late, it is difficult to manage cash flow. Functions that provide early warning of changes in payment patterns are valuable. The longer the project takes to deliver, the longer problems continue to occur.

It is possible to build some very sophisticated calculations based on time. For many organizations, it is sufficient to recognize that time has value and to use a rule of thumb to recognize this value.

Rule of Thumb:

Time costs of delay are often 25 percent of the project cost.

This is a hidden cost factor arising from lack of availability of the intended functions.

A project should have a payback period based on the results it is meant to generate. Delays to those results cost money. Few wish to actually calculate the actual costs that the project saves each year.

Those who prefer a simple rule of thumb use: "time benefits" of the project are worth 25 percent of the project budget.[1]

Cost of Funds

Money costs! Many projects don't consider the cost of the money invested. The funds come from somewhere—a bank, equity issues, or other forms of debt. Fortunately for most projects, this is something that the CFO and the finance team manage.

In investment terms, the project should generate value equivalent to the cost of funds. Seeing that many projects generate both financial and nonfinancial value, the returns from the project can be considered acceptable as they are approved by the project sponsor and steering committee.

Project delay adds to the cost of the project in that the capital invested in the project is not earning its expected return.

Functions

Your Data:

Average functional delivery by projects: ___ percent.

Projects deliver both financial returns and nonfinancial returns. Some of these will be specifically enabled by IT; some may require other support. The key thing is that there is a set of functions or capacities that the business expects as a result of the project.

On Functional Variations

It's tempting to say that no variations to scope should be allowed. Scope changes add to project risks and costs.

In practice, this needs to be taken with a pinch of salt and reality acknowledged. While there are sound project reasons to freeze requirements, since it is difficult and expensive to build to a shifting target, there are some circumstances where unfreezing scope is clearly appropriate:

- When a function is new, unknown, or complex, it is very difficult to get it right. Some experimenting and learning should be expected and built into the project. Prototyping, agile, rapid application development, and other methods are all useful for getting a sample to the business so that they can touch it and feedback. Few people can fully visualize something they've not experienced—and as much as "fixed" requirements are preferred—they may not be possible in that type of environment.
- Projects that take a long time to deliver—the real world has moved on, and business needs change. It's sensible to prioritize functions that have the greatest impact/demand first. Be prepared to review and adjust. Factor this into the budget.
- Weak functional specification. This is a different matter—it's not reasonable to expect someone to read minds. Nor can a project team reliably estimate project budgets and schedules if the goals aren't clear. *Solution:* clarify and document requirements properly.

From the point of view of the functional yield, poor requirements or goals are the same as a poor review of an investment. If what is expected is not clear, or is not reasonable, or is not based on a sensible risk review, then the project will fail.

Reductions affect the functional yield either by not providing expected functions (like my kitchen shelves) or by reducing quality (like my bench top).

Perceived Value

Customers have perceptions of what they got. In customer relationship management terms, the questions that need to be answered are "Are they satisfied?" and "Would they recommend us to other potential customers?"

In project terms, is the business disappointed with the results? Are the capacities being used? Did the business find the project experience pleasant?

Perception of value matters.

Your Data:

Average level of business customer satisfaction: ___ percent.

Sidebar—The Art of Shaving—The Value of Service Over the Product

Back in the Good Old Days of the manufacturing (or product economy), manufacturers used to say, "Build it," and they will come. Henry Ford offered cars in any color as long as they were black.

In today's service economy, most of the value is in the service. The value of physical assets is often significantly less than the value of the intangibles for most companies.

Why is this mentioned? Projects often overlook this major area of value.

Laurie Young writes about the factors that contribute to the successful transition from a products company to a services company,[2] and he shared this shaving story with me.

Yes, shaving. Men spend a vital part of their life shaving their face, and worry if they did a good job, or if they look scruffy. Gillette has made a healthy profit from this over the last 100 years or so. Yet, in most places, the price of a simple razor is around $1, or a fancy blade may go for $4. Even if a man changes blades every day, there is a limit to how many blades Gillette can sell and the profit they will make.

Then there is the Art of Shaving barbershop. "Ahh," said Laurie, who had clearly enjoyed his shave there. Set up with all the modern conveniences, it includes aromatherapy and the peak of the old-fashioned art of shaving. This is the manly equivalent of a fantastic facial. The Royal Shave sounded spectacular—$55 at the time of writing: personal service including a freshly sharpened strop blade.

This is Service. It marks the service premium that a good experience commands over an "okay" or poor experience.

If an IT project was evaluated in this way, what sort of shave would it be?

- A shave with a blunt razor in cold water?
- A Mach 3 shave?
- A Royal Shave from the Art of Shaving?

Service is about increasing the perceived value of the experience. After all, the result is still a shaved clean face, but the man who has received a Royal Shave is much more satisfied.

Service is an area for potential competitive advantage for IT service providers and project teams.

The Functional Yield in Reality—A Window into 3 IT Portfolios

This is where we actually do the numbers to see the overall effect of write-offs, under delivery, being late, over budget, and the quality of the service experience in business terms.

For those who like benchmarks—this is the performance reported by large groups of IT projects across many organizations. It represents the current state of the project management profession.

For those who wish to maintain ostrich-like innocence (in the political field this is called "maintaining plausible deniability"), skip the rest of this chapter and do not read Table 4.1.

Tables 4.1 displays three sets of IT projects evaluated by independent researchers. The data is rounded to highlight overall levels of performance rather than details. The service experience is considered "okay" for this benchmark.

TABLE 4.1
The Good, the Bad and the Ugly

Profile	**IT Organization 1 *The Ugly***	**IT Organization 2 *The Bad***	**IT Organization 3 *The Good***
Star projects delivering 20% extra	—	—	10%
Cancelled projects that are written off	30%	20%	10%
Remainder:	70% of projects	80% of projects	80% of projects
Average Cost Overrun	+90%	+40%	+10%
Average Functional Shortfall	–40%	–50%	–5%
Average Schedule Overrun	+120%	+80%	+15%
Real Functional Yields Achieved:			
Real Functional Yield (RFY) (rounded)	–80%	–60%	–20%
For every $100 invested, the return is	–$80	–$60	–$20

The functional yield of the IT investment in each case was negative.

Most organizations would be proud of the performance of the Good Portfolio, yet even this had a –20 percent RFY. The other two portfolios, the Bad and the Ugly significantly underdeliver with negative RFYs of –60 to –80 percent.

As investments go, these portfolios would need to show strong contributions to business goals to be considered acceptable.

As an executive who cares about performance, even identifying one major project that falls into the "Ugly" category has substantial business value. Early identification of a "Bad" or an "Ugly" project allows proactive use of the Keep, Kill, or Reconsider decision and lifts the overall business results from projects.

These three portfolios are benchmarks. See Table 4.2 for sources.

TABLE 4.2
Benchmark-Based Portfolios

Profile	IT Organization 1 *The Ugly*	IT Organization 2 *The Bad*	IT Organization 3 *The Good*
Portfolio	1	2	3
Based on	Standish 1994	Standish 2003	Sauer 2007
Reported by	Executives	Executives	Project Managers

Given the dates, the efforts to introduce widespread project management practices have paid off. The more recent projects show reductions in project write-offs, cost, and time overruns. That is good news.

Most want to dispute or deny this range of results. This is why it is better to get your own data and evaluate your own results track record.

Would you like to calculate the functional yield of your projects? See Appendix A for more details on the process.

What was the result of your functional yield calculation?

__________ percent.

Few leaders evaluate the project portfolio from the perspective of an investment portfolio. Most executive and project managers will evaluate a single project. The full portfolio is eye-opening. A 10 percent write-off does not seem so much until it is put in the broader perspective of the total portfolio. A delivery variation of +/− 10 percent in time, budget, and functions seems good until it is considered in the light of an NPP cost.

Remember that whatever results you find—and it may be that your own data is similar to the IT projects above—the fact you are looking at it puts you ahead of other organizations.

It takes courage to face the facts.

If your results track record is like those above, you are normal. This may not be good enough for you. Real successes are preferred, not results based on doing less badly than the next guy.

Every project attempts to succeed. If failures are normal, then the problem is not the individual—it's a systemic problem in the organization. This is good news—there are many opportunities to improve results.

You may choose to share a results track record with others. It may inspire you to focus on your project on being the greatest success it can be. Use **Probability** (Parts 2–5) to assess the results risk of your specific project.

Takeway

The functional yield on benchmark project portfolios is substantially lower than most executives expect.

By paying attention to the functional yield, results can be improved:

The first step is to acknowledge reality and assess the track record of the organization and projects in delivering results (in the next chapter).

The second step is to assess specific projects to identify if they are in jeopardy of failure (**Probability**).

Leadership requires courage to face reality.

Endnotes

1 Twenty-five percent as a rule of thumb is based on the general practice of businesses depreciating IT software

and hardware over three to five years. This implies from a financial perspective that the value of the software and hardware is extracted over that time period and it (the application) will be replaced after about four years.

2 Conversation with the author during his launch of "From Products to Services" in 2009.

Chapter 5
Diagnosing Productivity Health

Some would call this a benchmark—I call it a diagnosis—this is about **your** projects, not someone else's. It's **your** health that counts—not the guy next door's high blood pressure—and your health needs to be compared to a benchmark.

The Results Diagnostics

A diagnostic is a method of collecting data in order to assess the health of a patient—or a project.

Sidebar: On Health

Doctors are aware that health is the result of a combination of factors. Medical research has identified various indicators that are known to be associated with immediate or long-term health issues. A doctor collects a variety of data when you visit. They generally collect your current symptoms and a history, and order tests to obtain additional data. A good medical practitioner also investigates how you are feeling—your mental health.

Health is a matter of perspective. Some people say they are healthy if they don't have a cold and can get up to go to work. Their motivation and fitness maybe are low causing a lower quality of life than they could have. Others are super fit—they can win competitions. Yet they may be using resources that are hard to fix or replace. Many athletes find their joints wear out and require surgery in their middle years. Everything was fine before, but now major intervention is required.

We are familiar with general health factors for ourselves—that health is a combination of genetics, nutrition, mindset, exercise, and lifestyle. Organizations also find that a combination of factors affect their health.

For IT, productivity is the measure of the overall health of IT projects. In the previous section, we used the real functional yield to baseline the current productivity from IT projects. This was a top-down assessment of health.

In this chapter, we evaluate productivity health from the other perspective—the core components of project results. This diagnosis focuses on the core components that generate predictable, accountable results from projects.

Project Health Factors

Key factors associated with productivity growth from IT projects are those factors related to the success and failure of business results from those IT projects.

Summarizing the factors discussed in previous chapters:

- Project management and an experienced project manager;
- Organizational change management and an experienced change manager;
- Effective results risk management;
- Distribution of project success (the NPP rate);
- Business's perspective on the project:
  - How the business experiences the project
  - The need for business to contribute to generating results, since some factors are in the business's control
- PAR—are the results predictable and accountable?
- Are results of this investment probable? (See Parts 2–5.)

It all comes together to profile the productivity your organization gets from IT projects.

This profile is valuable. It is the company track record for successful projects and is a predictor of future success for your next projects.

Project Health Check

You've read the statistics. Projects often disappoint. Your own experience may concur. This may suggest that the project failure rate is costing your organization productivity.

Other people's data is interesting. ''Aren't their results dreadful!'' some say quietly to themselves.

Some leaders reflect, ''I wonder how successful our projects really are. Can I afford to continue at this level?''

For those who would like to evaluate their own data, use the following health check for Productivity From IT Projects.

If your project health is fine, great; your only decision is whether you'd like to be healthier by identifying actions to further lift the results and ROI of your project. For sick projects, action is recommended in the chapter ''Take action to lift success.''

When you read these sections, use your pencil. Write in the book. Work out your own initial estimates in the margins or on the back of an envelope.

The diagnosis has caveats:

> ''The diagnosis includes statements and recommendations. It is not a substitute for a professional assessment.''
>
> ''If your assessment identifies areas that may be of concern, contact a trusted professional who can do a full diagnosis.''

Data allows you to see the reality.

> Traditionally, in China, people paid a doctor to keep them well and stopped paying if they fell sick—quite a different approach to health and vitality.

This is about your organization, your business, and your results. Not someone else's health.

You can also complete this diagnostic for your project portfolio.

Use of Good Practices

What happened in your business with a recent important project? What were the actual business results after implementation of a recent important project?

Instructions: Put a tick in the appropriate box based on your experience in your organization (Table 5.1). Get verification by asking other people in the organization. Perceptions of ''how often we do this'' can vary significantly across an organization. These differences in perception are important. Survey tools to facilitate Project Success Diagnostic data collection and analysis are available from www.successhealthcheck.com.

TABLE 5.1
How Often Do You Use Good Practices?

Frequency/Discipline in Applying This Business Practice to IT Projects	Project Management	Organizational Change Management	Results Risk Management
1. Rarely—what is it? We leave it up to the individual project.			
2. Occasionally—it's suggested.			
3. Regularly—it's encouraged.			
4. Most of the time—it's used with varying degrees of rigor.			
5. All the time—it's how we do things. We track and monitor to ensure it occurs.			

Net Experience: Paradise – Jungle = _______

Is the left column the normal business practice? Typically, it is. Results are about more than the numbers.

This is your track record for applying the disciplines behind success.

Recognition of Business Experience with Projects

How many of the adjectives below fit your business's experience with projects or transformation? See Chapter 4.

Instructions: In Table 5.2, circle the ones that apply most frequently.

TABLE 5.2
Jungle or Paradise?

Jungle	Paradise
Slow	Timely
Frustrating	Fit for need
Disruptive	Enabling
Unproductive	Empowering
Expensive	Investment
Nightmare	Dream
Workaround	Works
Write-off	Results as planned
Unpredictable	Predictable
Difficult	Responsive
Total Circled:_____	**Total Circled:**_____

This is an assessment of intangible ROI, of the service experience delivered by the project.

If changes from IT projects feel like a jungle, they require more energy. There will be fewer successes. This has a cost in hard financial terms, in speed to market, in customer and partner relationships, and in employee morale and turnover.

Is the "nightmare project" a one-off event? Or is it more normal than you would prefer?

A one-off failure is one thing. A regular pattern of failure, even if it is only 10 percent of your projects, is something else.

Tangible Project ROI, or Hard Productivity Gains

Assess: How much have you spent on projects and related changes for this project or major program?

External costs: (a) ________ (cash paid out to others)

Internal costs: (b) ________ (value of all resources used)

How many projects/initiative/changes does this represent? (c) ______

Average project cost: (a + b)/c = (d) ________

Overall improvement to business observed: (e) __________ (these should be verifiable by financial or key metrics)

Net results: (e)–(d) _________

Is this a positive number or not?

Convert this into a percentage: ROI = [(e)–(d)]/(d): ________
Grade it in Table 5.3.

Many organizations don't calculate this regularly. It is a common blind spot and is one of the reasons why results don't get delivered.

TABLE 5.3
Grade Yourself

Grade	ROI Range	Implication
1	ROI is less than –15 percent	A real loss
2	ROI is between –15 and –3 percent	A marginal loss
3	ROI is between –3 and 3 percent	Essentially neutral
4	ROI is between 3 and 15 percent	A marginal gain
5	ROI is greater than 15 percent	A real gain

A range is suggested that reflects the reliability and robustness of your data. It is easy to install false confidence in data by attributing accuracy when in reality reasonable estimates are what is available. Project ROI in a business case should be a reasonable estimate. Projects that deliver within three percentage points of zero are essentially neutral while projects that delivery substantially over 12 percent (the 15 percent) are distinctly good or bad. Refine your ranges as your PAR improves.

Project Health Diagnosis

If you've done these assessments, then you've completed an initial health check of your IT project productivity.

In summary:

- Project Tangibles: Actual ROI?
- Project Intangibles: Jungle or Paradise?

What do you see? Signs of health? A flourishing organization? Signs of disease? Of struggle? Of stagnation? Or is it same old same old?

Get Your Data Together

If you've done the assessments on the previous pages, summarize them in Table 5.4:

TABLE 5.4
PAR Components

Business Scan #1 Assessment		Rating (1-5)
1 Use of Good Practices for Project Results	Project Management	
	Organizational Change Management	
	Results Risk Management	
2 Recognition of Current Project/Business Reality	Paradise—Jungle	
3 Actual Project ROI	ROI Category	

These assessments are powerful. They review the reliability of process (1) and the reliability of the outcomes (2) and (3). A fourth is included in Appendix B for a CIO cross-check.

Assessment 1 reviews the means—how a project gets results. It focuses on the reliable use of project management, change management, and results risk management. Project results are rarely repeatable without these disciplines. If these are not used reliably, it is rare to find strong accountability for process or results. Project results are also rarely repeatable without these disciplines.

Organizations with successful project track records usually rate all areas 4's and 5's. Those that report 3, 2, or 1 have increasing rates of project failure.

Assessment 2 reviews intangible elements of the means and the outcome, the ends. Organizations that regularly report that business benefits are successfully achieved from projects lean to the qualities of paradise rather than a jungle.

Assessment 3 focuses specifically on the tangible, financial elements of the outcomes.

When **Assessments 2** and **3** are combined, the health of the project and overall productivity from IT becomes clear (Table 5.5):

TABLE 5.5 *Health and Productivity of IT Projects*

	Basic ROI—Negative	Basic ROI—Positive
Paradise (+)	Project is strugglng	Project is thriving
Jungle (–)	Project is dying	Project is struggling

Everything you find in these assessments is good news. It puts you ahead of the competition—most organizations and projects don't take the time to reflect and don't have the data for action.

Project Health Diagnosis Summary

Based on your organizations track record (PAR components in Table 5.4), is project success predictable? (See Table 5.6.)

TABLE 5.6 *Diagnosis Summary*

Are good project practices applied at level 5?	**Yes/No**
Is ROI 3 percent?	**Yes/No**
Is it Paradise?	**Yes/No**
Is the track record for results at 4 or 5?	**Yes/No**

If they are all Yes, then the IT projects are PAR. Success is probable.

If not, then results are not reliable or predictable and unlikely to be positive.

Framing the Diagnostic for Decision and Action

Given your assessments, would you say the track record of the organization makes this project (or portfolio) highly likely to succeed? Might succeed? Or is it likely to fail?

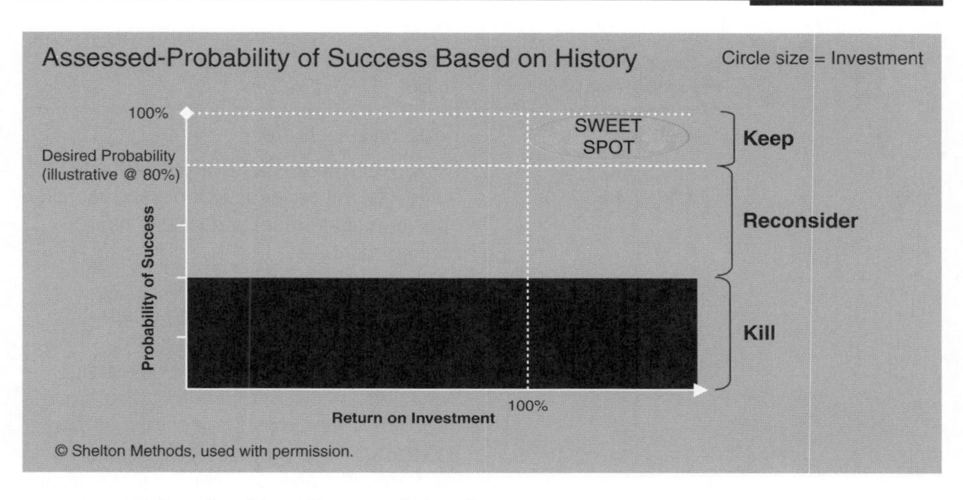

FIGURE 5.1 Mapping Your Expected Result

Use Figure 5.1 to map the probability of project success and the investment.

Draw a circle whose size represents the size of the investment. Locate the circle on the diagram based on:

- Horizontally: the ROI (return on investment) Negative, Neutral, Low, or Strong may be enough if you do not have detailed data at hand. A project should deliver sufficient results to cover the investment. Otherwise, the returns are negative.
- Vertically: the probability of success based on the track record. Highly likely to succeed as the organization delivers projects at PAR (all Yes), probably succeed (mixed), or likely to fail (mostly No).

Your decision and actions depend on where the project sits on the Results Probability map. Refer to Table 5.7 for the next step to take in improving the overall business results from projects.

If this project is using the same general approaches and practices to project management, resourcing, skills, funding, organizational change management, and results risk management as other projects, it is most likely to deliver the same way as the rest of projects in the portfolio unless it is specifically doing

TABLE 5.7
Project Health Diagnostic Action

Location on Results Probability Map	Action
Sweet Spot	**Keep** and celebrate!
In Top Band and Outside Sweet Spot	**Keep**—consider what might be done to lift the ROI by improving use of organizational change management and results risk management.
Middle Zone	**Reconsider** the project. Resources are scarce, and cynicism abounds from repeated failure. Don't waste capital (Rule #1 of investing). Don't needlessly contribute to corporate cynicism. If the project is required—it may be strategic or a project that is necessary for some regulatory or license to operate—complete a detailed diagnostic of the risks to results using Part 2: **Probability** and develop a risk management plan for the identified risks to results.
Black Zone	**Kill** it off. Put it out of its misery. Re-allocate resources to projects where success is probable.

things differently—like managing risks to results proactively. (See Table 5.7.)

On Results

IT projects get business results when IT meets the needs of the business executive at the operational level of the business—the white and the green worlds. If the intangible assessment of Paradise/Jungle is negative, this flags a critical area for project attention for both the white and the green world.

Acting to Lift PAR

PAR is about Predictable, Accountable Results.

Based on your results, consider:

1. *Accountable:* Is accountability for both tangible and intangible results clear? Are both business and IT fairly accountable for direct and indirect contributions to the overall success of achieving business results from the IT project? Do the necessary governance processes operate for effective keep, kill, or reconsider decisions?
2. *Predictable:* Regularly occurring results are predictable. Once expected outcomes occur regularly, there is a basis and a reliability on which you as a leader can really plan and deliver on substantive strategic change through IT projects. You have the confidence that IT can deliver its part of the equation.

Does the track record show that the results are consistent with your expectations? Consistent negative results are repeatable (and predictable), but not good for productivity. Is there a level of consistency that can be relied upon?

If productivity growth is the aim, *all* the assessments must be operating at a 4 or a 5 rating. Ratings of 1, 2, and 3 mean that processes are not reliably used and positive results are not reliably expected.

If processes are reliably used, yet results are not reliable, look at the quality and discipline used by these two processes. There is a world of difference between project management, organizational change management, and results risk management being done well or poorly.

Organizations that don't use project management rarely can track what's going on, where it's at, what has worked, or what hasn't. Project management is a fundamental discipline that is necessary for delivering accountable, reliable, predictable productivity growth.

Organizations that rarely use organizational change management set themselves up for failure and negative ROI. Few projects deliver business results without people behaving and doing things differently.

Organizations that rarely use results risk management are unable to assess the probability of success early, invest capital in risky projects, and are rarely able to reformulate projects to address risks to business results.

All three are necessary conditions for successful productivity growth from projects.

Results

Are the intended results occurring for specific projects? Are those generated as a result of several projects delivering their components to a bigger picture? Are both tangibles and intangibles delivered?

What does the business perceive?

What do IT and the project teams perceive?

Both need to be satisfied with their results and processes, or else the business won't get the results they want, and the project teams will burn out.

Lift Project Performance by Addressing the Failure Rate

The most effective way to lift performance is to identify the projects that aren't likely to succeed and apply those resources where they can do some good.

This takes sensitivity. People on the projects are working hard to create success. Those who set up the project intend to succeed. The organization that will use the capacities of the project requires success.

The reality is that projects and organizations are often not set up for projects to deliver results. Thus change and transformation fail. Strategy fails.

Given the intent, assess the likely success of projects AND look after the people. If you don't:

- People will actively avoid future projects as poisoned chalices to their career and reputation.
- The organization will play games to create or hide projects.
- Business cases will display feats of creative hope, rosiness, and unrealistic expectations to get funds.

Addressing failure rates and turning this into success rates is an organizational change—treat it as one. Both the white world and the green world will require attention.

Takeaway from Productivity

Business productivity growth is a result of an ongoing series of changes ranging from physical technology to M&A to mental technologies.

Independent data suggests that the vast majority of IT projects fail globally. They fail in the United States, in Europe, and in Asia. Only 7 percent deliver or exceed expectations, whereas 93 percent disappoint. This is consistent with the results reported by M&A projects.

The functional yield shows the impact of this IT project failure rate on a company's productivity. The Project Health Diagnostics provides a health check of productivity from IT projects. Many IT projects and portfolios deliver negative returns.

Action can be taken to improve success rates:

1. Admit success is not guaranteed.
2. Recognize the cost of accepting results that are a little under, a little late, a little over budget as not good enough. A NPP rate is costly.
3. Invest in reducing the risks to results.
4. Explicitly use results-based risk management to fund changes in the plan.

PAR is about predictable, accountable results. This requires considering:

- The project and the capabilities it delivers.
- The business context—the business capacity to get results from project capabilities.
- The mind game of the players.

Based on your track record, what is your expected project result? How does it compare to the benchmarks at the end of Chapter 4?

Does history suggest that the project is likely to succeed? Does it suggest that the project is likely to deliver results?

Business results and productivity from projects are lifted using results risk management (see **Probability**).

As an IT professional, as you read this book, you'll see that some of the issues and questions are addressable at the level of a project. Others require action by someone outside the project's official sphere of accountability. These need to be escalated.

As a business executive or CFO, the financial implications of project successes and failures are crucial. The capital implications are critical.

1. **Keep** a project that is likely to succeed.

   If a project is unlikely to deliver business results, there is a choice to make:
2. **Kill it:** Don't do the project. Allocate the capital to a project that is more likely to succeed.
3. **Reconsider:** Reformulate the project so that risks to results are addressed with adequate funding, accountability for resolution, and action.

As a CIO, the ability of IT to contribute to business results continues and becomes even more certain when IT increases its track record to deliver business results from project.

As a proactive project manager, you must manage for results as well as for delivery.

Part 2
Probability

93 percent of IT projects fail at some level

33 percent spectacularly
60 percent by just a bit
7 percent of projects are stars

Which is yours? What will you do about it?

Chapter 6
Talent Scouting—Spotting Success Early

100 Percent of Projects Intend to Succeed

In Part 1, Productivity, we explored the cost of projects not succeeding—the obvious costs of outright failure and the creeping incremental costs of delivering a little less, a little late, and a little over budget. Methods were to measure project performance. Benchmarks from other portfolios of IT projects were shared. The benchmark shows success is not normal.

Given the opportunity to benchmark your own productivity performance, are you satisfied with your current project performance? With the current productivity of changes? From here on, we focus on Results Risk Management™ data and diagnostics to identify potential successes, so you can invest resources in success rather than failure.

By spotting talent, the projects that are likely to succeed, you can focus on ensuring they do. And you can do what is needed to address risks of failure.

Here is the process of Results Risk Management in a nutshell:

Step 1: Assess the probability of project success. There are eight indicators of project success and research-based diagnostics to support this.

Step 2: Take action. There are three options, called "Keep, Kill, or Reconsider."

1. ***Keep*** projects that are likely to *succeed*.
   Recommended Action: Congratulate the team for a good project set-up. Pay attention to the project as it progresses so that it continues to succeed.
2. ***Kill*** projects that are likely to fail.
   Recommended Action: Don't do the project. Kill it off.

   Fall back: Only use this fallback for license-to-operate projects. Invest in reformulating the project for success and then proceed. If the project was likely to fail, it has a significant number of hurdles, each of which takes attention, time and resources to overcome.
3. ***Reconsider*** projects that are *likely deliver a little less than expected, a little late, a little over budget*.
   Choice:
   a. Leave it as is or
   b. Reformulate it so that it can really deliver value

   Recommended Action: Reformulate the project so that it delivers real results. Be wary of the choice to leave the project "as it is" as the cumulative costs of "a little" add up to a large NPP ratio.

There are two ways to make this assessment:

1. Use past experience as a guide for likely future performance.
2. Assess a specific project to see if it is healthy and set up for success.

Part 2 of the Success Healthcheck begins introducing Results Risk Management™ along with a short background to the method for diagnosing probable success found in the 8-Fold Path to Project Success. Chapter 7 provides an introduction to the 8 elements or folds in the 8-Fold Path, illustrating the use and value of the diagnostic with an archetypical project. Chapter 8 looks briefly at results delivery processes and maturity models. Project health, like maturity, is a matter of perspective.

Part 3: **Project** focuses on risks to results that primarily arise from the way a project is defined and set up. Part 4: **Presence** focuses presence of risks to results that primarily arise from the business context outside the normal direct remit of most projects. The final chapter completes the results risk diagnostic process with a health assessment. Part 5: **Performance** looks at the next steps you can take on the journey to better business results from projects.

Past Performance Predicts Future Performance

If your organization or the project team is used to delivering projects, then the first place to look for data is the track record.

Does the team or organization have a track record of delivering excellent results?

The project risk profile below shows the experience of most IT projects (Figure 6.1).

Generally industry data on the current standard of performance shows:

- Most projects deliver a little less, a little late, for a little more cost (light grey).
- Many don't deliver and are either very late or over budget (dark grey) or written off (black).
- Only a few projects are stars and deliver on schedule and budget, and meet or exceed expectations (yellow).

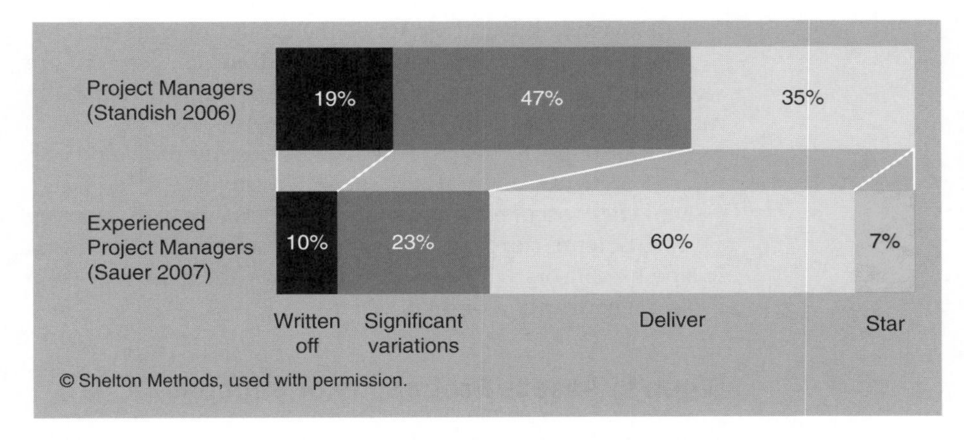

FIGURE 6.1 Project Risk Profile Based on Benchmark IT Portfolios

As a matter of comparison, people who measure mergers and acquisitions say that 80 percent of these fail to deliver intended benefits, too.

If you've completed the diagnostic in Chapter 5 of **Productivity**, you have a benchmark in the form of the track record of your organization. Past performance predicts future performance. If you keep the same habits, the prognosis will not change.

Moving towards the future, we now turn to ''how to predict success'' of a specific project. In practical terms, it is about doing a healthcheck for your project. Is *this project* healthy and likely to succeed? Or is it likely to fail?

Predicting Success

All projects have risks. The question is, are the risks sufficiently managed to make the investment worthwhile? If the risks to results are too great or not addressed, the project is likely to fail: the investment written off, people frustrated.

All Projects Have Risks

Risks are situations that may jeopardize a project's success. Some risks are caused by how the project is set up, others by the way the business perceives it. Some risks are apparent on Day One, while others crop up as the project progresses.

Possible risks to business results from IT projects are wide-ranging. For ease of reference, the most frequently reported risks are summarized in Table 6.1.

Each of these 10 risks can reduce or destroy the value of a project. They can occur at any stage of a project.

Some risks occur early in a project and act as an early warning sign of potential project delivery failure. Proactive PMs and business sponsors will keep an eye out for these and review a project when several of them occur.

When to Assess Probability of Success

Verify the quality of the proposed project investment. Consider the project business case and plan like a business prospectus.

TABLE 6.1
Top 10 Risks to Project Success

Risk Area	Questions to Ask Yourself
Clarity of scope and requirements	How clear is the end state?
Degree of business involvement	Is the business involved? Are they interested? Is there a sense of urgency or need?
Skill, experience, and motivation of project team	Are the right skills available? Is the team motivated to deliver? Do they have the information and tools they need?
Familiarity with the technology	How knowledgeable is the team with the technology? Are they committed to learning what is needed to be effective?
Commitment of executives to business goals that the project supports	How committed are they, really? This is a totally un-Politically-Correct question, but very important.
Appropriateness of planning and estimation, given the goals	How reliable and credible is the project planning and estimation, given project goals and the team's experience?
Executive and staff view of the project in the business	Does the business perceive the project as helping them? What sort of wins does the project bring and when?
Turnover of personnel involved with the project	How many key personnel changes are there on the project?
Volatility of the project charter	How many changes are introduced to project goals, scope, or functions? In the budget? In the schedule?
Volatility of the business	How much will the business needs change during the course of the project?

The best time to improve the quality and returns of an investment is before it's made.

There are four points when a business and a project can significantly reduce the risks to their success:

1. *When the project is set up.* This is by far the most important time to assess probable success—everyone hopes the project will be a success—there is lots of good will and optimism.
2. *When the project is about 10 to 20 percent complete.* This is an assessment of the early track record of the project.
3. *Pre-implementation.* Just prior to implementation, assess if the project capacities are actually up to scratch and whether the business context is ready and positioned to use the project capabilities effectively. Implementation is a major investment. It is a tough decision to kill a project at this stage, particularly if the project has delivered the required capacities, but if the implementation investment is doomed to fail, it is the correct appropriate decision.
4. *At funding gates.* Large projects tend to receive funding in phases. This is a good opportunity to see if the results are still probable. If the business context has changed, the business needs and project objectives may no longer be aligned. The project's track record may suggest significant issues in delivery.

With a business results focus, a set of potential risks are identifiable upfront. Of these, a distinct subset is visible when a project is initiated.

Proactive project managers and entrepreneurial executives will evaluate risks to results; they'll monitor for them—and they will act to address or mitigate them.

When a project is set up, the diagnostics focus on the signs of a healthy project—one that is likely to succeed. Just as high blood pressure is an indicator for potential heart attack, the focus is early signs of results risks. The diagnostics in this book focus on the risks identifiable upfront so that you can proactively manage for success from day one. All of these risks are applicable throughout the project—others arise as the project progresses. Register on the website www.successhealthcheck.com for diagnostics for other stages of project delivery.

Results and Success Take More than Delivery

Most projects focus on delivering the deliverables, not achieving business results. It is like buying a fabulous piece of software and then not using it. Software becomes shelfware.

Shelfware is delivery of a technically successful project that met scope, schedule, and budget. Like shelfware, it may not have achieved a business result.

Tools or technology only add value to the business if they are used appropriately to generate income, improve cost effectiveness, or reduce business risk. If the tools aren't used, business results aren't achieved.

Most project risk assessments focus on delivery.

The Results Risk Management™ (RRM) approach focused on risks to business results. The diagnostic is the 8-Fold Path to Project Success.

The 8-Fold Path—just like the Buddhist philosophy of living—evaluates: how aligned are we to the bigger vision, to the way of operating, to the rules we live by, and to the way we flow with time?

The Foundations of the 8-Fold Path to Project Success

The 8-Fold Path is a framework to assess indicator risks to business results. The version contained in this book focuses on the risks most apparent at project setup and initiation. It is built upon of decades of research by different researchers:

- CMMI, PMI, and Prince II groups, who identify the risks of IT software project delivery to time/cost/specification—the traditional project risks often addressed by the discipline of project management.
- Kotter, PwC/MORI, and others, who identify factors that contribute to success when dealing with the human component of change—these are usually addressed by the discipline of change management.
- Chris Sauer, Mark Keil, and others, whose research identifies factors that affect successful delivery of IT projects and factors that experienced PMs use to help deliver business results targeted by the project.
- Joanne Flinn, whose research at Templeton College, Oxford, and HEC (École des Hautes Études Commerciales

de Paris) identifies factors affecting the success and failure of large, multi-country projects in big businesses. These projects have additional levels of risk and complexity that are often overlooked.

The Complications of Countries

For those who deal with the multi-country, multi-million-dollar projects that many large organizations do, a little more on this. When a project goes multiple-country, complexity goes up.

Research shows that the most common point of failure is the belief that what works in the head office country (usually where the project is approved) will work elsewhere. It won't. As Dorothy once said, ''This ain't Kansas, Toto.'' The technology may be the same. It may be proven and work well. However, the people and business context are different in each country. Projects that assume ''we are all the same'' are highly likely to fail or to require significant additional resources to deal with the inevitable reactions that this copy–paste template approach creates. See Figure 6.2.

Additional sources of risks for multi-country project are found in Table 6.2.

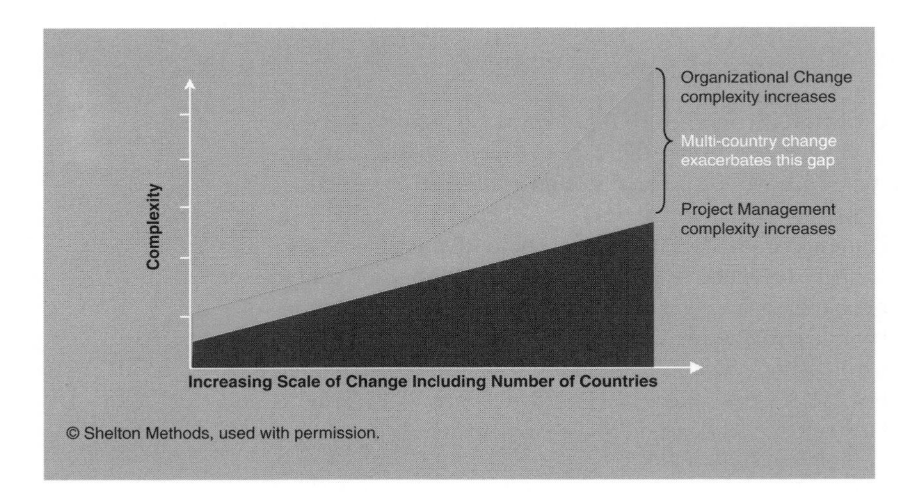

FIGURE 6.2 Impact of Complexity on Project Results

TABLE 6.2 *Complexity and Risk in Multi-Country Projects*

Source of Complexity	Risks Arise from Differences in
Multiple Business Units	Business issues.
Multiple Countries	Laws and regulations.
Multiple Cultures	World views, languages, and approaches to change and leadership.
Multiple Political Interests	Executive and managerial interests (the white world and green world interests).
Multiple Technologies	Integration with local legacy systems, contracts, and operations.
	Complex or new technologies being used to tie the data and processes together. Increasing need for external parties to support technology platforms or business processes.
Multiple Locations	Distance, time zones, not being able to easily meet.

Additional attention and resources are required to work with the extra dimensions of complexity found in multi-country projects. Those projects that choose to control the variations allowed in the technology configuration at the country level must recognize the additional investment required for change in business operations and behavior at the local level. Business operations require alignment of IT systems, people (skills and behavior), and processes to deliver reliable results. A change in one part of the business system will inevitably require change to align other parts.

Dangers in Overlooking the Obvious

Some things are so obvious that they are overlooked. The research made the obvious explicit:

1. Business results come from more than just IT deliverables.
2. Both project management and change management are necessary to deliver business results.

3. Setting up something not to fail is NOT the same as setting it up for success. Not failing is neutral. Success is better than neutral.
4. Projects need to consider the business context in which they deliver, and business context continually changes.
5. Many of challenges to success can be identified before project kick-off. The challenges reflect the way things are normally done by projects or the business.

Behind these was a series of related oversights.

IT projects usually deliver a tangible product like an IT system, yet business result is also the result of elements—like more effective customer service or a measurable outcome like a percentage increase in sales or sales margin.

Yet, the activities that convert tangible capacities of the project into elements of business results are rarely included in the project budget or plan; thus they are rarely done.

No wonder it is common to fail to achieve business results.

The two core professional disciplines that deliver change, project management and change management, have different, related goals:

- Project management delivers "deliverables"—tangible products that can be assessed and signed off.
- Change management focuses on the human dynamics of change.

Yet, it is very rare to find an effective partnership of change management and project management.

Given the goals of the two disciplines, it is obvious that projects require both project and change management. After all, project management helps to plan and manage the journey, and change management helps to influence and prepare people for the new way of operating.

My own research began here . . . just what elements of project and change management did executives find that substantially contributed to success and failure?

I interviewed executives whose responsibilities ranged from country management to the boards of global companies. They operated in Asia, Europe, and the Americas. Their roles ranged from business to IT, finance, HR, and marketing. All use IT projects to improve their business functions. They spoke about the factors that contributed to success and the factors that contributed to failure.

The wider perspective provided by the executives was: Projects are rarely set up for success; usually the view is "not to fail." Executives are getting what they asked for—hoping that a project would not be too painful.

Yet, executives say they want success.

They knew it when they saw it. Each shared their experiences of the dream projects that had stood out above others and what held projects back from regularly succeeding.

The headline findings—what holds projects back from "success?"

1. Project goals are usually technical. They are rarely framed in terms of business results.
2. Project quality processes are often underutilized. The desire is usually to "just get into it."
3. The business context in which the project needed to deliver is rarely considered.
4. Business cases were simplified and underfunded financially, yet optimistic and glowing in potential benefits. Neither part was realistic.

What contributes to successful projects?

1. Specified project goals that are business goals. Goals include intangible elements in the business, not just the IT systems.
2. Projects followed project quality processes:
   a. Business cases and business plans are developed and subjected to thorough tire kicks to test robustness.
   b. Project risk management processes were used to keep ahead of risks to business results. Assumptions were recognized and tested.
   c. Projects and executives considered the human reaction to the change as of Day One. Many considered possible reactions from people before projects were even kicked off.
3. Projects considered the business context:
   a. The IT project is aligned to the current business context of strategy, leadership, and culture. Many IT projects are used

to introduce change to the ways people work. The bigger the gap between the current reality and the intended goals, the less the project is aligned to the current reality. Executives said that *successful projects explicitly recognized these gaps and addressed them as part of the project.*

b. For projects introducing something new, projects specifically recognized the effects of the historical operational procedures and addressed them in the project.
c. Projects considered the organization's history. Organizations and people have memories that affect how they receive particular projects. The project recognized the historical reality, good and bad, and specifically structured the project to work with the issues created.
d. Projects paid attention to the type and volume of changes that affect any one business area or role to reduce team or organizational burnout.

Deeper still, the executives spoke the politics, the silences, and the conflicting interests that stood in the way of projects delivering business results. These too are part of the reality that a project must face for success.

The final finding was that many of the problems that could affect project success were visible and identifiable when the project was set up.

How to Set a Project Up for Success

Many of these "challenges to success" can be diagnosed up front and the risks to business results reduced. After all, when a project is first discussed it is possible to:

1. Assess the goals—are they deliverables or results?
2. Assess the organization, sponsor, and project manager's record of success (or failure) in delivering project results. Track records are early indicators of future performance. Doing the same thing and expecting different results is the definition of insanity.
3. Evaluate the business context and check that the project budget and plans are appropriate for the issues that may be faced.

Otherwise it's like building a house without thinking about the land that it's on. Imagine not looking at subsidence or underpinning. Or building without funding the reinforcements needed to hold walls up against the local climate.

Successful projects did this assessment as part of the decision phase. In many cases, it was done before the project was kicked off.

I've used my research and business experience to develop a structured diagnostic to help lift project results called the 8-Fold Path to Project Success. In management terms this is Results Risk Management™. Think of it like a recipe or the *I-Ching* of project management, harking back to the 5,000-year-old Chinese *Book of Changes*.

The 8-Fold Path diagnostic asks:

- What risks may contribute to failure? How do we spot them, assess their impact, and reduce their impact?
- What factors can help success? How do we spot them and work with them to maximize their impact?

It is a structured way to look at projects being set up for success. Few entrepreneurial executives want to be associated with the sorts of failure rates or write-offs discussed in **Productivity**.

A word of caution as you read. You are likely to recognize many of the risks and challenges. You may say "that's obvious." What it takes to be healthy is well known, yet, we don't always have the disciplines to apply and do what we know is necessary. This is why diagnostics and methodologies exist. They provide a framework for checking that we are not skipping vital steps.

A regional executive for the Asia Pacific business of a well-known fast-moving consumer good was working with the diagnostics and said of one section, "Yes, that is obvious." I asked, "Yes, but are you actually doing this in your projects?" The answer was a sheepish, honest no.

Another executive in a major global investment bank said, "I just reviewed one of about 600 projects that we have, I know the project is going to face problems as it does not deal with the risks to results." I asked, "Are you prepared to begin with a single step? Being disciplined builds step by step. Start with this one."

If you feel something is common sense or obvious, my question to you is "are you doing it? Are you doing it with quality and discipline?" If not, use the 8-Fold Path diagnostic methodology to help your project.

I want you and your projects to succeed. I want to hear about how your teams come and say, "Wow, what an experience." How the business (white and green worlds) say "I'm more effective as a result of your project."

Why Start with Productivity

Before a problem is solved, we need to recognize that there is a problem. To realize that there are alternatives. To realize that it could be better.

If the current project failure rate is acceptable to the business and CIO, then companies and executives won't focus attention on doing projects differently. Bandwidth, attention, and funds are limited. They will question why your project is resourced differently. You are making the active choice to invest in success as this has greater value (financially and in people's motivation and productivity) than underinvesting in a failure.

It helps to explain to a results- or financially-oriented person that the choice is:

a. Invest x with a high risk of failure.
b. Invest x y with a high risk of success.

There needs to be an incentive to change. Part 1: Productivity provides a structure that allows you to raise the awareness of the problem through the cost of the NPP rate and in the PAR assessment—failure is very costly.

Productivity showed how to calculate the costs of the current practices—and to work out the probability of failure based on your historical record. It makes the case for change.

Probability (Part 2–5) provides the basis for assessing if a project is likely to succeed or fail. It also includes a list of the investment costs needed so that the budget is more realistic in supporting success and ROI evaluations more reasonable. See Figure 6.3.

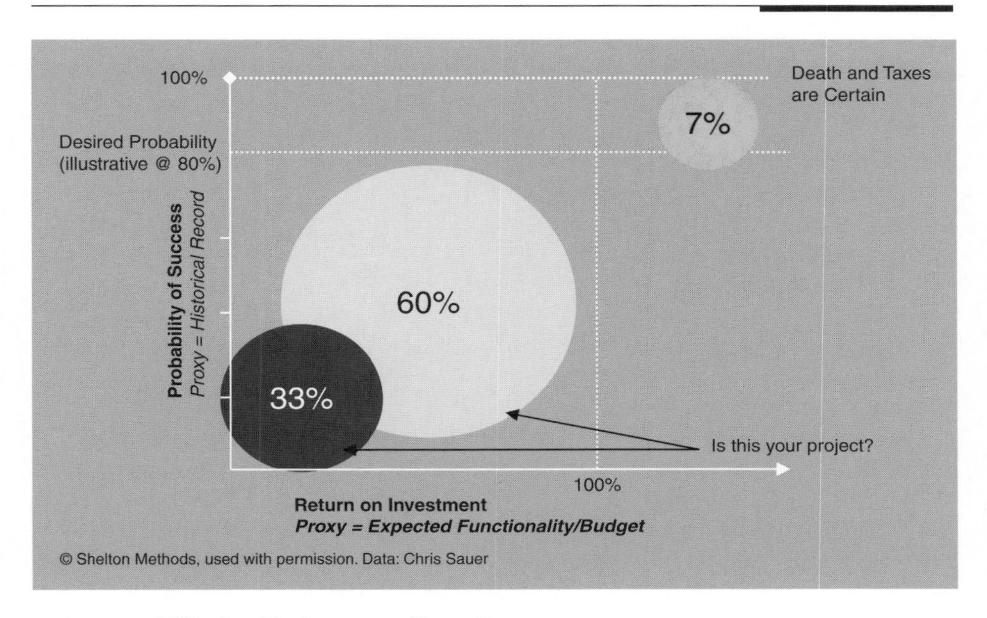

FIGURE 6.3 IT Project Performance Overall

Chapter 7
The 8-Fold Path to Project Success

The 8-Fold Path is a diagnostic framework of the factors that help or hinder a project's delivery of business results.

Simply, a successful project is one that delivers the value the business intended. This means that:

- The project delivers what was wanted, when it was wanted, and for the amount agreed.

  And

- The business uses the capacities delivered by the project to generate business results.

These two statements structure the 8-Fold Path.

Sidebar: How Robust Do I Need to Be?

Some say "Oh, 8 parts, that's too much for me." This is fine. Small projects need a simpler test like a pulse check. Look at Path 1. Intent is Clear.

A project that doesn't know where it is going is like a person without a pulse.

Some projects need more diagnostics, like an annual health check. Others still, due to their size, complexity or criticality, need the full executive health check.

Project provides a risk to success diagnostic for projects like an annual check-up. It focuses on the first 4 Folds to Success.

Presence provides the additional diagnostics needed for the executive health check. It focuses on the remaining folds.

The 8-Fold Path begins with the project **intent**.

1. What does the project intend to achieve?

   This is a combination of tangible and intangible results (outcome) and the project's interaction with the business (process).

   To adapt a phrase from Performance Management, "If it's not stated, it won't happen." If the intent is fuzzy, it's easy to miss or to have different interpretations of what's wanted.

Next there is the robustness of the process that delivers results.

2. How robust is the **business case**?

   Project decisions, particularly "Do we do this project?" depend on the quality of the business case. There are a wide variety of elements that need to be covered if the decision making is to be based on good data. It's like applying for a loan; yes, we'd like it to be simple and easy, but the bank needs information to see whether we are likely to repay.
3. How reliable is the results delivery **process**?

   This is about the process that delivers results in the business. Many organizations make simplifying assumptions to ease project planning. Not all of them hold true. The assumptions, if unverified, create a gap between the reality the project faces and what it does. It's like assuming a path is smooth, when the reality contains detours or pits. If you know about them, you can plan around them; if you don't, it is a bumpier journey than expected.
4. Will people be **motivated** to accept or reject the project?

   Few IT projects can deliver results if people in the business or if customers refuse to use the capacities provided. What is the "rejection" risk?

The final stage of assessment is the presence of results risks arising from the broader business context in which the project expects to deliver:

5. Are the factors needed for success **aligned** with the business's strategic context?

   Most projects intend to change the status quo. It's rare to do an IT project to simply replace a function with no change. The business results from the project come more easily if the factors that generate change go with the grain of the current business direction, leadership, and business culture.

6. How will **operational** policies affect project results?

   There are policies in IT, finance, and HR that were developed for good reasons to manage the status quo of the business. As an unintended consequence, some of these policies can make it harder for projects to achieve results.

7. How will the **flow** of business history be addressed?

   Every project faces the history what's come before it. This history includes memories, good and bad, of projects that have succeeded spectacularly or failed dreadfully. As the project progresses, events will occur that affect its capacity to deliver business results. A project's business results depend on its ability to keep up with the flow of events.

8. What is right **balance** between change and stability?

   Each project adds turbulence into an organization. This turbulence is necessary for change. But with too much turbulence, people find they are overwhelmed by change, and they become less effective. Too little, and the organization stagnates and loses its capacity to adapt easily to new circumstances, and it falls behind. A project that pushes too fast or not fast enough affects its business results.

The Results Risk Management ™ healthcheck (Table 7.1) in the 8-Fold Path to Success focuses on:

TABLE 7.1 *Coverage of the 8-Fold Path Healthcheck*

Assessment	Purpose/Outcome
Clarity of **intent.**	Clarity of the intended results of the project
	Awareness of the intended results of the project
Robustness of business **case.**	Completeness of investment requirements
	Risk and mitigation for results delivery issues
	Qualitative assessment of project plans, budget, and business case.

(continued)

TABLE 7.1
(Continued)

Assessment	Purpose/Outcome
Reliability of results delivery process.	Maturity of a monitored process to measure results Maturity of an accountable process to measure results Use of simplifying assumptions that regularly undermine results
Motivation is energized.	Project is aligned with motivation to move White world–Green world alignment
Alignment to strategic position.	The pressures on the project that result from the strategic context of the business The degree to which the project intent aligns with the current strategic context
Operational controls support project intent.	The extent to which IT, people, HR, and finance practices may help or hinder project results The impact of the cumulative effect of misaligned operational controls on project success
Flow of history favors the project.	The hidden traps that come from the history of the organization that could affect project results Identification of those business units most likely to be at risk
Balance aids project success.	Evaluates the potential for sudden changes in the tolerance of change in the business Identification of those business units most likely to suffer from change burnout and thus jeopardize project success

What Does This Look Like?

Business results come from a project when both the project and the business work effectively together to achieve the intended goal. Visually, the diagnostic report represents the risks in two parts (Figure 7.1).

The left-hand side shows the health of the project side of the results, while the right shows the presence of risks from the

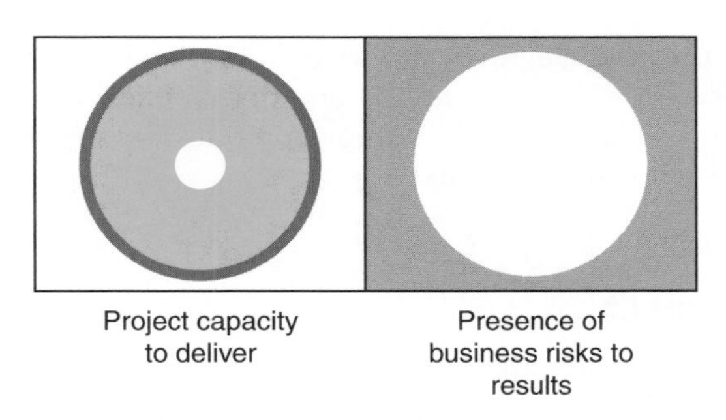

FIGURE 7.1 A Project That Is Likely to Succeed

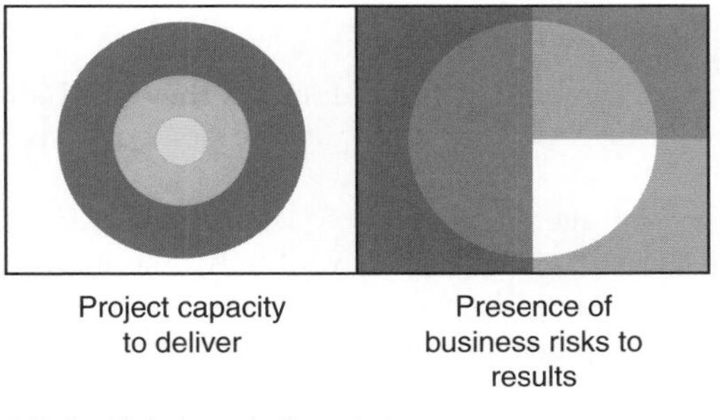

FIGURE 7.2 A Project That Is Unlikely to Succeed

business context. A project like this is clearly healthy. It is likely to succeed.

Contrast it to Figure 7.2:

The intended goal is not clear (the white dot in the project is almost invisible). The grey of risks outweigh the gold. The business context is dark.

This project is unlikely to be successful.

An Archetypal Project

Before we go into each component of the 8-Fold Path in depth so that you know what to look for, let's look at how an archetypical project uses the diagnostic framework to assess probable success. The project in question is one that applies a traditional technology that has helped improve productivity in small businesses for several millennia.

The Project

''I want to buy a donkey,'' said John.[1]

His companions were surprised. ''What on earth for?! What would you do with it?''

''I'd give it to a village.''

''Don't be silly, John, what would a village do with a donkey?''

''They'd use it.''

''But don't they have all the donkeys they need already?''

''Maybe not,'' said John. ''I'm sure someone could use a donkey.''

John loved travel, he loved people, and he loved adventure. He studied and travelled, and eventually, like many explorers before him, he found Kashgar.

Kashgar. A place of ideas, of wealth, of people. Trade routes, markets, a giant melting pot of people, of ideas, of culture, of technologies over the centuries. Kashgar was old when Alexander was Great and his men marched through on their way to India. It was old when Genghis Khan's younger brother led the Mongols through the Silk Route. And older still when Marco Polo passed through Kashgar and its surrounding villages.

There are many markets in Kashgar, including the largest animal market in Central Asia. Horses that race across the steppes. Camels that trip across the deserts. Pigs that rummage in the mud. And donkeys. The traditional beast of burden. Those carriers of what is needed.

In Kashgar, a donkey is useful.

John and his companions talked some more. What would they really do with the donkey?

One of them had an idea. ''What if we give the donkey to several people so they can share?''

''Yes! That's great, then it's not so much work for any of them, but they can use the donkey when they need to.''

"So, how do they decide who uses it when?"

Gosh, this one donkey was getting more complicated than they thought.

"But I still want to buy a donkey! And I want to give it to someone who really needs it," said John.

"Okay, so, who really, really will get the most from the donkey?"

"Why don't we ask the village elder? He is likely to know who is in need."

They consulted the village elder. He'd met John before and knew John was familiar with the village.

"A donkey?" he asked. "Who would need it the most?" He thought. "There are several widows here that could certainly use the strength of a donkey to help them carry firewood. But they don't know how to look after one. That's a man's job. Giving it to just one could create envy and resentment in others in the village."

"Perhaps there is a man who could have the donkey and lend it out to the women when they need it?" one from the group suggested.

"Hmm," said the elder. "That's a possibility. Mr. Khan is steady, responsible, and he already has a donkey. So he knows how to look after one, and he has space for another. He is well respected. And the women trust him. They'd go to him to ask for the donkey when they needed it."

"Great!" said John, "We can buy the donkey! It's going to help people, and we can enjoy the market."

John and his friends went down to the market. They soon realized there was more to buying a donkey than just going "That one looks nice." They learned from the donkey broker how to look at a donkey and to see how strong and fit it was. One of them learned how to judge a donkey's personality. Stubborn and grouchy wasn't the sort of donkey they wanted. They did the health checks and made sure the donkey had had the jabs it needed to prevent local diseases.

They'd realized the widows were poor and had limited funds. They added enough money to feed it for a year. Donkeys eat.

They negotiated and bought a donkey. They took it to the village.

Mr. Khan was a bit overwhelmed. The donkey was a responsibility, a compliment but a responsibility. He was concerned. As a pious man who thought deeply about his soul, he asked the elder, "Is it permissible to accept gifts from outsiders? Are they believers?"

John looked at his companions. None of them had considered this. "Yes," he said, "We believe. Maybe not in the way you do. But we believe in the goodness of the human spirit."

The elder nodded then told Mr. Khan to take the donkey.

The widows looked on, wondering, "What will this new donkey really mean for me?"

• • •

Stories like this usually stop at this point with "and they all lived happily ever after." But business is not like that. It continues.

Many IT projects begin with a good idea. IT is often a great source of new ways to improve productivity.

In this short story, it was John's idea to give a donkey to a village. To help. A simple idea. A simple change. Yet one with complex ramifications.

To achieve real business results, the village had to learn new skills, change roles and expectations of people, and consider additional budget expenses like feeding the donkey. For the change to succeed, it also had to deal with people's psychology, beliefs, and history. John, the elder, Mr. Khan, and the widows each had their own history and concerns that affected how they responded to the donkey.

A project is usually declared a success when the donkey is delivered.

From the business perspective, the project is not yet successful. Results have yet to be delivered.

If the project was reviewed to assess its probability of success, we would find that results were not certain even though the project been well thought out and well managed up until this point.

8-Fold Path Results Risk Assessment

The pre-implementation review of the Donkey Project using the 8-Fold Path diagnostic framework would have found three areas of high risk. (See Table 7.2.)

TABLE 7.2
Donkey Diagnostic

8-Fold Path	Donkey Project: Short Assessment	Confidence in Achieving Results
Right Intent	Goal was clear: a new healthy donkey for a group of people who could benefit from it: the widows.	Good
Right Process	A well thought-out and executed process that incorporated the key elements of project and change management.	Good
Right Case	A reasonable assessment of the project costs and its run costs after implementation. A decision that the investment was appropriate. Funds were available to see it through to completion.	Good
Right Motivation	It would appear that the widows' lives would be better. The skills and social issues behind the acceptability of the donkey in the village were considered and addressed.	Good
Right Alignment	The village elders knew John and knew their villagers. It was consistent with what they wanted to see happen in the village. Leadership was aligned, and it was handled consistently with the local cultural norms.	Good
Right Operations	It is not clear if this is consistent with other practices in the village.	**Unknown**
Right Flow	It is not clear if there is any record of how the leaders will follow up and see that results are delivered as expected or if resources will be reallocated to other priorities.	**Unknown**
Right Balance	It's not clear whether there are other changes going on that put pressure on the widows or Mr. Khan.	**Unknown**

One of these unknowns could undermine the project's results. Fortunately, once John or the elders realize that these factors could affect the intended results, they can check to see if there may be issues that affect the potential business results.

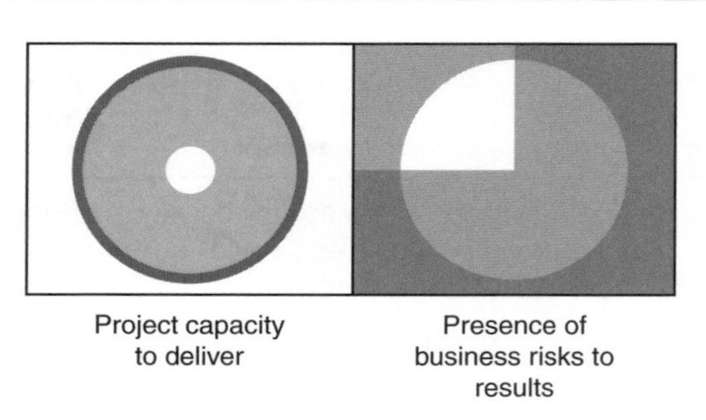

FIGURE 7.3 8-Fold Path Assessment: The Kashgar Donkey Project

Diagnosis

The project's probability of successful delivery is high, while the probability of business results is moderate. This is shown visually in the diagnostic summary in Figure 7.3.

There are risks in the business context that need to be addressed if long-term business results are to come from this project.

Opportunity Lost

For many businesses, IT projects feel like the Donkey Project. There was potential. Yet there were not necessarily results.

Someone spots an opportunity where technology can add value. They do something about it. Money, time, energy, and passion are invested.

A potential is created—a new idea, a system, a direction. Then it dissipates or is under-used.

The investment is lost.

Doubt and even cynicism begin, particularly if the failure was high profile or affected many people.

Then additional effort is needed to deal with that negativity.

This becomes a project cost for the next project.

What Are *Your* Real Results?

When implementing IT projects, getting business results can have the feel of an adventurer putting on a pith hat, saying, "Go there,'' ordering the luggage bearers into a line, and then sending out scouts to find a path through the wilderness.

Business leaders want to see those results. They anticipate these results as part of their business plan.

All IT projects' purpose is to deliver business results. Yet the medical phrase ''the operation was successful but we lost the patient'' can describe the reality. Technical delivery successful, business results not achieved.

All projects say they will succeed. They won't. Assess the risks to the project in the same way good medical practitioners assess risks to a patient before surgery.

Trust and Verify

A project is initiated because you trust that it will deliver results. The 8-Fold Path is your process for verifying that successful results are probable.

Endnote

1 A real story—yes, it did happen. A group of Westerners were traveling through Kashgar in 2006. One had done the research for a Ph.D. thesis in that region, and the rest is history. Or in this case, the gist of the story. Yes, names of individuals are changed. A picture of the donkey can be found on the Success Healthcheck website.

Chapter 8
Business Results Are a Process

You've got smart, diligent people in the project teams. They are working hard. They are enthusiastic. They are experienced. They use well-respected project management methodologies. Your project sponsor is a leading panther in the ExCo pack. You use business cases sensibly. The project team understands priorities and strategy. They are a partner, not a millstone. Military analogies and sports metaphors fly around to keep it interesting.

Projects are delivered.

Yet results aren't.

"Easy change" seems to be an oxymoron.

The process that delivers results also needs attention. It needs to deliver predictable accountable results, too.

A key step in the process of reliable delivery of results is the recognition that the delivery of results can be seen as a process.

If the occasional project delivers success, for the business it is like the random luck of winning the lottery rather than good practices and discipline. The latter is referred to as the maturity level of a process.

Results Delivery Process

The Results Delivery Process works alongside normal project management processes. It focuses on the results. If projects operate a business benefits realization process, the results delivery process adds to maturity, reliability, and the results actually delivered (see Table 8.1).

The more frequently results delivery processes are used as part of the business's project management approach, the more predictably success is achieved.

TABLE 8.1
Phases and Processes

Project Phase	Critical Result Delivery Process Actions
Conceptualization: The idea of "what we want," vision, or goal definition.	Evaluation of the idea, initial business proposal, key areas affected,[1] anticipated funding approximated.
Initiation: Approval to proceed, resource (people, $) allocation, accountability accepted.	Business case completed, qualities of goals set ("we will know we have achieved it when . . . "), anticipated funding estimated by phase. Initial results risk assessment and mitigation plan completed along with "As Is" situation.
Blueprint: Design of the results delivery plan, identification of dependencies.	Blueprint (the "building plan" for functions) and their dependencies over time. Includes: Meaningful release packages for the business. Use of methods like RAD and Agile to bring IT's delivery of benefits forward. Business capacities required. Be explicit about the business testing required and the needs. Multiphase plans including foundational needs aligned to business priorities and timing. Multilocational/country issues addressed. "To Be" design completed.
Development: Project builds or acquires the capacities needed.	Monitoring of current reality. Consider if qualities and capacities are still appropriate, given lead times and any changes in current reality.
Testing: Project tests and proves the capacities are ready, at the appropriate quality to be deployed.	Risk assessment of quality of deliverables as well as the business's readiness and capacity to extract value from the new capacities.

Results Achievement: Project deploys capacities in the business.	Introduction of new capacities to the business. Monitoring of results, refinement of capacities and deployment process.
Completion: Project teams close out work and hand over to "business as usual."	Key results of "To be" evaluated, learnings identified for future programs.

Maturity

IT folk are familiar with the concept of maturity. Maturity describes predictability, the reliability of a process delivering its intended product.

In project terms, maturity affects:

1. The reliability of a project delivering.
2. How effectively project resources are used.

Sidebar: Maturity and Reliability

The higher the maturity, the more reliable the delivery process is, both in the way it works and in the results it delivers. The original maturity models were developed at Carnegie Mellon. There are now several different models addressing different components of technology delivery. These days, maturity models are found from software to people management to innovation.

There are "negative" maturity levels. These occur when either the business or the project team is sabotaging, cynical, or distrusting. Stephen R. Covey calls this "the tax of distrust."

The positive side of maturity is like the process of growing up.

The eager stages are pre-puberty. These are all about being heroes—preferably rescuing maidens or fighting dragons. The bigger the crisis, the better. Dramatic for the hero, but not very reliable for the business.

There are the teenage years of some reliability and the adult years of reliability.

The 8-Fold Path is a risk assessment diagnostic that supplements maturity model processes.

Poor results are often an indicator of immaturity of the results delivery processes.

Maturity and Results Deliver Processes

A results delivery process provides structure. It allows a project to pick what it focuses on now.

Maturity-based structures were used in **Productivity** to assess three fundamentals of success:

1. Reliability and quality of project management.
2. Reliability and quality of change management.
3. Reliability and accountability for results reflected by project governance.

The business's track record is the first place to look. It is what is likely to happen again—unless deliberate steps are taken.

If the results delivery process is showing signs of immaturity, consider this an ongoing tax on the ability of projects to delivery predictably and reliably. Consider addressing it.

Endnote

1 This is an organizational change management evaluation of the capacity of the project functions to deliver value in the business given its currently reality.

Part 3
Project

The indicators of project success identified four risk areas:

1. The clarity of the intended goal.
2. Inappropriately simplifying assumptions about the process needed to get results.
3. Business cases that omitted key necessary investments.
4. Ignoring the motivation (or lack thereof) to change as and when the project would be implemented.

The next four chapters look at the risks to project delivery that are assessable up front by the project team or by the project management office.

Because these chapters are diagnostic in approach, they do suggest action. They recommend cross-checks. They ask questions.

They all help you get data that allows you to draw a conclusion in respect of the specific indicator. Is the project healthy or not?

When you summarize your insights, you'll have a diagnostic that looks like the ones on the next page.

At this stage, in **Project** we assess risks primarily arising from the project context. The risk assessment of the project focused risks are shown on the left hand side while Part 4 **Presence**, focuses on risk arising from the business context (shown on the right hand side).

Project capacity to deliver

Presence of business risks to results

© Shelton Methods, used with permission.

or

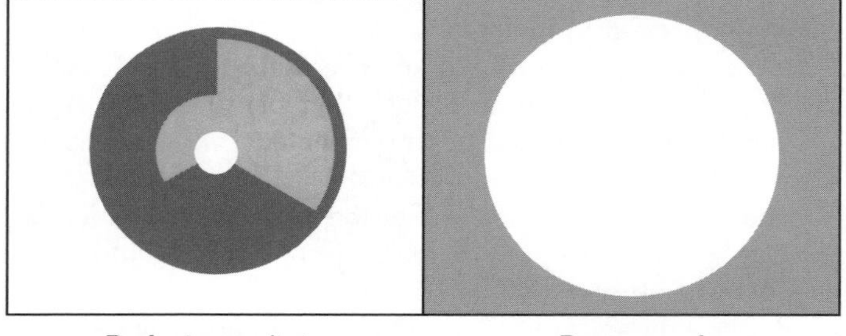

Project capacity to deliver

Presence of business risks to results

© Shelton Methods, used with permission.

Assessment: Highly likely to succeed.	**Recommendation:** Reconsider project set-up.
Presence of business context risks not assessed.	Business context risks not assessed.

You will also have a list of risks to your business results.

Let's get into the next things we need to look at to see if the four project folds are healthy:

1. Intent is clear.
2. Business case is robust.
3. Results delivery process is robust.
4. Motivation is energized.

Chapter 9
Fold 1, Intent Is Clear

Intent. A deliberately broad concept. The opening question to the 8-Fold Path to Project Success is "**what do you intend?**"

The clearer the intent, the easier it is for the IT team, for the project, and for the business to:

- Understand what is required of them;
- Understand the changes that are needed;
- Identify the capacities that need to be built;
- Recognize what is acceptable as it currently stands.

Eight Elements of Intent Contribute to Success

1. What are the tangible outcomes intended?
2. What are the competitive positioning outcomes intended?
3. What are the intangible outcomes intended?
4. What are the short-term intentions?
5. What are the long-term intentions?
6. What qualities do you intend the process of the project and change to have?
7. What are the intentions in respect to each stakeholder?
8. What are the intentions in respect to external, global issues that affect the big picture of business?

Results Are . . .

IT projects have a **tangible** result—a physical IT system and the information it produces. The financials.

They also have an **intangible** result—a business outcome. It might be bottom-line results. It might be a strategic capacity.

There are unintended results—a frustrated or an unsatisfied organization.

Most reasonably-run IT shops can deliver an IT system that fits the stated requirements. Yet the business does not declare the project a success. The IT system works one way; it may not be how the business works; the project may require new skills or bandwidth that is not available. Tangibly the IT system is there. It works. Yet the intangibles don't.

Intangibles determine success in the eyes of the business at both the white world level of the executive and green world level of the shop floor that operationally delivers results.

It is like going to a restaurant. It's not just that the food served was what you expected. Did it live up to what you had wanted? Flavor, service, ambience. . . .

Many projects have tangible results: a financial outcome, a business acquired, a shift in average customer value.

Many more have intangible results. Ones that determine if the project is a success: a vision acted on, customer satisfaction, employee morale, shareholders, or owners who are satisfied with the company's performance.

Return on Investment Implies Results

What sort of results are you looking for?

Are you after financial results? Or other results?

If they are not stated, they won't exist. This is as true for tangible results as it is for intangible results.

Results Are Clearly Specified

If the intended results are not clearly specified, they will be misunderstood.

It helps to have other parts of the organization read them and say what the words (or diagrams and pictures) mean to them. Interpretation occurs. Check what they are.

Let's use a rice farm as an example. It is a simple business organization. There are lots of them. Rice farms are the backbone of many an economic system.

If you are like any farmer, you have goals that reflect your intent for the year's harvest. The farmer's more detailed goals include:

- Getting the rice to market;
- Number of seedlings that germinate;
- Getting the field prepared for the new crop;
- Cost of inputs and the price received for the rice;
- Yield from the rice field;
- Overall profit for the season.

He may include other goals like:

- Whom he involves in the harvesting party;
- Seeing skills developing in selected staff so that they are better able to help him for the next harvest;
- Quality of the rice wine he makes on the side;
- Having the time and energy to take his daughter to her coming-out party.

After all, being a successful farmer is about more than just producing a rice crop. The farmer's results will be a mix of financial and other goals.

A farmer has a plan for all the different things he wants to achieve with his rice farm during the year. As a farmer, he's naturally dealing with projects—seasons and weather create a continuously changing environment, while market pressures put constant pressure on the farmer achieving higher yields and productivity.

Generating Results

There are three ways that value can be generated:

- Financial;
- Competitive capacity;
- Intangibles.

All of them imply that the business side of the organization has to do things differently. After all, bottom line, the business gets money from the customer. The business creates the inflow.

IT projects generally enable a business result. They are rarely in the position to be fully responsible for a business result—this also depends on business decisions and business actions.

Financial Results

There are three[1] core financial value drivers[2] managed by the business:

1. Revenue increased;
2. Costs saved;
3. Time to market.

How specific is the project about these? Are they documented in the project charter or project plan? Do they say exactly where, how, and when? What are they dependent on? Who is accountable or owns this result? What assumptions are necessary for this to hold true? What is the implication of a change in the economy?

Table 9.1 displays typical tangible results:

TABLE 9.1
Tangible Results

Tangible Results	Examples
Increase Revenue	Customer representatives increase their sales by 5 percent.
Reduce Costs	Cost of sales decreases by 5 percent due to automation saving staff time.
	Costs reduce due to reduction in errors and rework.
	Customers can complete a process without using a sales or support person (costs of time to complete the process are transferred to someone else who is not on your books or balance sheet).
Time to Market	Service response is 50 percent faster.
	Straight-through-processing or online processing delivers "instant" response or service. Being first in the market with a killer application or service or new product.

Each of these can be quantified in terms of the business impact expected.

These are all about getting to the ultimate bottom line, Profit and Loss, the Balance Sheet, and Cash Flow Statements. This is when shareholder financial value is created.

Check that the project plan or project charter has clear answers to these questions. Are the assumptions behind the results projections credible? How sensitive are the results to changes in the economy?

CASE STUDY

FROM REAL LIFE

Khen Meng reviewed the CRM business case. It was well developed. Each of the seven different businesses that were part of the project had identified operational and financial KPIs. Six months into the project, there was a major economic downturn. Khen Meng identified which parts of the business case were dependent on upcycle assumptions. Then Khen Meng identified new functional priorities that suited down-cycle conditions.

Results from Competitive Capacity or License to Operate Requirements

Projects may be done so the business has a strategic choice—hard revenue/cost figures are not expected on each program.

Strategic capacities facilitated by IT projects could include:

- Development of software-enabled business capacity.
- Building an IT function in the interest of creating a strategic option.
- To cut off the competition by being fast in the market.
- Building capacities and teams to swiftly and effectively integrate a strategic growth path based on mergers/acquisition and their integration.

Required capacities vary depending on the actual business strategy.

Delivery of license-to-operate requirements driven by regulatory bodies and legal requirements also add intangible value.

What are these specifically?

CASE STUDY

FROM REAL LIFE

Thomas reviewed the recommended set of projects arising from a scenario-planning strategic program. He found that 80 percent of the recommended actions and thus the IT initiatives were common to most scenarios. This provided the basis for prioritization and definition of the core IT program. This also helped the selection of the specific project actions that were unique to specific scenarios.

Intangible Results

Intangibles are an increasing percentage of corporate value.[3] Projects play a critical role in contributing to the growth (and destruction) of this value. Few projects outside of marketing explicitly define outcomes and results in this area. IT should.

Yes, many of the intangibles require business action if they are to be achieved. If the need for them is not recognized and accountability for them is ignored, then business results won't result. That is failure.

> *What gets measured gets done.*
>
> —an accepted maxim of business, usually attributed to Peter Drucker

The practical corollary of this phrase is that what is not measured is not done or not done consistently.

Leaders who recognize this get specific about:

- Quality and process effectiveness;
- Employee morale, learning, and innovation;
- Organizational vision, direction, and values;
- Qualities of customer relationships.

Each of these has been associated with long-term corporate success. They are lead indicators of bottom-line results.

If they are not included as part of the project objective or ROI, they just aren't done. They are not part of the project's desired outcomes.

They are invisible. They become nonexistent.

"Paving the cow path" is an IT phrase. It means to automate an old process without substantially improving it. Quality and freshness of milk in the local market are not affected by paving a cow path. Challenge the value of just paving a cow path.

CASE STUDY

FROM REAL LIFE

Donald was head of operations in a major international retail bank. Mimi was CIO. They were concerned with an IT transformation program that would jeopardize his business. They added a project ROI a metric of "Zero operational problems on Day One." That is what they got. Unlike the other 16 countries facing a similar IT transformation. The other countries each faced hundreds of thousands of dollars of operational costs after implementation.

Note: Assumption: there is an intention for the project to get results. This usually requires people to do things differently. Few projects are solely about implementing a process or vision or IT system as such. It is about achieving the business result—the actions taken, the effect on performance.

If this assumption does not hold true, consider challenging why the project is being done.

Intentions of the Project Process

An IT project does not exist on its own. Project teams work with the business or customer in several ways to:

- Refine what is to be done (scope and requirements);
- Identify the trade-offs that may be required (cost, time, function, risk);
- Quality assure the product (testing);
- Refine the product based on the business experience of using it (early on through the use of prototypes, or as part of implementation and software change releases);
- Use business staff who are often key experts or members of the project team (project staffing).

A business and the project team may have easy interaction, or it may be frustrating. The project could burn out the team in one phase at the expense of later phases where staff resignations add to results risk.

The qualities explored in the Jungle/Paradise assessment in **Productivity** are very relevant. They described the quality of the experience that the customer has with the project: in this case, the business with the IT project. Each major party to the project may like to describe the qualities it considers most important to their process satisfaction.

Like going out for dinner, priorities may vary based on what you need. Speed of service matters some days but not others. A surly waiter may or may not be important. Cheap may be more important than quality for one meal but not for another. Predictability of staff usage may be more important in some periods but not others for the restaurant manager.

See further in Chapter 11, Fold 3: Results Delivery Process Is Reliable.

Intended Time Frame for Results

This is not about how long it takes to get the intended result. It is about how long you want the result to last.

Long gone are the days where "cheap = breaks down" or "expensive = lasts." In the manufacturing area, Sony and other Japanese companies showed us that cheap and reliable go together.

So too it is with projects. How long is the result meant to last? It may be that a single quarter is all you need. It may be that the particular project is to deliver something you would like to see last for several years.

Say so.

If a project is short-term, then make it clear how the longer-term solution will be found and implemented.

Intended Quality of Result: Quick Fixes or Strategic Change

Some projects are meant to be quick fixes. They are Band-Aids to deal with a current issue. The sad thing is that, in many cases, the Band-Aid stays on and is not replaced by either a better fix or by healing the underlying problem. Over time this practice leads to an IT environment and business processes that are complex. Complex as in messy. Often they don't need to be.

In IT, tactical responses tend to add to the spaghetti ball of systems interactions. Tactical responses are rarely consistent with the IT architecture. It's the old contradiction of a short-term fix.

If you have a bigger picture that you are building to, such as a particular business strategy or IT architecture, that broader goal needs to be reflected in the project.

The project intent needs to be explicit. Is it working within the framework of that broader plan?

Is the intent tactical or strategic?

Do keep in mind that many tactical changes make it harder to achieve the strategic objectives if they are not consistent with the strategy/architecture.

Intended Impact to Stakeholders

Many projects focus on the delivery of the goods—the tangible factors covered earlier. Other consider the quality of the experience—will it be a dry shave or a royal shave?

Successful projects consider what is in it for all stakeholders. The project evaluators work out their intent so that where possible, it is a win, or at least neutral, for each stakeholder.

Successful project managers have learned that it takes only one small group of people to be against a project for results to be reduced.

CASE STUDY

FROM REAL LIFE

Roger was introducing a new IT system to support a process that would link all the departments that served a particular customer group. Many new services were planned. More efficient processes were designed. Two small groups in two different departments, about 9 percent of the staff affected by the project, decided they did not like the new process and reverted back to their old manual system. It took a year to address this problem. A year in which the business results were reduced and delayed.

How does the project expect each stakeholder group to respond? What would be desired? This is the intent. See further in Chapter 12, Fold 4: Motivation Is Energized.

Intent's Impact on the Broader Picture

Many projects focus on factors that are internal to the organization. In this day and age, projects need to state their intent in terms of a broader picture. There are several drivers that push this as part of the success story.

- Integrated supply chains mean that impact on the rest of the supply chain may help or hinder overall business results.
- Partners who supply services.
- Triple bottom-line commitments.
- Big picture environmental impacts.

Replacing hardware implies that some hardware will be turned to waste—that is environmental. Or a new cable may affect a heritage building.

Changes to business practices affect external parties.

Changing business needs affect the services needed from business partners and the supply chain. A project can intentionally have significant impact on these groups that helps or hinders the project results.

Does the project intent consider and decide what it is about in respect to these elements?

See further in Chapter 15: Fold 5, Project Aligns to Current Strategic Position.

Takeaway

If it's not stated, it's unlikely to happen.

Intent is more than a set of numbers. In the end, business results may be assessed as financial. However, there are critical contributing elements to achieve those end results.

The eight elements of clear intent provide a framework for assessing the clarity and completeness of the project's intended outcomes.

Testing Clarity: Will those who need to understand and interpret the intended goals the same way?

> This is a short exercise to experience just what may be required when checking intent. It is easy to have different interpretations . . . and the results are not as expected. How often have you heard "I thought I was clear . . . ?"
>
> An illustrative exercise—here are the instructions. Do it with colleagues or at home with the family. The solution is in an Appendix E.
>
> Take a piece of paper. Fold it into two. On the outside draw three circles in a triangular formation in the middle of the page. On the inside, on the opposite side, draw two circles next to each other. Draw a small circle beneath it and then draw a curve facing upward. Draw a square around them.
>
> We often use words to communicate a concept that may be easier seen or experienced.

The level of detail that is required for goals and visions is often radically underestimated and underfunded. Creative professions do mock-ups and drafts so the customer can see what is planned, not just have to imagine it.

37 Signals and many IT commentators recommend the equivalent in IT projects . . . Agile, RAD, prototypes, use of fourth-generation languages, small builds/releases are well-established methods. It is much cheaper to correct and align different interpretations in a demo than in production.

Warning Signs for Project Objectives and Goals

- They are not clearly documented.
- They are not commonly known. **Test:** Can peers who are not close to the project tell you the gist of what the project is for?
- Are they dull, uninspirational, or hard to understand?

Having established the goal the project intends to achieve, the next step is to evaluate the robustness of the business case. What investment will be required to achieve the intended goal?

Endnotes

1 Those deeply involved in the value field will know that there are seven financial value drivers. I have simplified the ones in the assessment to the ones that most business managers have some influence over: turnover growth, cash profit margin, capital expenditure, and competitive advantage period. The remaining three value drivers are usually managed by finance. These are the cash tax rate, working capital costs, and weighted average cost of capital.

2 The role of "value" drivers is well established by Joel Stern (EVA) in Joel M. Stern and John S. Shiely (2003), *The EVA Challenge: Implementing Value-Added Change in an Organization.* (John Wiley & Sons, Inc.); Michael Black (shareholder value); and Michael Hammer (re-engineering) in Michael Hammer and James Champy (1993), *Reengineering the Corporation: A Manifesto for Business Revolution* (Harper Business).

3 The importance of these intangible results to long-term business results are well established by James Charles Collins and Jerry I. Porras (2002), *Built to Last: Successful Habits of Visionary Companies*, HarperBusiness Essentials and by Robert S. Kaplan and David P. Norton (1996), *The Balanced Scorecard: Translating Strategy into Action* (Harvard Business Press).

Chapter 10
Fold 2, Business Case Is Robust

Results of Investment: What's the Bottom Line?

To be blunt, most projects underestimate the investment required. When projects are unclear on what they want to achieve (Fold 1—Intent Is Clear) and/or weak on the reliability of post-implementation results achievement (Fold 3—Results Delivery Process Is Reliable), the business case is dubious and the decisions based on it are unsound.

Business Case Quality is a result of:

- The results intended (final outcome and the process of getting there. The End and the Means. See Path 1—Intent).
- The Process of achieving those results is credible (if the plan is not credible, results are not likely).
- Resources required (financial, people, facilities . . .).

A business case should focus on the adequacy of resources for success.

The real investment is usually documented in a project business case.

A good business must answer the question "What will it really take to get the results we desire?" This will be a combination of:

- Financial resources;
- People resources dedicated to the project;
- Subject matter experts seconded to the project;
- The business's will to see it through, also called political resources or managerial bandwidth.

This fold focuses on the financial resources. They act as a proxy for the other three.[1] If there is not enough money, then the people and the experts won't be found internally or externally. If there is not sufficient political will, the funds won't be found.

The **test** is "show me the money" or another valued goal.

Sidebar: A BS Detector for Project Proposals[2]

Project proposals and business cases are marketing materials—they have one goal—to convince those who have the funds to part with them for the project. It's up to the reader of the proposal to identify whether it is robust, worthy, and a reliable reflection of future reality.

The truth is that few proposals will say outright that they will fail. I've seen many that I know will fail—the plan and the funding overlooked critical elements of success.

Now BS is not necessarily an intentional outright lie. It's more often a favorable telling of the truth. Possibly with a few unfavorable details overlooked.

Here are eight steps to detecting BS in proposals:

1. Expect it, particularly when the aim is to convince you of something.
2. *On the concept:* Ask, "Why should I believe that statement?" What are the facts? The independent or experienced opinion? The data that supports this? Any due diligence?
3. Ask them to explain it to your intelligent six-year-old. This is a great cleanser of confusion and jargon. If pressed, a ten-year-old will do. If it looks weak in this form, then the BS index is high. Plain English is good!
4. *Consider:* What could go wrong? Is this is the best case? What else could it be? Constructive skepticism.
5. Ask for the devil's advocate. What is the other side of the question? Be curious. There are usually several options—and several sides to any question.
6. *On the Plan:* Kick the tires of the idea and plan. Holes the size of Mack trucks are danger signs.
7. Track record: Do the parties have a record of successful delivery or not?
8. *On the numbers:* Challenge the budget and the assumptions behind it. Use rules of thumb to test reasonableness.

What Is the Real Investment?

There are three sets of investments.

1. Direct costs to design, build, or acquire a capacity so it is ready to use;
2. Implementation costs to deploy the capacity in the business so that it is used;
3. Pollution costs—those costs that are picked up by other business units because of the choices made by this project.

The term ''investment'' is used since this is about investing to get a result—not simply a cost or expenditure for no outcome.

Ignoring any of them shoots the investment component of your ROI calculation in the foot. Costs have been ignored or hidden.

If you want quality numbers, you need a full and honest picture of the investments required. You need a process that generates reliable estimates.

It's about avoiding the ''garbage in, garbage out'' syndrome—in this case, project investment decisions based on inappropriate and misleading data.

Health Warning: When you complete these calculations, you may find the numbers a surprise or even a shock. They often are when you begin to add it all up. It's why some people avoid doing it. It's pain avoidance—in the short term. Writing off all or part of a project is more painful in the long run.

This is why it is good to verify the financial component of the business case.

Quality of Business Case

You can approach this next section in several ways—read it and add ticks and crosses. Or smilies ☺ and frowns ☹ as you consider a particular project or set of projects in your organization. You can get out an envelope and jot down numbers.

Try this as an exercise to make it more relevant. Reading can become pretty theoretical.

Pick a project that you are familiar with.

First, what do you know about how the costs were estimated in the first place? Is the method reliable? Is it reviewed? Is it based on experience? Are estimates completed top down and bottom up against a goal-directed plan? Are they WAGs (wild-assed guesses)?

Evaluating the Business Case Financials

The financials should cover:

- *Direct costs:* What it takes to build the capacity so it is ready to deliver. Some of these capacities are non-IT.
- *Implementation costs:* What it takes to realize value from that capacity.
- *Pollution costs:* Costs passed on to other parts of the business without their agreement.

Use the back of an envelope to calculate these for the project. There are 16 core cost components. Use the long side of the envelope.

Cost Group 1 = Direct Costs

Objective: To get the project to a point where it is ready for delivery: for instance, a house fully built or remodeled. Or a car on the driveway. It includes foundations, walls, plumbing, architects, quality assurance, government inspections, tiling, painting, decorating, and furniture.

Estimate

1. What was/is the project budget for the hard direct costs?
   For example: IT: hardware, software, licenses, customization, communications, infrastructure upgrades, staff, consultants? What is the cost of adjustments to test-beds and pilot/proof of concept environments? What are the resourcing costs? What are the future upgrade implications?
2. What are the costs for data clean-up and conversion?
3. What are the costs for process engineering and design?

4. What is the cost of the business staff and their experts to specify requirements, review documents, test systems, trial processes? What is the cost for developing new training, procedure documents, help, coaching support, role definitions? What is the cost of equipping learning and training environments? What are the ongoing training and qualifications implications? How does this affect recruitment? Can these skills be easily sourced in the local market? What does this do to the number of people required? Does it create new roles? Does it eliminate roles? What does this mean for staff acquisition, retention, and release?
5. What are the costs to buy/lease new space? What are the costs to refit locations, if that is required?
6. What are the marketing/PR-related costs? For example: Marketing: campaign, collateral, agency fees?
7. What are the legal implications and costs of our locational choices? What is the tax impact?

CASE STUDY

FROM REAL LIFE

Fred was evaluating a project proposal that moved the operating location of transactions from one state to another. He'd heard that the "location of decision" could have tax implications. He investigated and found out that the location in which the managers made a decision affected which state would tax the transaction. He included the tax differential as a factor in his Real ROI assessment. This is a process design decision for multilocational processes for Shared Services.

8. What do we need for quality assurance during the process and of the integrated solution prior to delivery? Experts, testing, assessments, quality assurance reviews? How will Front-to-Back or full business process lifecyle tests be performed?

These are the core investments needed so that the business will have the potential of reaping a return.

CASE STUDY

FROM REAL LIFE

Paul considered his project. It was to implement in three different countries; he wanted it to work. He engaged an independent review of the project to identify where it was. The two questions asked were "Is the solution robust for the business? Is the business ready for the solution?"

For one country, the review concluded that the infrastructure would not support the business processes effectively. That country's implementation was deferred until a viable solution could be found.

In another country, the business process created an unacceptable operational impact. The business process and supporting IT application were adjusted to make it more effective.

The third country was fine and proceeded with implementation.

Cost Group 2 = Implementation Costs

Objective: To implement the project so that it operates effectively in the business or with customers. This is like actually moving in, settling, and living in the new house. Or getting into a car and taking it for a drive.

Estimate

1. Costs to physically deploy software, install new hardware, and to set up communications infrastructure.
2. Cost of customer and external communications to align these with the new ways of working.

   The need to communicate with customers, regulators, partners, and shareholders is well recognized. Budget for this should be included in the project budget. So should joint accountability with the business executives responsible for that stakeholder.
3. Cost to be ready and able to operate with the new capacities:
   - Costs to have staff in training, time to progress the learning curve to full productivity (Trained to Productive);

- Costs of relocating, redeploying, retraining, or acquiring staff as required by the business results;
- Costs of workarounds, live data clean-up, and manual reporting;
- Costs of deployment support and staffing.

IT + OO = EOO or the value of being ready to operate

Use the "back of the envelope approach" of average person day rates for your first-pass estimate. Take your payroll costs, divide by the number of staff, and then by 200 days (that's an average number for the productive days you get a year from a person).

Estimate the number of days of training on the basis of 1 day minimum training for each new process or function.

Double it to reflect the learning curve and support time they will need until they are fully productive. This actually is a fast learning curve.

Example: For 8 new functions and processes (pretty standard for a small system) and a set of 200 people affected, with an average on-cost of \$500/day = 8 functions × 2 days until productive × 200 people × \$500/day = \$1,600,000.

Did you just hear someone say "ouch!?"

If people are not trained and effective, then you have:

IT + OO = EOO

IT + Old Organization = Expensive Old Organization.

There is often a temptation to avoid the "ouch" in recognizing these costs.

These costs are ones that require acknowledging. They are part of what it takes to get the business side of the organization up to "trained and productive," which is the practical definition of being ready to operate.

Underinvesting in the organizational readiness component of project success is a key contribution to poor results.

In **Productivity**, we looked at the McKinsey research,[3] which shows that it makes the difference between a 35 percent ROI (i.e., a 65 percent write-off) and a worthwhile ROI of 143 percent (i.e., a 43 percent return over investment). Good organizational change management makes the difference. It takes resources and investment to get this additional ROI.

CASE STUDY

FROM REAL LIFE

George calculated that one large ERP implementation resulted in a 5 percent increase in staff turnover. It cost on average $5,000 to replace a person and to get the replacement up to speed. Across the region, this translated into 1,500 extra people who needed to be hired and integrated into the organization—a cost of $7,500,000. Awareness of this would have justified an investment by the project and the business in staff retention-focused actions.

Implementation costs can easily be three to four times the direct costs of the project. Certain failure, on the other hand, is even more expensive. It is a certain write-off.

Cost Group 3 = Pollution Costs

Objective: To quantify the implications to the business of some of the intangibles of how the project is done. This is about recognizing the hidden costs of poor project processes.

In the perfect world of economic theory, the "best decision" is made, in such a situation; the alternatives are, by definition, worse.

In the real and often messy world of projects and business results, there are various ways in which results can be delivered. Each option has different costs associated with it. The "best" choice for the broader business might not be the obvious "cheap" choice for a particular business unit. A project is often considered frustrating or a failure as it results in costs now carried by other parts of the business. This is pollution.

CASE STUDY

FROM REAL LIFE

Robert reviewed his business results. They were okay, but not as good as he'd expected. He dug into it. Reviewing his staffing plan for the previous year, he realized that a large project had affected his operational area of the business.

The project had originally projected that it would need 0.5 people for 3 months. When he looked at actual resource usage, the project had used 1.5 people for a year and was still running. The project business cases had not considered the support cost of ongoing releases and process upgrades. Robert's business ran lean. The project had absorbed his capacity to do the extras that would grow the business.

The going-in position for projects, should be that the impact of the project on other parts of the business is, at minimum, neutral or positive. If a project introduces a change that has a negative impact elsewhere, it has the same effect as pollution—a negative response.

This is not about risk or contingency estimation. This is about acknowledging the (negative) flow on effects of the project to other parts of the business.

Estimate the costs to other parts of the organization for flow effects:

1. Cost of delay/time in terms of market opportunity, lost sales;
2. Cost of customer retention;
3. Impact on brand and reputation;
4. Cost of unplanned staff turnover;
5. Cost to staff morale and productivity;
6. Costs of operational downtime, delays in operations, and overtime.

Each of these has hard, bottom-line impact.

If a project has a negative impact on any of these, it is a cost to someone's bottom line in the business. It is a cost to the staff whose lives have been affected as well as a loss of customer satisfaction. It is a source of frustration and lower productivity for those involved. In fact, some say the only good point of overlooking these costs is that it is a gift to your competition!

Cutting corners on a project's business case is costly. Failing to fund the activities required to deal with these intangibles is a transfer charge to the line of business that eventually loses productivity when something like this goes wrong.

CASE STUDY

FROM REAL LIFE

Alice was asked by a CEO why the organization should invest in organizational change management for a big project. She calculated the costs associated with data clean-up, of management distraction, and of staff overtime.

The clincher to funding investment was an assessment of potential impact of poor organizational change management to customers in terms of lost business and customer defection under several scenarios:

- Staff "resisting";
- Staff being "neutral";
- Staff "adopting" the new business practices.

As a balancing item also consider the value to other parts of the organization that you create—serendipity and synergy are possible. Only count these in the business case if another part of the organization is really interested and excited by the new possibilities. As a control item, it is good to have them sign off on their interest.

Bottom-Line Value

By looking at these costs and, in some cases, opportunities for revenue, you can express the bottom-line value of making strong business decisions, decisions that are based on a realistic view of what it takes to get successful results.

Business cases need to consider the net impact of the project on the business. If a change requires fewer staff with more systems, it may sound good—until the total cost of owning and managing the system is considered or the change in skills required of staff and the availability of those skills in the local market.

Real business results require a broader perspective, as these real-life situations show.

CASE STUDY

FROM REAL LIFE

Khun Nalinee recommended that the business invest in a full business test for a new IT system. It required everyone in the business to come in on the weekend. The CEO approved it.

Why? Their colleagues in another country had found problems when they had implemented that IT system. It had cost them $500,000 to clean up. Knowing this justified the investment in risk avoidance.

CASE STUDY

FROM REAL LIFE

Hiro-san approved implementing a customer services support system that produced customer letters. Some of the letters were not correct and were sent out. It was considered a level 4 problem meaning that no direct costs were associated with it and a manual process could deal with it. However, the Country Manager had to apologize personally to each of the customers.

Recognizing the social impact of leaving this problem could have justified fixing the problem and saving the "embarrassment and shame" in the eyes of customers—and the time of the Country Manager.

Now, a Secret . . .

Many, many executives know about these costs. They have felt the pain of them. They understand this dynamic . . . but they don't include them in the business case. They rarely formally review and approve implementation as a separate decision. That's because of other aspects in play. The executive is being rational even though he or she is setting the project up for failure.

Yes, it is dysfunctional for the business—all the capital written off, all the employee frustration and cynicism.

Why do smart executives do this? The business context creates the incentives that drive this behavior. See Folds 5 and 6 in Part 4: **Presence**. It is often better to try and then blame failure on some circumstance than to actually set a project up to succeed.

Working Around This Secret

Some Entrepreneurial Executives and Project Managers use risk management processes to deal with pollution cost-based issues because they don't want to jeopardize their business case. That is good. Make sure that funds needed to deal with this risk are available to the project without delay. As sponsor, you'll want to be sure that risk management processes are effective.

If something is foreseeable but not certain, a contingency budget is required so that the risk is mitigated. It still requires recognition and resource allocation.

Key Points About the Business Case Quality

- Even simple businesses like a rice farm have multiple goals for their projects.
- Value is more than money.
- What is ignored won't exist. What is defined as a goal, may.
- Business cases need to be credible—would you take this one to a bank manager for a loan?
- Transferring costs to another part of the business by ignoring the need for those resources is a great way to annoy that part of the business and contributes to project failure. It is polluting.

Project Results Sensitivity

To continue the application of good credit practices begun in **Productivity**, banks ask for lots of information when they grant loans: industry, products, track record of management. They even ask for collateral.

While internal projects funding doesn't usually have such rigor, there is one element that is worth adopting. It is sensitivity analysis to external events. Like an economic upturn or downturn. Or a major competitive shift.

Good banks use industry assessments as part of their portfolio management process.

If an industry is looking as though it may have a downturn (or an upturn), they can simulate the impact on the portfolio. This is risk management in action.

This sort of sensitivity analysis is particularly useful to larger projects.

If it is not possible to do an impact analysis of major changes in the business environment at the project level, it is hard for the project and thus the business to adapt—to keep up with the times. A business needs to choose when, where, and what to reprioritize to get results that are relevant to the changing environment.

The assumptions that the project makes about the business environment should be documented as part of the project plan. Then if things shift, it is easy to see which projects are delivering results that are most likely to be affected and focus in on them.

Takeaway

Begin with the end in mind.

—Stephen Covey

The business case is the beginning. It is the foundation. If it is weak, if estimates are poor or issues avoided, the business case will be built on rocky ground. Poor foundations don't lead to strong buildings.

The Goals, the Plan, and the actual Results must be clearly specified in business terms.

Projects have three phases of delivering benefits:

1. Projects are usually seen to deliver a capacity.
2. The capacity is implemented or deployed.
3. The business applies itself to using it to generate results.

Investment costs and effort are comprised of three parts:

1. Direct costs;
2. Implementation costs;
3. Pollution costs.

Documenting the assumptions behind the business case aids future analysis of the effects of changes in the business environment.

Estimates need to be reasonable and reliable, not an optimistic "if it all goes well." They need to be realistic.

Warning Signs for Business Cases

- ☠ Costs are not recognized.
- ☠ Estimation factors are not credible.
- ☠ Dependencies are undocumented.
- ☠ Sponsors have track record for not attending meetings.

The impact of these factors can be seen on time, cost, and quality in Appendix D.

Endnotes

1 If you are assessing a project that is underway, check these out too. Lack of resources—be it time, skills, bandwidth, or money—all contribute to failure.

2 Inspired by Scott Burkun's "How to Detect Bullshit." http://www.scottberkun.com/essays/53-how-to-detect-bullshit.

3 "Change Management that Pays," *McKinsey Quarterly* (2002).

Chapter 11
Fold 3, Results Delivery Process Is Reliable

Departments are frequently told to keep projects lean. Lean becomes starved when the project is so simplified that it cannot deliver expectations.

In practice, it is irrelevant if the business wants something as fancy as rococo or as simple as Zen. Intent needs to be clear; resources need to be adequate.

If appropriate resources are not available (see Business Case, Fold 2), the appropriate response is to adjust the Intent (see Fold 1, Intent Is Clear).

The next step is to look at the process it is using to get results. If the process is not reliable, then results are less likely to be delivered. If the process is under-resourced, it may be too lean to deliver results.

How Reliable Is the Results Delivery Process?

Many organizations allow projects to fail, because they don't measure or monitor project results. They don't hold executives accountable for the project investments they make.

An investor who makes investments and fails to track performance will be unlikely to succeed over time.

A mature results delivery process effectively monitors project results and provides transparency to the:

- Reliability of the governance process that aligns IT projects to the portfolio and company strategy;
- Maturity of the results risk management process;
- Maturity of the results delivery process.

If results are tracked and executives held accountable for their commitments, fewer projects deliver in the "hero-in-a-crisis" mode.

Simplifications Undermine the Results Delivery Process

"Keep it simple" assumptions are often used to simplify the process of project setup, design, and implementation.

These simplifying assumptions frequently cause problems due to inappropriate specification of the intended goal or the transfer of the real costs of the change to other departments or organizations. The receiving organization, often unconsulted in the project decision, rarely supports the change. The result is failure.

KISS: 6 Keep It Simple Symptoms

KISS is a quest for simplicity.

However, KISS creates simplifications that are not reflective of reality. For example, it only takes three rules to simulate birds flocking.[1] When we try to simplify projects and organizations down to a few KISS assumptions, projects can overlook reality.

Six KISSes, like those in Table 11.1, can be considered project danger signs.

Let's look at these in more detail. They appear simple, but the effects of project results are substantial.

A Vanilla KISS

Vanilla has the appearance of simplicity for IT projects.

TABLE 11.1 *Dangerous KISSes*

KISS Description	Simplifying Assumption
Business Needs = Vanilla	The budget and schedule indicate that a "vanilla" or "out of the box" software implementation is the right choice for the business.
Scope = Functionality	The project perspective and the scope of technology functions are the full solution.
Confidence = Capacity to Deliver	Undemonstrated confidence in capability to deliver and utilize an exciting new technology, which will bring tremendous benefits.
Location = Identical	The business is a single object with minimal variations that can be managed by templates and minor variations.
Plan = Certainty	A fixed delivery date without caveats or flexibility. Negligible or no consideration of "What might happen?"
Delivery = Benefits	Success is the delivery of the physical results, not the business outcomes. For IT projects, this is delivery of systems rather than successful business operations.

Vanilla is meant to be fast and cheap. Buy the package, load the disk, and voilà, there it is. The only little, eenstsy-weeny problem is that it doesn't always work quite as expected.

Ever loaded MS Office that way? I have. It was easy . . . and then I've spent the next few days working out where the functions had gone . . . and wondered why I've lost control of things that I used to be able to control easily. Then I spent hours working out how to get back that sense of being in command—over two days of down time for a power user with an incentive to get over the hurdle.

All this for just a simple application like MS Office.

Pick a complex business program like ERP or CRM or BPM that is costly to buy and more costly to configure to your needs. A vanilla project allows for no adjustments. The business has to adjust and compensate instead. The business picks up the down time of adjustment.

In addition, the business operation isn't vanilla. The cherries and chocolate—may be reports and information that help deliver services to customer segments or allow them to serve other parts of the organization without effort.

The customers may not change their requirements; the regulators still have their expectations. Other parts of the business may not change their needs. How will the operation get done with only a vanilla implementation? A vanilla project may significantly increase the cost to run the business effectively.

Vanilla projects have benefits. The business often asks IT to reduce the costs of building new functions or of owning them. Package applications, be they proprietary or open source, are valid solutions.

The business needs to consider the trade-offs of vanilla projects:

1. *Fast technical implementation with standard functionality.* People often change their practices. The business challenge is: Are these cherries really adding business value, or do they reflect some historical decision which is no longer appropriate?
2. *Effort to change people and skills to suit the package.* Is it more effort to customize the application to meet the business needs or more effort to change the business processes and people to suit the IT package? Which is more cost-effective? Where is customization or configuration critical?
3. *Are all the functions available in the package really required?* Is some of the package decorative functionality? Does the package deliver core, standard functions that your organization requires? Does it provide an easy pathway to higher value services to customers?

Vanilla is not a diet option. Vanilla projects can generate hefty cost transfers to the business when the costs of adjusting the business (people and processes) to using vanilla are not considered.

A typical conversation between the business and the project team:

Business: ''All I get is vanilla?!''

IT project: ''Vanilla is all we can afford!''

Business: ''I was fine with my old system.'' Thinking to himself, ''Without my cherries, it will be so much extra effort and cost to run the business. I am not happy. I've just picked up lots of costs.''

A Health Warning

Projects are always under pressure to reduce cost. The most sensible and obvious method is to reduce the cost of systems and maintenance—an out-of-the box project with no customization allowed. This approach may add significant cost to the business to adjust operations.

The savings of a vanilla project are often a cost transfer to another part of the organization. The implications to ongoing business operations must be considered to fully cost a project.

Scope = Functionality

Take a moment and pick up the project requirements document—the one that says what you wanted—that describes what it will be like when the project is successfully completed.

1. Was it signed off? Who by?
2. Is it understandable by others?
3. Are the non-functional specifications adequately deep?

Sign-off needs to be by an appropriate cross-section of people—those with experience in the business, in finance, in HR, in project management, in change management—to show the requirements design is credible and complete. Does the project documentation consider flow on effects in other business units?

Is it understandable? Would a manager from business or process know what it's talking about? Would your significant other say it makes sense? It takes effort to bridge the languages of business and IT. That's why business analysts are worthwhile.

Few people are mind readers. The requirements, the description of the "future," and the results of integration need to be understandable to:

- Those who wrote them in the first place;
- Those who will build tools and the capacities to support the transitions;
- Those who will use them to operate in the business after the project is complete.

The requirements document often focuses on what business functions are required, but often overlooks business practicalities that drive non-functional specifications like:

- Impact on other business units;
- Effect of job roles, skills, or training;
- Effect on customers or business partners.

The detail in the requirements document should be appropriate for the intent it is trying to achieve. The requirements for a strategic project will be different from a software specification, but all documents must be understandable both to the sponsor/business and to the project team acting upon them.

A project that intends to deliver results defines an integrated solution—requirements that cover people, process, data, and IT systems.

A Health Warning

Documenting and agreeing on requirements appears time consuming. It requires thought, effort, and decision making. Many prefer to minimize it or avoid it.

Project teams can't read minds. If requirements are vague or unclear, the project team will define the scope and requirements that makes sense from their perspective. They may have explained the possibilities to the business, but they may not have the right frame of reference to understand the ramifications of the options.

Use approaches like RAD, Agile, prototypes, usability labs, case-drama,[2] and stories to illustrate what the business will look like when the project is implemented.

Improving Your Success Rate

For Business: Write requirements in your business language. Use visuals and prototypes. Be open to alternative ways of expressing your needs.

For the Project: Add "translation notes" to put business needs into project frames of reference. Footnotes, sidebars, and paragraph references . . . you'll find a way.

CASE STUDY

FROM REAL LIFE

Graham linked roles, process design, and system requirements into a requirements document. It covered premiums, commissions, and payments for a life insurance system. Everyone knew what they had agreed to including the Chief Actuary, relevant lines of business, process, organizational change, and technology teams.

This document provided a basis for a business prototype walkthrough that identified issues, which were resolved upfront (cheaper) instead of late in the testing process (more expensive).

This very successful project was showcased to the Princess and the Finance Minister of Thailand.

Confidence = Capacity

Part of the attraction of working on projects is the opportunity to work on something new. Even if a project team sounds confident, check that there is the appropriate level of proven experience on the project team with people who are respected.

Confidence is not a substitute for capacity or capability. There are big benefits to using experienced project managers, as shown by research data in Part 1: **Productivity**. Project management is a profession with apprentices, journeymen, and masters. Large or complex projects require masters.

An attraction of working in technology is the chance to work with new technologies and their possibilities—a constant stream of new toys. It is seriously exciting and a fertile area for creative thought.

Caution—the excitement factor can add risks to a project. Fear can lead to avoidance. Consider technology choices dispassionately:

1. An exciting tool or a software may or may not be appropriate for the business.
2. An exciting technology may not mean the project team or the business has the capability to use it effectively.
3. Uncertainty about a technology does not mean it should be avoided.

CASE STUDY

FROM REAL LIFE

A stable project team successfully utilized several new technologies. Several additional technology capacities were identified as key to the IT architecture and strategy. With the latter, the project leader was outside her comfort zone, she felt the risk and complexities were beyond the teams' capability, and that it was too much risk to use the new technologies. Fear of failure stood in the way.

This team avoided the adoption of a new core element of the overall IT strategy. It resulted in delays of several years to the delivery of required technology capabilities and added millions of extra costs to the business transformation program.

Simple = Identical

Businesses may have the same objectives, yet components and approaches are rarely identical. Even in a single country—each sales, finance, operations, customer service, and management group has their own taste and texture. When there are multiple countries, so do every location and country.

A project is setup for failure if the assumption is made that what works in one part of the business achieves identical results in another part of the business.

What are the needs of the different components of the business? Is the basis historical or focused on the future (growth, competition, regulation, partners, strategy)?

Two related assumptions reduce project success:

1. "All people and places are the same."

   This assumes what we do here will work elsewhere. In reality, customers, business issues, staff, and regulators vary. Market dynamics vary by location.

   Variations can be substantial for organizations with multiple geographic locations. Doing business in China is different in India, France, Brazil, or the United States.

   Projects and productivity improvements with a large geographical spread often have multi-year deployment programs—and must respond to each of their shifting markets.

2. "People are like computers; they won't react until we turn them on."

   The assumption is that implementation can be planned later, when the project is ready to deliver. Implicit in this assumption is that the business has no idea about the project and so is not beginning to react to it. An assumption of secrecy, while attractive, rarely holds true. A good internal information network is a survival skill in the corporate world. It is better to assume that the grapevine and bamboo telegraph is effective and to start considering peoples' reaction to implementation when the project is kicked off.

CASE STUDY

FROM REAL LIFE

Jesus was advising an IT transformation program, one that is often associated with job instability. The nature of it required teams from across the business to contribute to the decision making—46 people in the kick-off. Knowing this, he advised the project sponsor to formally brief the staff about the program and the potential impact as soon as possible.

The Sponsor did—the day after the kick-off. Even by then, staff in other countries had heard rumors of the project.

Information moves fast these days.

Improving Your Success Rate

For the business: Identify critical competitive market needs. These are usually driven by regulations or the requirements of a specific customer segment. Identify where people in the organization may be sensitive to change. Each location will have its own organizational history and culture that generates local responses. Ensure the requirements or the project plan addresses these as needs or as risks.

For the project: Factor the need to have local variations from a functional perspective and from a business change perspective into the project plan requirements and funding.

Improving Your Success Rate

For the business: Consider KISS implications during requirements evaluation and approval. If these functions are not delivered, what is the cost to the business (direct financial costs, jobs, staff turnover)? What will the business need to do to cover these risks?

For the project: Consider the incremental cost and return if the project is more than just KISS. Focus on results to be achieved, rather than short-term tasks or deliverables.

Plan = Certainty

There are some things in this world that should be engraved in stone. Michelangelo's David. Rodin's sculptures. The cathedral of Chartres or the temples of Angkor Wat.

Stone is a wonderful medium for art. Not for project plans.

Does your organization act as if the project plan is carved in stone?

One of the things we know about plans:

No plan survives its encounter with reality.

— Duke of Wellington

A good project plan is neither stone nor Jell-O. It is impossible to build something on ground that is constantly shifting.

A good project plan is like an agreed menu, with the recipes and key ingredients established first. Then, as business conditions change, the project and the business can work out the implications of the change—the impact to resources, products, and time.

Good project plans include an element of "what if" scenarios, contingency, or slack. Good leaders recognize that things may not go according to plan, so they plan contingencies accordingly.

The absence of particular terms is a warning sign—are terms like "adjust," "dependency," "contingency," and "ahead of time" acceptable in your organization?

"Contingency" and "slack" are terms generally used in IT to refer to the allocation of spare resources (people, time, money) to the project to provide capacity to respond if reality shows the plan is not correct.

There are two similar terms:

1. Dependency—what must occur before we can start.
2. What-if—If "x" occurs, then we need to do "y."

A starved project can't respond easily to environmental changes. A lean project has reserves for the challenges at hand, but not for dependencies and contingencies

If certain terms are unacceptable in your organization, like "possible," "risk," "mistake," or "error," this is also a warning sign—that the project is unlikely to have adequate contingency reserves.

If the term "learning" indicates that someone was wrong or inadequate, this can also be a project warning sign.

Improving Your Success Rates

For the Business: Identify project dependencies and allow for "what-if" contingencies. Allocate budget and time. Discuss possible actions to mitigate during the project planning phase.

For the Project: Identify project dependencies and work out contingencies. Evaluate the project plan and identify "go–no go" points. How far can you go before it is too late to change direction?

CASE STUDY

FROM REAL LIFE

A Business Process Management project faced a fixed four-month deadline. Sarah asked the business. "What if you only have a week to pilot?" "What if these functions are not available?" She explored "what if" things go badly and "what if" things go well.

This changed the critical path—several apparently minor functions were reassessed as key to reducing the risk of operational failure due to the tight time frame. One was the need for a final date for staffing decisions so security could be adequately tested.

A Health Warning

In some organizations it's like being Typhoid Mary if you admit to dependencies and contingencies—and worse still is admitting to risks, errors, or failure. In other organizations, these things are seen as opportunity.

Know your organization and find a way to get the contingencies needed for the project to manage normal uncertainties and unpredictability.

Delivery = Results

The business usually begins to generate results when a project delivers a capacity.

But delivery is not the same as results. Effort is required after delivery. Is this results delivery part of the project plan? Is it credible?

The way the business chooses to use the new capacity depends on a variety of factors. To return to our Archetypal project from Chapter 7, which scenario below feels truest to your project or experience?

CASE STUDY

RESULTS SCENARIOS—4 OPTIONS

"Thanks for the donkey, John," said Mr. Khan and the widows. John and his friends felt good. Donkey had been delivered.

But had real results been achieved?

The widows wondered. The donkey was meant to help them, but what would this donkey really mean to them?

What happened next?

This is a key question for most projects. It's about what really happens once the project's capacity is available to the business.

Let's explore how the story might unfold.

Scenario 1

Mr. Khan led the donkey to the four widows, "This wonderful animal is for you."

As they were asking Mr. Khan what to do with the donkey, Mr. Khan was called away to celebrate.

The women could not move the donkey, and they gave up in frustration. They hid the donkey outside the village and only pretended to use him. The funds to feed the donkey for the first year were spent elsewhere by the elders. The widows struggled to use the donkey and to feed him. The widows were berated by Mr. Khan and the elders for wasting the opportunity.

Scenario 2

The widows were not convinced the donkey would really change anything. They'd seen it before. Promises made to widows don't count. One of the men would take the donkey for other purposes.

Indra asked, "Shall we try? It might be better this time."

On the first day Mr. Khan showed them how to care for the donkey.

On the second day, Mr. Khan used the donkey to take corn to market. On the third day, Mr. Khan told the widows to feed the donkey.

The donkey's food was soon finished. The extra funds to feed the donkey had been reallocated to another village project.

Scenario 3

Jane said, "We can try different things now. Life might be easier." May was not convinced.

Over the next few weeks, they worked out a schedule to use the donkey, and Mr. Khan provided coaching on how to care for the donkey.

While they politely thanked John and his friends for the gift, they had other things on their minds.

Over the next few weeks, they worked out a schedule to use the donkey, and Mr. Khan provided a little coaching on how to care for the donkey.

Scenario 4

The four widows were brought over to meet John and the donkey. They were curious. Mr. Khan had shown them how to work with a donkey. They discussed who would look after the donkey, how they would use him, and when Mr. Khan would use him. They'd even borrowed Mr. Khan's other donkey and taken him out for a day.

(*continued*)

(continued)

Jane wasn't excited about cleaning up after the donkey made a mess in his stall. Juanita didn't like the extra work at the end of the day when she was tired and her children needed feeding. However, the widows agreed on a plan because the chance to collect more firewood was better for all of them.

A few months later over a cup of tea, Mr Khan explained how to care for the donkey during the winter, and they discussed ideas on how to feed the donkey next year, when the feed money ran out.

When is a project declared a success? Upon successful delivery?

From John's perspective, he'd done what he set out to do. Yet depending on the scenario above, the village may or may not view the donkey as value added. A project may represent extra work or an opportunity to improve the business or an opportunity to use funds elsewhere.

Each of the people reacted in part due to their past experiences.

The four scenarios show the different sort of results that the same "product" (the donkey) can have in the same business (the village) due to the different histories and decisions made by those who received the projects. See Table 11.2 for a summary.

These simple stories reflect common project experiences. Sadly scenarios 1 and 2 are common. Only scenario 4 addressed the human issues, resources, and activities required to respond to reality. It is often easier to declare a physical product a success and to ignore complexities and realities of what's needed to get real results in the business.

Is Success the Donkey or a More Productive Village?

The what-gets-measured-gets-done approach requires tangible results. The do-it-now approach says find a product that is easy to install. The don't-hold-me-accountable-for-someone-else's-actions approach encourages a definition of success that is within the project's control.

The project was delivered, a donkey in the village. His photo is on the website. For John buying the donkey was the exciting

TABLE 11.2
Story Summaries

Scenario	Staff were (the widows)	Funds to support capacity were (Donkey)	Results
1	Untrained with new capacity.	Reallocated to other purposes.	Capacity wasted
2	Minimal training. Cynical based on past experience.	Reallocated to other purposes.	Likely to fail. Inadequate resources. Results depend on whether the staff were motivated to make it work.
3	Some training and support. Discomfort ignored.	Applied to purpose.	Results undervalued in the business.
4	Trained and supported by management as they took on the new capacity.	Applied to purpose.	Results achieved. Created future opportunities.

bit and helping someone was the valuable bit. What's not known is if the donkey really helped the village.

This situation frequently occurs in the technology space. IT is often looking for a home for new cool toys—so they can use and play with them. The same situation happens when entrepreneurs explore new products or markets.

Experimenting has its place if the project is managed and is recognized as experimental. A business can budget for that. It is not a good investment if a project is really about an expensive cool new technology without a solid business case.

Test the business case for your project: does it help generate real results? Perspectives may differ—as they did in the village.

A Health Warning

Acknowledging reality and how people might react can be sensitive—to the individuals and to those who lead the decision.

CASE STUDY

FROM REAL LIFE

Alice listened to a CEO's presentation to his top 200 people. He'd recently cut head count by 10 percent. He announced a forced pay cut of 5 to 10 percent across the managerial ranks, and he announced new objectives. A few days earlier, the media had reported that the CEO and his executive team had received a bonus of $10 million. At the coffee break people were saying, "I know where my pay cut went."

Later Alice implemented a customer relationship system. They'd provided basic training and support. But after the announcements, employee reactions were full of doubt, resistance, and cynicism. Bottom-line results were rotten.

A pre-implementation review could have identified the continued effect of the announcement and led to the appropriate additional investment to mitigate the impact on the project results.

Improving Your Success Rates

For the business: Use an organizational change management plan to help transition people to the new way of doing things. Evaluate the impact other events may have on your project.

For the project: Work with the business to provide opportunities for people to experience the new methods before it goes live.

How a group reacts is partially due to the organization's history, partially due to the group's history, and partially due to individual experiences.

When reality is acknowledged, expect some pain. For many in an organization, it is a fairly reasonable assumption that change means job uncertainty, job loss, or an increased workload from covering multiple roles—there is a reason for cynicism and fear. Be prepared for positive reactions too. Good leadership and teamwork can be found in any environment.

CASE STUDY

FROM REAL LIFE

James realized the most effective way to help people learn new ways of doing things was to provide them a way to try it—without fear of punishment, laughter, or looking like a fool. He evaluated the effectiveness and costs of different approaches to this change management question.

He decided a business lab would be useful given the number of people impacted and the sort of problems that could occur. He also arranged for a simulation that allowed people to try different processes and decisions independently or with others without putting the business at risk.

CASE STUDY

FROM REAL LIFE

Alex was running a program across five business lines. He assessed the organizational health to see where there might be pain or where there might be positive points that could affect his change program. In one department, despite a large, recent retrenchment, morale was high and acceptance of the need to change was good. In another department, far less affected by recent business changes, staff were doubtful and unwilling to explore new ways of working. He structured his change management plan with this in mind.

Takeaway

Real ROI is a team effort. The business and the project team must work together for effective project results delivery. It is naive to assume that KISS is enough or that results will magically happen upon delivery of a capacity.

1. Real ROI requires the project and the business to work together to deliver results.
2. Every organization is good at some things but poor in others. The symptoms show where to focus improvements.
3. Deeper issues can underlie failures or lack of health. Part 4 describes underlying systems that must be healthy and aligned to achieve ongoing results and productivity.

Predictable accountable results (PAR) is a deliberate, mature focus of business leadership—from the top level down. Anything else is a continuation of the hero-in-a-crisis approach or a continuation of the practice of investing in projects for the sake of reputation, rather than for results.

An executive should track four aspects of results maturity:

- Reliability of the governance process that aligns IT projects to the portfolio and company strategy;
- Maturity of the results risks management process;
- Maturity of the results delivery process;
- Presence of simplifying assumptions and practices.

Warning Signs for Results Delivery Process

- ☠ The business leader sees his/her role on the Steering Committee as sitting there and accepting delivery.
- ☠ The project plan is to be completed after project initiation.
- ☠ Risks and Contingencies are "not applicable."
- ☠ Implementation is out of scope. It is "someone else's problem."

Endnotes

1 If you are interested in seeing the "boids," go to http://www.red3d.com/cwr/boids.

2 Case drama is an approach that role plays how the business will operate. It is used to link the process/systems tools with the knowledge/psychological needs of the staff in new design.

Chapter 12
Fold 4, Motivation Is Energized

Motivation is the driver of human activity. It seems obvious, yet few projects formally evaluate and deal with the impact of the project and the project intent on the motivation and performance of people in the organization. The question to ask is **"will people be motivated and energized?"**

If people will really be energized, brilliant! More often, a project is lucky to get a neutral response. More often it is negative.

Setting a project up for success requires looking at this squarely. In this fourth fold, we evaluate the likely reaction to the intended results. This is the most consistently identified reason for a project's failure to deliver business results.[1]

Risk: Accept or Reject—People Are Part of the Business Results Equation

"Will people accept or reject the intended change?" This is the basic dynamic to consider. It requires attention and is assessable upfront.

Tactically, projects often look at an organizational change management stream of work to deal with this response. The project plan then includes activities to deal with the three Don'ts:

1. "Don't know about it." Action required: Communications: Tell people of the change so they know about it.
2. "Don't know how." Action required: Training: Provide adequate training and opportunity to learn how and to become competent.

3. "Don't want to." Action required: Resistance: Understand the underlying reasons for this and address it.

Projects that deliver results address these three elements with adequate resources and attention. Check that the business case is adequately planned and funded.

Let's get deeper into motivation. There are three unexpressed aspects that have direct bearing on project results. The wow success stories addressed these additional elements directly. They paid attention to:

4. Adaptability—the capacity of the people in the organization to take on changes or operate under conditions of uncertainty.
5. Motivation—maintaining or improving the things that motivated performance in each role and dealt with any project impact to that motivation.
6. Approval—humans are social creatures and seek approval. They will choose to follow the lead of authority figures even if it is not rationally sensible. They will often follow subliminal cues given off by leaders.

Successful projects understand the dynamics of what makes people in their organization tick, and actively worked to keep energy focused and high, to keep people motivated in the business.

This fold focuses on these last three elements of motivation as key risks to business results. It is about people and their responsiveness to change. Projects can choose to operate and introduce change in a way that improves motivation within the organization, one leading to higher overall performance. Or they can follow traditional methods—the ones that result in the business saying "we survived." This usually results in a dip in people's performance.

The focus at the time of project set-up must be on how this project is likely to affect motivation. Motivated people are more likely to try something new, to learn and thus to change. People who are unmotivated or turned off are less likely to change.

The "accept or reject" dynamic plays the leading role in achieving business results. This dynamic describes motivation—are people for or against the project? It is also called resistance. Resistance is the term used when someone doesn't want to do what we want them to do.

More correctly, resistance is the failure to recognize and address dynamics that arise from the psychology of groups. These dynamics affect the perception of the project and affect people's motivation to make the changes required by the project.

The early indicator of possible failure is the degree to which the project's intent is likely to affect motivation and performance in the organization.

Team energy is important. Good project managers and leaders pay attention to the motivation and energy of their teams.

This risk assessment broadly evaluates the motivation of those affected by the change. This group is critical for results delivery.

. . . the Likely Response

What sort of reaction do you get from peers when you explain you are on a project? Depending on the historical track record of project success or failure, the reaction could be excitement, sympathy, or condolences.

What does a historical project failure rate mean to the performance of your organization?

A new project may then cause people to feel frustrated, distracted, and stressed, and cynical. Bottom line: It means reduced performance and lost productivity.

A new project may also make people feel that jobs are less secure. Best case, their job may change, worst case, their job is lost when new technologies may automate the job or cause it to be located elsewhere. The implication of the project to the individual is often uncertain.

What does uncertainty mean for project success?

Adaptability

People who are more comfortable with uncertainty find it easier to take on new tasks than those that need certainty.

For organizations, it means skills that increase our personal ability to adapt, to learn, and to work in different ways help projects deliver change more effectively.

Personal adaptability is important for the organization. If people are not adaptive, they will struggle to change the new ways of working that flow from the project. Projects often require new ways of thinking about how business is done, which translates into how each of us works and behaves. At the organizational level, adaptability is the ability to respond to varied customer needs and market pressures. Adaptation is affected by:

- Methods that project deliverables are introduced into the business;
- Surrounding business processes and organizational culture;
- How skilled people are in adapting.

Bottom line, if a project introduces a change that is not in the apparent interest of individuals, they are unlikely to accept it. If the organization is not adaptable, they are unlikely to have the required skills to cope with uncertainties and changes.

CASE STUDY

FROM REAL LIFE

A project implemented world-class CRM software but was rejected by the sales staff, because it added another hour of daily work.

Recognizing reality, the business initiated a proactive assessment of the likely business results, and this problem was identified as a critical risk. The business decided to change processes to reduce the impact, which resulted in a successful CRM program.

CASE STUDY

FROM REAL LIFE

A business process management program was challenged by a highly centralized and autocratic decision-making practice that resulted in process bottlenecks.

Recognizing reality, an executive knew this bottleneck would escalate as an issue on the first process to be "facilitated by BPM." The business had to address the underlying issues in order to respond more swiftly to the market.

Resistance—Psychology Not Taught at School

People perform best when motivated. Yet, the reality is projects are often associated with job insecurity and job loss. For many, this is not motivating; it is distracting.

Combine this with other dynamics, including the war for talent, the impact of the project on motivation and retention, and retention costs can become critical for project success.

A moment on talent: Gallup's[2] research shows there is potential for most people to be "talent." Yet headhunters say "talent" is the top 3 percent of people who do things, can be relied upon, and are leaders with heart and integrity.

Most of us would like to be described this way. Do many people say, "I'm going to the office to be a dead weight?" Probably not.

Do managers and leaders try to be like Mr. Burns in *The Simpsons*? Do you set out to frustrate people and stress them? Probably not.

Assume that all the sociopaths and psychopaths have been weeded out of the office; then most people would like to say they like coming to the office, look forward to work, and enjoy contributing something worthwhile. Conceivably, many people could be talent.

Projects can choose to pay attention to the things they do that reduce motivation, personal and team performance, and uptake of capacities. This attention can focus on reducing the risks of people not using capacities and how to improve motivation to help performance.

Business results usually come from people using new capacities provided by a projects delivery. If people are insecure or unmotivated, uptake and results will be slow. If there is a track record of projects creating job losses, people will be distracted. Talent either underperforms or leaves.

Projects that wish to mitigate risks that affect motivation and human performance need a deeper understanding of "resistance."

Resistance Can Be Sensible

There is a North American expression: "Don't expect the turkeys to vote for Christmas." While the turkey has pride of place on the dinner table, it is not in the turkey's interest. Many big changes result in lost jobs or lost competency in their current jobs because new processes must be mastered to be competent when the project is implemented.

Why would people want to lose their jobs or lose competency? Resistance can be sensible. It is irrational, both logically and emotionally, for the turkey to vote yes.

Recognizing and dealing with the risks that this issue poses to project results upfront is the focus of dealing with the "don't want to" reaction. Don't want to can be sensible in the eyes of the green world.

CASE STUDY

FROM REAL LIFE

Mark led an IT transformation from applications silos to IT Lite—a services/customer-focused approach to delivering IT. Roles completely changed for 30 percent of staff, partially changed for 15 percent, 65 percent were outsourced to a new employer, and 12 percent headcount was reduced.

Mark ensured the human dynamics were understood. He also used the additional diagnostics in **Presence** to facilitate project acceptance and results delivery. His focus was to help new ideas, ways, and approaches integrate into the organization, rather than be rejected as alien life forms.

Motivation Is Multifaceted

Moving on to lifting results by keeping motivation up.

It is widely **assumed** that money is the only motivator. If pay stays the same, people will continue to perform.

Factually this is not so. A change in what we do or in what is expected of us can change our motivation. How a change is introduced affects motivation and thus business results. Projects can choose to pay attention to potential negative reactions that demotivate, reducing personal performance, and act to reduce these risks. Projects can also choose to look for opportunities to create positive reactions to improve motivation and performance.

Maslow's hierarchy of needs and other more recent advances in the psychology of motivation provide a frame of reference that a project can use to assess impact of intended business outcomes on motivation. This may require consultation with an experienced organizational change strategy practitioner or a organizational development practitioner. Both of these professions focus on people's performance, motivation, and values. Business transformations that wish to affect values or behavior as part of their business results are highly likely to affect motivation.

To get business results, a project needs to consider the impact that the changes will make to motivators and address areas where the impact may impact project results negatively.

The spectrum of needs[3] that business projects are more likely to affect are represented by five segments of the circle in Figure 12.1. At the center of the circle is self-orientation; the

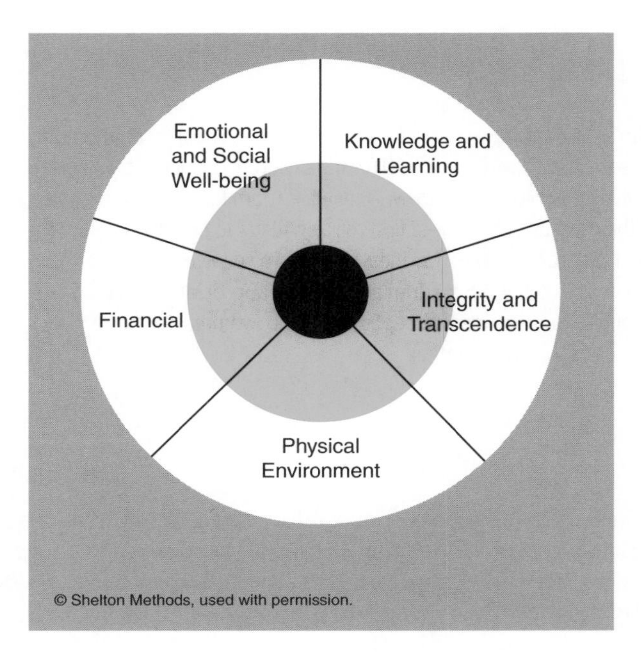

FIGURE 12.1 Facets of Motivation

mid circle is where motivation is about interaction with others; while the outer circle reflects where motivation comes from relationship to a broader community. These three levels influence the appropriate response.

Assess what drives your own happiness and motivation. Have you seen the way teenagers put infinite energy into something they love? Wouldn't it be great to feel that way about work?

Energy can seem boundless when we are motivated.

Projects that pick up on these differences can construct their change processes so that they reduce the risk of negatively affecting a key motivator in a group or can improve the results of a change by deliberate enhancing something that motivates a group.

CASE STUDY

FROM REAL LIFE

Inspired by a child with leukemia, Jane created a program called Shear Inspiration; 20 women shaved their heads and raised $312,000 for the Children's Cancer Foundation. More than enough to fund a sterile bone marrow transplant room their first-year goals. In their second year, they had two objectives: first to raise funds to help those families who struggle with the resources it takes for their children to receive chemotherapy, and second to raise awareness that the children and families appreciate even a simple gesture that shows you've noticed and accept them. The women do this for the intrinsic reward—not for cash payments.

Successful leaders recognize this diversity of motivations and work with it. Consider the impact of various motivations for your project and ensure you have the resources to work effectively manage them.

Table 12.1 makes the differing motivations and the required intensity clear. The five domains of motivation are in personal terms as motivation is personal.

TABLE 12.1
Domains of Motivation

Dimension	Immediate (Self)	Extended (Family, Friends, and Local Community (FFC))	Global (Communities Elsewhere)
Emotional and Social Well-being	I am happy to be me.	I enjoy my FF&C. They are well.	I contribute as I desire to other groups.
Knowledge and Learning	I'm confident in what I know and in learning what I need to know.	I get to learn and try things that interest me regularly.	I'm challenged and stimulated in new areas.
Integrity and Transcendence	I know and live by my values.	My values are consistent with those around me.	I actively follow and grow my spiritual well-being with others.
Physical Environment	I'm fit and healthy, physically safe and comfortable.	My local environment is healthy and pleasant.	My decisions and actions are consistent with a sustained healthy environment.
Financial Well-being	I get by. I do a fair day's work for a fair day's pay.	I have what I need financially.	I've freedom to contribute financially to others.

Evaluate your own sources of motivation and energy.

Scale of 1 = Dreadful and 10 = Fabulous!

Motivations in personal life: How strongly do you rate your work life? Your personal life? Work is not everything, but it is about half our waking week.

Motivations in professional life: How many of these sources of motivation do you or your company **actively** use to help people perform better at work?

From project perspective: How many of these motivations are consistent and aligned with the intended goals of this project?

Some companies overlook the power of ''big'' motivators, while others have found great success by paying attention to it:

- Google's ''Do no evil'' is an example of integrity and transcendence aimed at the community level.
- Al Gore's *An Inconvenient Truth* focuses on environmental global issues.
- Nike's supply chain learned the value of social global issues.
- Many design companies focus on learning and knowledge.
- Cadbury and Hershey were founded on the basis that a company should contribute to and support a healthy local community.
- ANZ bank's competitive repositioning in the 2000s, based on living up to values, led to outstanding business results.

CASE STUDY

FROM REAL LIFE

Steve reviewed plans for major organizational changes. He reflected on the nature of the roles in the organization and what motivated people. He found that:

- People on the front line service area were highly motivated by their role in the community.
- People in the IT team were interested in technology, learning, and toys they could play with.
- People in marketing were sensitive to any action that suggested changes in the values of the organization.

He reviewed his plan and made changes to ensure that these sources of motivation were retained.

CASE STUDY

FROM REAL LIFE

Jacky and her HR team regularly reviewed the organization to identify dominant motivations. They looked at positive, enabling behaviors and cynical, disabling ones. They used this understanding of their culture to structure HR and leadership programs that led to a major shift in business results.

They become number one in the market in customer and employee satisfaction. The share price reflected their achievement—it showed the most significant growth of companies in that industry.

Key point: People are motivated by many things. Work ignores much of it. Lack of "motivation to change" is usually called resistance.

Projects often implement change with no consideration to:

- How motivation is affected by changes to systems, processes or roles;
- How motivation is affected by the process of implementation.

Poor motivation = resistance = results failure.

Hint for better results: given the intent of the project and the motivations of the people who will need to change, what they do or say if the project is to deliver; is the project likely to improve motivation or not? Be realistic. Recognize both the risks and the opportunities upfront.

Where Do Interest, Engagement, and Energy Go?

More on maintaining motivation and performance. The hidden dynamic of approval comes into play at a level below conscious awareness. Ignored, it reduces project results;

recognized, it becomes part of the way more effective projects deliver results.

Why is it that individuals can show passion and genius in their personal lives but rarely do so in the office? What might projects pay attention to as they consider how they introduce a business change?

People—we are trained to respond in specific ways. Some of these affect project results negatively. Three great scientists provide useful insights: Pavlov, Skinner, and Milgram.

Simply: Pavlov showed that dogs and people respond to stimulation. And they associate. Feed a dog, ring a bell. Dog salivates when fed. Repeat. After a while, the dog will salivate when the bell is rung. Stimulus, response.

Skinner showed that people respond better to positive feedback (things we like, praise, and respect) than negative feedback (things we don't, rejection, and pain).

In school we got praise for the right answer and bad marks for the wrong answer.

By the time we join the work force, we are well trained: we do what is asked and not go outside the boundaries. If we do well, we get a good review and pay packet; if we do poorly, it's a bad review, poor pay packet, and increased job risk.

When a project introduces a change that requires different behavior, it is risky for people to go out of their learned safe zones.

There is a second element—we are social beings. We like to be accepted—to be part of the group. Stanley Milgram's experiments strongly demonstrated this. Two aspects are relevant for project success:

1. We will do things to conform, even when we don't agree.
2. We will follow authority, when we don't agree, even when it harms us.

Milgram suggests that the appearance of freedom of action that many organizations think exist, may not be so. Our training in corporate survival gave us an internal, unconscious, "don't rock the boat" perspective. If our boss doesn't show support, we won't either. If those around us don't like it, we are likely to go along with their views.

This is strongly authority-based. Leaders must model the desired behaviors and practices by "walking the talk" if they want people to "rock the boat."

Note: We all have "personal radar" developed early on in life. We use our radar to determine whether a person is sincere. If leaders talk without belief or behavioral integrity, we will discount the words and follow the actions. When Gandhi said, "You need to be the change you wish to be," he was referring to this depth of internal consistency of personal belief and its reflection in the words and actions of the leader. Projects that require changes in values or in behavior must look at the capacity of leadership to model and walk the talk; otherwise results are far less likely to be delivered.

Combined, people are less likely to adapt new practices and behaviors if:

- Leadership does not walk the talk.
- Leaders talk and behave inconsistently with the future practices.
- The required behaviors take people out of their safety zone.

Projects need to make a realistic assessment of the ability of key leaders to model the required future behaviors consistently. Inconsistent leadership actions with the stated values and behaviors of the projects undermine results.

From the project perspective, assessing the organization's programming takes sensitivity. It can be career limiting to say that a project's high risk is due to leadership traits and practices that undermine the credibility of the change.

CASE STUDY

FROM REAL LIFE

James worked for a group of executives to deliver a large cross-business unit IT change program. He assessed leadership styles and altered his change introduction processes accordingly. One executive was irascible and regularly changed his mind. Others were more consistent. One executive stood out to staff; they saw his values, words, and action as consistent and representative of the desired future way of working. James worked more closely with this executive to create a track record of successful change in that business unit before moving onto other parts of the business.

Later when the political moment was right, he escalated the concerns to the appropriate sponsor for attention and action.

Conflicting Interests: Rational Dysfunctions

An action is taken here. Another decision is made over there. Each is rational. However, at the organizational level, combined, they create dysfunctions.

These are called **rational dysfunctions**. A few were mentioned earlier in **Productivity**.

Rational dysfunction is behind many project failures. They most commonly occur when two organizational systems are not in sync. Something makes sense from one point of view or set of goals, but not from another.

For example, some organizations have a practice of giving a negative comment or increasing the risk of not getting a good review when a person does not get something completely right. Feedback is useful. However, if it gets to the point that people fear trying something new (like a new process) as they fear doing it imperfectly, then projects find it more difficult to introduce changes. From the project perspective, people should try and learn. Yet if people want to avoid the pain of "poor performance," they may choose to stick to the safe old ways of doing things. Rational for the person, dysfunctional for a project.

CASE STUDY

FROM REAL LIFE

Dick was torn. His line of business faced customer dynamics different from the rest of his organization. A large project moved all the businesses on a common platform. He had the choice of paying for extra coding and resourcing for the new IT system, or supplementing his operational base for functions that were not supported by the new IT system—both of which added to his cost base and operational complexity.

The easier option was to go slow on the system adoption so that the next executive to run the area would have to deal with the question. Dilemma.

Fear and embarrassment of failure make it hard for a person to try something new. People prefer the safety of known processes. Consciously or not, they will delay or avoid doing things the new way. This is rational for the person, but dysfunctional for the organization. It causes the project to fail to deliver results.

Rational dysfunctions abound.

Why do smart executives define IT as the project when they know that IT alone is not likely to get business results?

One reason is that in many organizations it is better to kick off a project and be seen as taking action than to do nothing. The fact the project is likely to fail or does fail is irrelevant. Few organizations track results tightly.

In this context, it can be rational to kick off an IT project even if results are unlikely. It is dysfunctional from an investment perspective.

Addressing rational dysfunctions requires understanding the dynamics that underlie what appear to be sensible decisions on the part of the various parts of the organization, an assessment of the impact of the dysfunction, and the political will to realign to a broader goal.

In the case above, it would require a high-level business commitment to delivering results from projects, an accountability process that tracks project kick-off and results delivered. It also requires changing the HR practices that reward the glory of initiating a project and balancing this with a commitment to delivery of results.

People Choose to Act or to Ignore the Project

Business results come from people doing things differently. They come from people using the capacities created from IT projects.

If people chose to block (resistance), or to be passive, to be bystanders, or even undermine the project, business results are reduced.

It's got to be rational for people to change in their eyes.

Part 1 **Productivity** presented the differing viewpoints of the white world of management and the green world of staff. Projects usually only deliver business results when change is rational in both white and green worlds.

Note: There is a fear-based school of leadership: "Do what I tell you or I'll fire you." Fear can be an effective psychological motivator for a short sharp action. Over time, physiologically, fear creates dullness and reduces initiative in most people.

To get long-term performance and productivity, twenty-first century psychology and neuroscience focus on positive psychological dynamics.

Key Points

- Resistance—other people don't do what you want them to do.
- Projects are a source of stress: "I am uncertain how my job will change" or "I might lose my job."
- Personal resilience and adaptability is a useful skill that businesses can develop to improve results.
- Motivation leads to energy to do things differently. Motivation is multi-dimensional. It is more than money.
- Projects need to consider the psychology on the ground.
- Acceptance is affected by unconscious processing and training.
- People are usually rational from their own perspective—even if it is dysfunctional for some other part of the organization.
- Business results come from accepting the reality of rational dysfunctions and working to resolve them.

Takeaway

Projects need to deal with the human reaction to change. Attention and resources are required to:

- Ensure people know of the change.
- Have the skills they need to operate effectively as a result of the change.
- Have an interest in taking on the change.
- Ensure motivation within the organization is maintained as part of the change process.

People choose to change. The ultimate basis for results and productivity comes down to rational choices people make.

1. A history of project failures results in disbelief and cynicism about future projects.
2. Project leaders must pay attention to motivations in the business for change, if they are to generate sustainable ROI.

3. Project leaders must notice and address dysfunctions, if they are to generate sustainable ROI.

IT project leaders are serious about getting successful results in the white world, but to get results they must resolve the green world issues raised in this section. Many of these issues are outside of IT; this is not a reason to leave it unactioned or accountability unassigned.

Motivation Warning Signs

- ☠ People in the organization have a reputation for resistance.
- ☠ Privately other parts of the organization are viewed as cynical or ineffective.
- ☠ Project leaders do not pay attention to motivation in the organization.
- ☠ Leadership practices are not consistent with the motivations needed to deliver results.

If motivation in the organization is not well understood by the project or the impact of the project on motivation has not been assessed, circle all four of these. Lack of real data is a "no."

If the project does not have a well-established organizational change management plan either as part of this project or as a parallel project, circle all four warning signs.

Note: IT projects that are not set up for success under Fold 4 are highly likely to produce shelfware.

Endnotes

1 Kotter, PwC-MORI, McKinsey, and my own research keep coming back to this point. Failure is significantly a people thing.

2 Gallup's First Break All the Rules, and It Only Takes One.

3 This model draws on several sources: Maslow, Barrett, and Seligman, who focus on motivation. Ethology provides other insights to motivation from biology.

Chapter 13
Part 3 Takeaway

All four lead indicators of a project's capacity to deliver business results should be healthy:

1. Intent is clear.
2. Business case is robust.
3. Results delivery process is reliable.
4. Motivation is energized.

Use Table 13.1 to summarize your assessment of each of the four project focused folds.

See Appendix C for a summary of the warning signs.

In a nutshell, the diagnosis is:

> ***Red Flag:*** Poor health. The project is likely to fail, materially miss delivery, or be rejected by the organization.
>
> ***Okay:*** Average health. The project is likely to "deliver a little less for a little more, a little late" as tolerated but not a wow result.

TABLE 13.1 *Success Checklist*

Project Likelihood of Success	Red Flag Several Warning Signs Circled	Okay 1 Warning Sign Circled	Set Up for Success 0 Warning Signs Circled
Intent Is Clear			
Business Case Is Robust			
Results Delivery Process Is Reliable			
Motivation Is Energized			

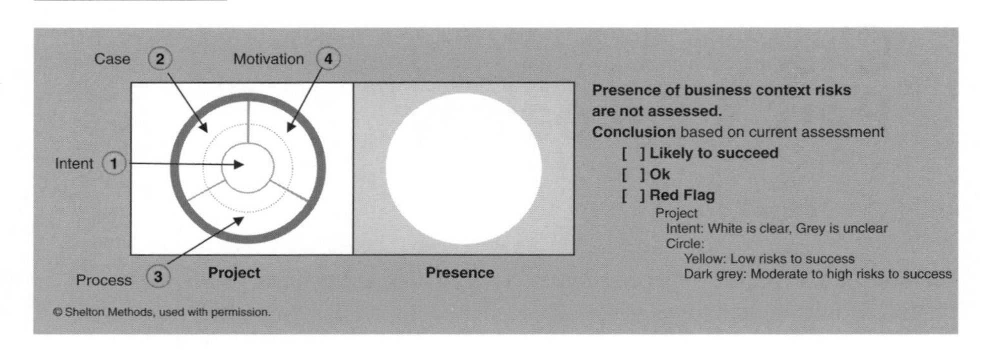

FIGURE 13.1 Business Context Risks

Set-up for success: Good health. This project has a good likelihood of delivering the desired results. At school, this would be an A or a B grade.

Figure 13.1 allows you to see quickly where the project is on target to get results and where it is weak.

Focusing on the left side, which shows the **project** assessment:

- The center reflects the clarity of the intent.
  If it is dark, the intent is not clear.
  If it is clear, then the intent is clear.
- The three segments of the circle reflect the assessment of the Business Case, the maturity of the Results Delivery Process, and the Motivation of the business to change.
  If a fold is set up for success, it is all yellow (good).
  If it is rated okay, then part of it is yellow (good + risk).
  If it is not set up for success, then it is dark grey (risk).
  The circle is outlined in black to denote a element of risk.
  Figure 13.2 shows three project assessments using the 8-Fold Path.

The circle on the right hand side reflects the assessment of the risks to results that arise from the business context. This is covered in Part 4 **Presence**.

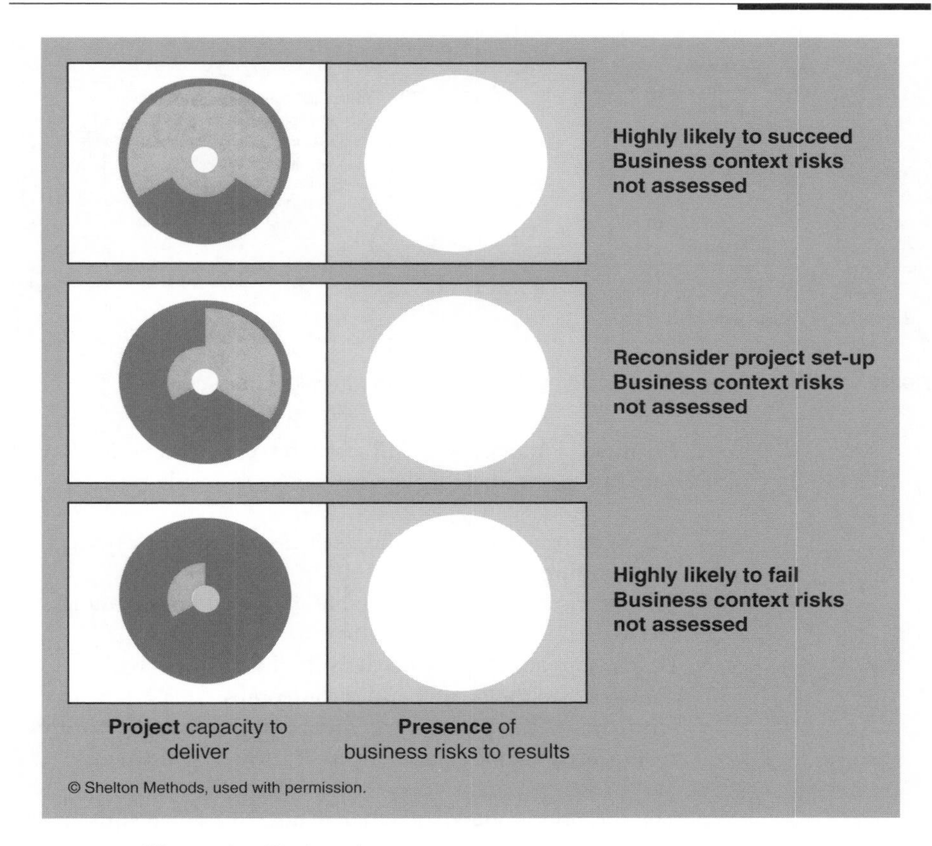

FIGURE 13.2 Illustrative Project Assessment

Your Assessment

Use the blank diagram in Figure 13.1 (see Figure 13.3) to summarize your project assessment. If intent was not clear, grey the center. Fill in the three segments using a grey pencil. For more impact, use color. If the project is okay, fill the inner segment of the circle with a yellow highlighter. Use a red pen to color the rest of the segment.

When the indicators are grey, particularly dark grey, hidden costs or resistance are likely to harm the project negatively.

Many factors that affect project results are in the control of the business. This context affects projects.

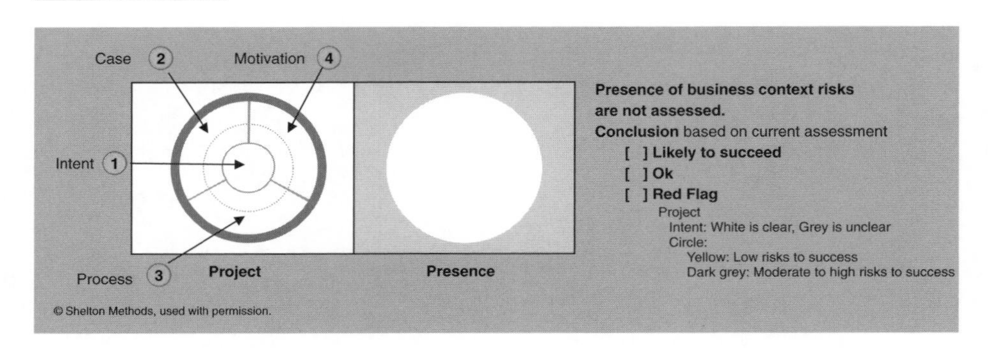

FIGURE 13.3 My Project Assessment, Business Context Risks Unassessed

Business, Finance, and HR each have key roles to play if projects are to predictably deliver business results:

- Financial practices affect the business case quality, budget, and funding.
- HR practices affect resourcing, rewards, and motivation to change.
- Leadership affects how proactively the business will contribute to the project and its outcomes.
- Ultimately, each party is accountable if predictable, positive results are to come reliably from IT project investments.

This broader context of what it takes to get results in the business is the focus of the next section Part 4 **Presence.**

Part 4
Presence

Avoid the failures.
Lift the successes.

The business context of a project has four risk areas:

1. Project alignment with current strategic position.
2. Operational context supports project intent.
3. Flow of history favors the project intent.
4. Balancing dynamics aid project intent.

The next six chapters look at the risks to project delivery that are assessable up front by the project team or by the project management office. Chapter 14 recaps the book so far and provides a broader context to these four risks, while Chapters 15–18 discuss the four sets of business context issues that create risks to results. Chapter 19 provides a basic form of Success Healthcheck Diagnostic for your use.

Make notes, highlight potential risks that face your project success. Circle the warning signs that are relevant to your business context and project.

Complete the diagnostic.

Every project faces risks from the business context—the question for each project is "have we recognized it and dealt with it adequately?"

The diagnostic structure helps you get data that allows you to draw a conclusion. Is the project likely to deliver results in the business or not?

Chapter 14
Background to Part 4

A quick recap of the book so far:

Part 1: **Productivity** focuses on three business problems:

1. Are we getting value from IT projects?

   The short answer is: "No, 93 percent of projects fail at some level." Commonly, when a group of projects is benchmarked as an investment, the portfolio shows a negative rate of return.

   Projects commonly deliver less than expected, for more than expected, later than expected.
2. How can the value from IT projects be improved?

   IT projects must be considered as a portfolio. The aim is to have as many projects as possible succeed. Reality being what it is, some will fail. The challenge is to reduce the failures.

   The 7 Keys to IT Portfolio Success provide a quality assurance process that immediately lifts the overall results from IT projects and investment.
3. Problem: **93 percent** of IT projects fail at some level.

   Hindsight is always too late. Project managers, CIOs, and business executives need a way to identify risky projects early.

   Research has identified a set of factors that are early indicators of success. The risks to business results from IT projects can be reduced using Results Risk Management. The 8-Fold Path is a diagnostic used to assess the likely success and failure of a project.

Part 2: **Probability** outlines Results Risk Management as a process.

Part 3: **Project** assesses the four indicators of successful project delivery: clarity of intent, robustness of business case, reliability of results delivery process, and the motivation of the organization to accept or reject the intended business changes.

Part 4: **Presence** assesses the business context and how it affects the likely business results from the project.

These diagnostics saved me not long ago on a major project with a global client. I asked questions; I gathered background on the project and the client. The risks that were apparent were tremendous. It seemed that there was no way that the project would deliver business results. For many, leading the project would be a career-limiting move. I asked if the project executive was willing to address the risks, and I put two risks forward as a test. It turned out that politically, they couldn't touch these problems. The project was doomed. We closed down the project and moved focus to projects that could succeed.

Wisdom is often about knowing what to do and what not to do.

Bottom line—in growth or recession, a project only adds to the business if it contributes to productivity.

In Part 1, **Productivity**, we benchmarked the actual results from IT projects using the functional yield of a set of IT projects.

Yield is a term investors (and farmers) use to see if an investment generates more that it costs. IT projects are productive if they add to the overall results of the business. Many organizations set their IT projects based on their IT strategy, but few actually track the yield, the results of their projects.

Each project is part of an overall investment that:

- Should deliver what was agreed, when it was agreed, for the price agreed.
- Needs to be assessed and managed in terms of the likelihood of the project delivering results. Realistically, not all investments turn out winners. Use the Functional Yield as a benchmark or as a basis for comparing and evaluating overall performance of IT investments.
- Generates greater results when the 7 Keys to IT Portfolio Success are used.

A well-managed investment portfolio evaluates which investments are likely to deliver a return, and which won't. These are avoided. IT project investments are no different.

Projects fail when:

1. They fail to deliver what was expected, when it was expected, for the price expected, *or*
2. The capacities of the project are either not used or are ineffective in the business.

Potential failure can be identified from risks that can be diagnosed up-front, just as a doctor can diagnose a risk of heart attack from blood pressure, cholesterol, and lifestyle factors long before the heart attack.

Likewise, a business executive or project manager can diagnose the risk of project failure based on research completed by experts in project results.

In Part 2, **Probability**, the basis of Results Risk Management™ and the 8-Fold Path to Project Success were introduced. Founded on research into project success, a set of risks to the health of project results identified the eight factors in the 8-Fold Path to Result Risk Management. Four apply primarily to the way a project is set up, and four apply to the business context in which the project delivers results.

A project delivers results when it works for the business.

Project focuses on the risks to the project delivering. The four key factors are:

1. Clarity of **intent**.
2. Robustness of business **case**.
3. Reliability of the results delivery **process**.
4. **Motivation** (to change) is energized.

The diagnostics to assess these risks are found in Chapter 13 in Part 3 **Project**.

This part, **Presence** focuses on the broader set of critical risks to results. These are overlooked or ignored in the focus of getting on with the project.

1. Project **aligns** to current strategic position.
2. **Operational** context supports project intent.
3. **Flow** favors project intent.
4. **Balance** and dynamics aid project intent.

These contribute to failure as much as project risks. They can be assessed as part of the project initiation process—before substantive time, resources, or energy is committed to a project.

Many projects (including those run by many third parties) assume that what was done on the last project will work for this project. This is rarely the case. The business continues to change as it responds to changes in the market place and in customer needs.

You can't cross the same river twice.

—Heraclitus

Process: Success in the Business Context

A project needs to deliver results in the context of the business. A four-step process is used to identify the areas that a project effectively addresses and those that are not. Risks that are not addressed jeopardize business results and increase the probability of project failure.

Step 1: Consider what the project intends to deliver and:

- Identify gaps between what the business currently does and what it needs to do to reach its goals.
- Consider the project like a journey—are there any potholes, ravines, or avalanches that the project may face? Anything that gets in the way of the project being able to smoothly and easily slip into the business reduces the likelihood of getting a result.

Step 2: Decide either to:

- Take the appropriate action to address the gaps and issues identified.
- Ignore them and fail.

Step 3: Document the decision made for each gap in the project plan and business case.

- Gaps that are addressed will require resources and activities in the project plan.
- Gaps that are not addressed should be recorded as risks that are managed as part of the project Results Risk Management process.

Step 4: Review the project results risks assessment to see if the project is likely to deliver value given the revised business case. Either

- Approve the revised business case and project plan, and *then* re-initiate the project now that you have set it up for success.
  Or
- Reconsider the project in light of its probable success. Consider the need for a Keep, Kill, or Reconsider decision. If there are risks to results that are not adequately addressed, the project is not likely to delivery results. This makes it a poor investment.

Given limited resources and budgets, it helps the business and the project if gaps and issues are identified upfront. Resources to address the gaps and issues can then be identified. If it is too expensive to address an issue which will make the project likely to fail, it is better to advise the business and the project of the issue, than to risk certain failure.

Business Results from IT Projects Require Continued Presence

Once a project has been set up for success, it is likely to succeed.

But we can't assume that success is guaranteed. The business world is a turbulent, dynamic environment. People will change in response to changes in the business environment.

If a project runs over a couple of years, as many large transformational IT projects do, then the project needs to keep current with changes in business needs and thus project priorities.

Projects, like other parts of the business, do not have 20/20 foresight. Projects need to stay in touch with the current strategic needs of the business.

Either may require the project to adjust what is needed, when it is needed, or the amount it costs. These are legitimate variations. Changes to the project scope, schedule, or budget on these grounds are a sign of success. The project is still capable of delivering a result that adds value to the business. It would be a failure in this context to let a project run to deliver results that only deal with old and now irrelevant business needs.

IT projects can fail at the point they are delivered. Projects assume that the organization and people in it will respond as the project wants them to. In reality, most business operations are set up to deal with other business needs. These are not always consistent with the intended goals of your particular project.

Present to Future Implementation Issues

The project implementation process often assumes that:

- The organization[1] can be managed and described mechanically.
- The project will fit into the organization like a piece of a jigsaw puzzle.
- The project is separate from the business, so that what goes on in the project doesn't affect the business—and vice versa.
- The reality we see now is the reality that will be there when we implement in the future.

In real life, we know these assumptions are not valid. They miss a vital reality: People respond.

For some, people's responses appear chaotic and unpredictable. In practice, there are patterns that can be observed and worked with. For example, a simple change is needed if I'm running late for dinner. My partner may not be impressed. If I call ahead and apologize, the response is different. If I am regularly late for dinner, there will be a different response again.

The business will respond to the project. The responses of people in the organization to an intended change are predictable, when you know the dynamics that drive their behavior. My dinner partner expects me to respect the time and effort that has gone into preparing dinner. When I don't, it is predictable that my partner will be upset.

Frequency (how often I am late) plays a part in determining what response I'll get.

Human systems like a business organization are predictable—there are patterns of behavior that emerge. In being late for dinner, the response I get depends on how early I call, the tone and words I use when I say I'm late, and how frequently I call to warn my partner and how frequently I don't. Memory plays a role too. So does the current situation. If the particular dinner is at the end of a long week, the response is different from the response I would get if it were an anniversary dinner.

Juggling the dynamics of being late for dinner and our partners' response is a skill most of us learn. We also know that what we do now will affect how our partner will respond to us in the future.

The dynamics that affect results are observable and predictable.[2] My research identified four dynamics in the business context that affected business results from IT projects:

1. **Alignment** of the project to the business strategy;
2. Consistency of project with **operational** context;
3. **Flow** of the project with the business history;
4. **Balance** of change and stability in the business.

IT projects can generate successful business results when they work with the dynamics in the organization. When the IT project doesn't align with business strategy, people will ignore the capacities of the project once it is implemented. This is failure, even if the project delivers exactly what it was supposed to.

Collateral Damage Costs

The military term is "collateral damage," the economic term is an "externality," the business term is . . . "someone else's problem." For projects, externalities create risks and costs to business results. In Chapter 10, Business Case Is Robust, costs that are transferred to other parts are the business were called "pollution costs."

To get business results from IT projects, the business and the project need to identify anything that will impact the project but looks like someone else's problem. Often if something is not within the project scope, the PM will say, "It is not my problem." This approach simplifies life for the project, but it adds unnecessary risk to the business results.

For IT projects, the most frequent causes of reduced results come from overlooking (or ignoring) the need for the business system to work effectively.

IT projects deliver capacities. People use the capacities to deliver business results. The people may be staff within the organization, customers, or business partners.

If it is "someone else's problem," it is unlikely to be done.

For IT projects, the areas in the business that are most frequently considered someone else's problem are changes to:

- Processes and procedures;
- Skills or culture within the organization;
- Jobs, roles, and staffing levels;
- Customer or partner interest and incentives to use the new capacities.

These elements are usually addressed by organizational change management and organizational development.

In Part 3, **Project**, the implications of ignoring these elements of the business were considered as part of the business case in Fold 2 and by their impact on people's productivity and motivation to perform in Fold 4.

If the business wants results from their IT projects, then projects need to address the whole business, not just the technology component.

Successful organizations manage cross-functional program risks by setting up an overall program that manages their total portfolio of projects (IT projects and other projects), so that the delivery of the different components of the business solution (technology, processes, people) are aligned.

If the IT project delivers successfully and another project in the program fails, then the overall business results will be jeopardized.

An Archetypical Business System

The executives I interviewed shared many stories of what works and what does not. Patterns emerged.

Their stories took me back to discussions I overheard as a child growing up in Nigeria and the Philippines where my father worked as a research scientist raising agricultural productivity. The goal of the Institute was "to lift farm productivity so that starvation is a thing of the past."

This was a big goal, one they thought was going to take decades to achieve. It took less than 20 years to address food production issues.

The scientists started working on the farm as a system. They realized that the whole business system had to work effectively with technology for farm productivity to lift.

A rice farm is a set of interconnecting systems. If water isn't flowing well at the right time, the rice won't grow. If the rice variety is wrong for the location and soil, it fails. If the farmer is worried about social unrest or his family, he cares less about his rice crop. Any of these affect the success of his business and the happiness of his family.

Juan de la Cruz, a rice farmer on the hills of Banaue in the North of the Philippines, gets results from his technology projects when he considers them as part of his business system. Over the years, technologies he has added to his business have included:

This breakthrough became known as the "Miracle Rices."

Numerous research findings came together to generate transformation in rice farm productivity. The varieties and yield of the rice, fertilizer, engineering, storage, logistics, marketing, and even greater understanding of how the soil physics and chemistry affected the yield and led to sustainable business results on the farm. Farmer psychology, communications and business economics also played a part in leading to sustainable business results on the farm.

- Improved yokes so his water buffalo work more effectively.
- New tillers that turn soil better.
- Mobile phones that allow him to call other farmers to see if they could release water needed for irrigation.
- Mobile phones also allow him to contact the man who takes the rice to market so they can agree on times for pickup.
- New breeds of rice—more disease-resistant or higher nutritional value, which lift the yield from the farm or the quality of his rice.
- Information that helps Juan target the amounts and timings of fertilizer and pesticides more effectively.

Each time Juan evaluates new technology, he knows that it has benefited someone else but wants to know if it will benefit him. He is not a bleeding-edge adopter. He realizes that changing one element of his rice farm affects other parts of his business:

IT has colorful terms for technology adoption:

- Bleeding edge;
- Leading edge;
- Fast follower;
- Well proven.

Each of these has implications for technology risk, project risk, and cost to maintain. A business should appreciate the implications of where "bleeding edge" truly adds competitive value and the value obtained by letting someone else iron out issues, build skills, and generally make a new technology well established. Technology adoption should be a conscious part of the IT and business strategy. The more edgy the technology, the greater the technology risks to results.

- A better yoke might improve productivity of the water buffalo because it sits better on its back, but will the water buffalo actually do more work as a result?
- A tiller or rice variety that works in one environment may not work on Juan's farm due to differing soil or water levels.
- A phone is useful if other people that Juan connects with are also connected and if Juan's relationships with the other people are good.
- Fertilizer changes may create long-term problems, like more weeds and more effort to clear those weeds.
- Fertilizer could also mean problems for the farms further down the irrigation stream and affect those relationships.

As a businessman, Juan wants his investment in new technology to work effectively with the rest of his business. He knows that some problems will become obvious later on. In the meantime, he looks at the indicators of project success in the business to see if he should proceed with the project.

Diagnosing the Business Context for Success

The business gets results from IT projects when the whole business system works.

Results Risk Management using the 8-Fold Path looks at the business system. The diagnostic reflects the following:

- Each project has its own goals.
- Each organization is different from the next.
- The same organization changes over time—so what works for one project is not necessarily effective for the next project.

Project managers need to assess organizational context for every project.

Each project needs to assess the business context in light of the project goals to check:

1. Project **alignment** to current strategic position.
2. **Operations** support project goals.
3. **Flow** of history supports the project.
4. **Balance** of change and stability is sustainable.

The next four chapters focus on these business systems. Each concludes with a short checklist tool for you to informally assess the effect your business context is having on project results.

As a leader, you are likely to be familiar with many of these. Life experience is relevant to projects. A disciplined diagnostic structure allows you to review risks with a methodological, reliable approach—this is valuable.

Use a pencil, take notes. Flag the risks that strike you as relevant to your project and its capacity to deliver business results. Ask yourself critically, ''Are we really doing something about this risk?''

At the end of each chapter is a short set of warning sign risks. Circle the ones that you see as applicable to your project.

The final chapter of this part provides a basic diagnostic for the probability of project success.

Endnotes

1 Morgan's wonderful book covers over 20 different ways of looking at an organization—as a mechanism, a brain, a psychotic. The analogy that best fits here is that of an ecosystem. An ecosystem is a series of systems that interact and broadly create a living, dynamic environment that can collapse, die, struggle, survive, grow, or thrive as it responds to changes internal or external sources.

2 Case Study of Organisation Applying Complex Adaptive Systems: http://www.bioteams.com/2005/07/29/an_organisation_ase.html. For More on Management Theory Associated with This Behavioral System, see Ralph D. Stacey's book *Strategic Management and Organizational Dynamics: The Challenge of Complexity.*

Scientifically, these dynamics are studied by the fields of complexity chaos and systems theory. There are specific qualities of these nonlinear dynamic systems—they are called complex adaptive systems.

As most readers will want to get to the point rather than the science, the focus of this book remains with the business issue ''how to spot potential failure and success . . . ''

Chapter 15
Fold 5, Project Aligns to Current Strategic Position

Projects exist to help move the business in the desired strategic direction. Projects succeed when they work effectively to close the gap between the current strategic situation and the desired strategic situation.

Bigger gaps require more change and therefore are more risky. The project needs to pay even more attention to bridging those gaps.

Think about your current business, the desired strategic goals, and what it will take to achieve them. Is the strategic journey:

- A short journey?
- Are there any detours, ravines, or minefields along the way?

A short journey is not necessarily easy. Political minefields or ravines are best crossed with bridges—these require investment.

Projects that aim to create strategic shifts face larger results risks than those that don't. The critical element for these projects is to identify the areas where there are differences between the current organizational state and the strategic vision. These are the gaps. The integrated project plan must address these gaps, else they ''become someone else's problem'' and a risk to results. IT alone will not cover all the gaps.

IT projects are part of the organizational performance system. Other parts (culture, policies, finance, HR, etc.) also play a role. All need to align and integrate to get sustainable results—even Juan needs to have all parts of his farming system—soil, water, seeds, workers, and his own motivation in alignment if he is to have a successful year on his rice farm.

What do projects need to consider when they are introducing an IT project that affects the strategic context?

Three strategic systems[1] affect business results from IT projects:

1. The external forces on the organization and the corporate strategy;
2. The leadership and vision of the organization;
3. The culture and politics of the organization.

These three systems must function effectively together for organizations to grow and projects to deliver results.

The strategic business environment affects the project's ease of delivering results. Contrast the ease of delivering business results in an organization that has clear direction, leadership that walks its talk, and happy, energized staff to one where strategy is not clear and consistent, leadership is weak or poisonous, or vision is poorly established, or where focus and effectiveness of people are eroded through misalignment and cover-my-back activities.

Weak direction or a negative culture means direct economic costs to the project through additional effort it needs to address the effects of disinterest, neglect, or even sabotage.

In general, an organization with clear strategy, a positive culture and motivated people outperforms an organization that is lost, and fearful.[2]

Risks to Business Results from the Strategic Context

Many leaders will be familiar with these systems. Specific components impact business results from projects.

As you read, ask yourself, "Is my project addressing these issues proactively or are we hoping that someone else is?" Verify that the other party is. If they are not, flag this area as a risk to results.

Strategic Context Affects Results

Strategic context is important, and several components are specifically relevant for project success:

1. Forces in play and the business strategy;
2. Economic context;
3. Movement along the strategy curve (S curve).

These strategic components determine the larger, longer-term context in which the project operates. If the project does not move the organization forward—to the future of the organization—the relevance of the project should be reconsidered.

Projects need a strategic focus, not merely a tactical fix, even if the time frame is short.

The Forces in Play and the Business Strategy

Today several forces drive business strategy. In addition to Porter's five forces (Figure 15.1),[3] technology and capital markets drive an increasing pace of change. In some industries, community, NGO, and regulatory pressures are also an increasing source of change. Each of these forces contributes to the

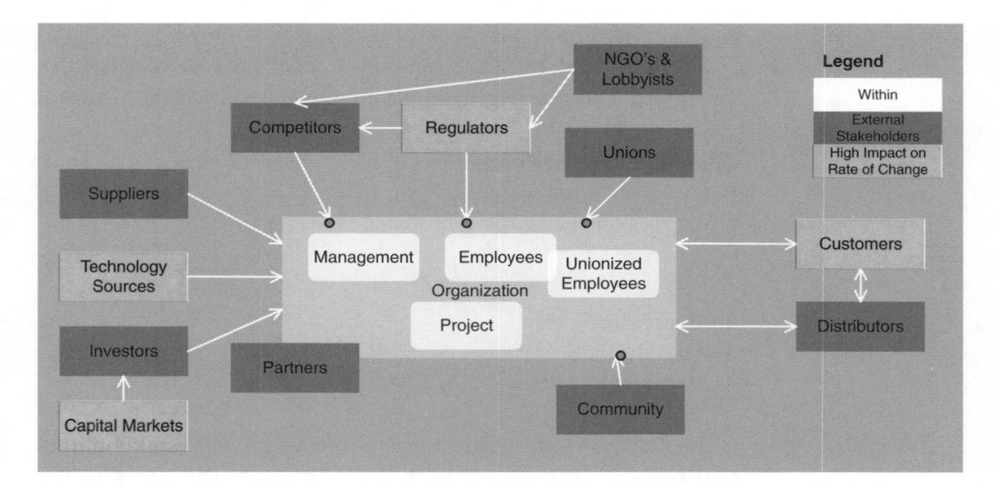

FIGURE 15.1 Twenty-First Century Version of Porter's Forces

business context of a project and may drive the type of requirements or the urgency for their delivery.

The forces also reflect the impact of an internal action on the external world—if a project impacts the business so that services are disrupted or reputation is damaged, there is a business cost.

CASE STUDY

FROM REAL LIFE

Mike reviewed a regional IT project that had completed the first country implementation of a logistics system. The project was designed as an internal IT project, but business implications to the supply chain and customers had been overlooked. The country was unable to ship product for a month as they sorted out operational problems. The bottom-line cost impact to distributors, customers, and to the business was substantial.

Forces influence the organization's strategy and projects designed to achieve that strategy. The more explicitly the forces are recognized and linked to project objectives, the more aligned a project will be to strategic direction and context.

Projects need to move beyond tactical fixes to consistently considering the strategic landscape that faces the organization.

Specific External Forces

External party relationships affect project success. Four are often critical for IT projects:

1. Customers;
2. Regulators;
3. Shareholders;
4. Partners.

Projects can consider these parties' strategic stakeholders and require a Strategic Stakeholder Analysis. This assesses the possible benefits and impact that the project has with each stakeholder and then factors appropriate tasks and resources into the business case and project plan.

Customers Are the Source of Profit and Thus Benefits

Customers are often overlooked by projects. Customers are obviously important. They are the ones who decide to buy more of the services, accept a higher average price, or buy less. Or they defect totally. The customer's impact on revenue generation is critical.

If the project has a real downside impact—it slows things down, makes processes more difficult, or causes operational issues—it will affect customer services, which affects revenue generation.

In many industries, the cost of customer acquisition is a good chunk of the first year's profit from that customer. In others the cost of acquisition is 10 times the profit on existing customers. In this context, paying attention to customer impact becomes crucial.

Frequently, projects fail to consider the potential impact of an internal project on customers. Even CRM projects, which intend to improve customer service to generate more revenue, rarely pay sufficient attention to the impact on customers.

Ask, "How will/could this project affect the customer?" and then "What else can we do to have a positive/neutral impact on the customer?"

Regulators and License to Operate

Regulators prescribe data, processes, risk management, and other outcomes that the business must adhere to.

Clearly, dealing with regulator and legal needs is a basic for project success. It's how it's done that contributes to project success or failure.

Some projects overlook the effect of regulatory requirements until the end, when it's "Oops, we have to do what?" This leads to delays, extra costs, and reduced business benefits. This is a fairly obvious error and correctable.

The other aspect of regulatory requirements is a tendency for people to assume "this is what we always have had to do to meet regulatory requirements," or "just do it" without robust discussion about how to achieve the requirement more effectively.

In some businesses, a regulatory check or review occurs just prior to implementation. Auditors want to see the final product and don't want to waste time before that. Projects then guess what is needed or ignore it until the audit report is complete and requires fixes to problems X, Y, Z before the project can be implemented. Project leaders panic, and there are additional costs and delays.

Regulations must be addressed. There are many options to meet legal and regulatory requirements. The tendency to is formalize a rock-solid process, which adds to projects costs and delivery time—and to organizational sclerosis or blocked arteries.

Better to explore options to meet regulations first and then decide the approach.

Practically determine the intent of the regulatory requirement and determine the best method to effectively meet the regulations. Work with the auditors to align and agree on your approach early.

A good process consultant and balanced regulatory advice can really add value.

Project leaders who ignore regulatory issues, or wait for a pre-implementation audit, put the project results at risk. If the auditor or regulatory liaison contribute to upfront planning and design reviews, their commitment will reduce the risk of project failure.

Shareholders and Providers of Capital

Shareholders and the financial markets provide a powerful set of incentives for good financial discipline in many companies. Interestingly, this group does not cast an eye onto the endemic failure rates of projects or the economic equation of project results. Shareholders should care about project failure rates at 93 percent.

However, it may not be a blind spot that business executives want to continue banking on.

Taking meaningful steps including tracking the track record of project results and demonstrating continued improvement in the delivery results are an appropriate proactive action.

Partners, Outsourced Services, and Key Suppliers

Many businesses rely on partners, outsourced service providers, or other key suppliers and distributors. Each of these is in business. Their management teams are likely to get their bonuses based on the service they provide you and the overall profitability of the business relationship. In the long term, each of these parties must make a profit in order to survive.

Projects, particularly larger ones, need to consider the project's implications on partners and suppliers of services:

- Does the project pass business risks to the partner that, if they occur, might jeopardize business results?
- Is the partner relationship one of flexibility and mutual support, or are you dealing with a volume, cost-based process commodity service?
- Does the contract allow variations in service levels or service volumes? What is the cost implication? Does it make economic sense for the partner?

Partners and major contracts can materially affect project results.

The Economic Context

The implications of the economic cycle are rarely evaluated in projects. Some large programs deploy one version at a new site, while rolling out an upgrade to an earlier site.

Leaders must be clear if the project intent is for up-cycle growth or part of down-cycle containment—this will clearly affect urgency and timing as conditions change.

Economic conditions and the economics of globalization continue to change. Projects must check that their raison d'être is still valid.

Position in the S Curve

The concept of the S curve comes from Boston Consulting Group's assessment of company lifecycles. The S curve is used to illustrate the cycle of business growth (and decline). As the cycle occurs, the challenges faced by the organization change.

The four inflection points indicate where the nature of the business challenge changes. This affects the nature of projects in

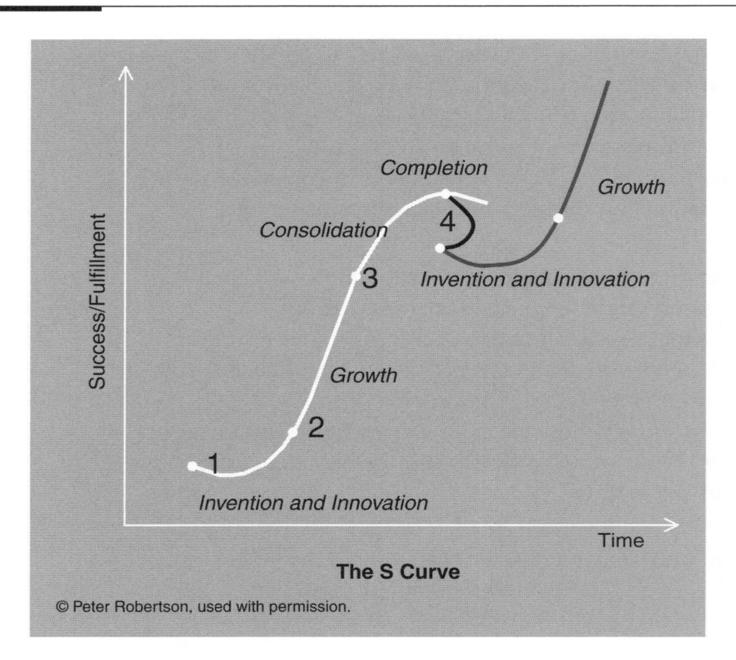

FIGURE 15.2 The S Curve

the organization as projects are used to shift the organization through these inflections (Figure 15.2). A project to build new capacities faces different challenges to a control and cost containment project.

The inflection points are the points of the greatest change. Risks to project success increase if the business lifecycle is not considered. Each inflection point has a new challenge:

1. The challenge for a new venture, start-up, or green field is about creativity, innovation, and getting someone to buy your product or service.
2. The challenge of moving from start-up to growth and leverage is about conversion of a prototype into a scalable, replicable set of business processes or products.
3. The challenge of moving from growth into consistency, consolidation, and value extraction is about efficiency and cost reduction.
4. The challenge of ''leaping the curve'' as one part of the organization moves from one curve (white) to the next

(grey) focusing on innovation while other parts of the organization focus on value extraction. The challenge here is about balancing the interests of extracting value with the dynamics of growth and building the next phase of success.

The S curve can show where an organization, a division, or product is in terms of its growth and maturity. One of the greatest strategic challenges for an organization is how it moves from one S curve to the next.

At any one time, a business may find that parts of it are operating in one part of the S curve, while other parts are operating in a different part of the S curve. In industries with rapid transformation, S curve transitions come rapidly and are seen as a core competency.

IT projects can be used to enable the transition up the S curve or across to a new curve—provided the project is aligned with the strategic goals of the business and caters for the shift in focus that occurs when the organization moves up the S curve.

There can be multiple projects with different goals to help the organization move along the S curve. Efficiency projects can affect the same business units as other innovation and creativity projects. When the different nature of these needs is acknowledged, it becomes easier to ensure projects are not in conflict.

It helps the success of a project if a company's S curve goals are clear, explicit, and communicated to the project team.

Leadership and Vision Affect Results

Leaders set the standards and the direction of the organization.

The quality of leadership and vision impacts projects and their capacity to deliver value and results in the business.

Three elements stand out that affect business results from IT projects:

1. Leaders as role models;
2. Leadership team consistency with the S curve;
3. Quality of communicating the goals.

Leaders as Role Models

Leaders are the Chief Role Model of many, many things. For projects, how they model values, decisions, and accountability is critical. If the leadership style is expedient, numbers-focused, and makes gut-based decisions with little follow-up on the results of a specific decision, then that is how projects will be run and delivered.

If the leadership style is reflective, considers implications, consistency, and calls for reviews of decisions and progress, then that is how projects will be run and delivered.

CASE STUDY

FROM REAL LIFE

Contrasting two leadership styles. A very numbers-focused executive took over from a more collaborative leader. Consider the impact their styles had on projects.

When leadership shifted to the "what are the hard numbers?" approach, there was a strong tendency to ignore the people elements of the project and to reduce the focus on the robustness of the results delivery plan.

The previous executive would ask questions about the people side of things and expect to see them addressed.

Better project decisions were made—ones that led to more solid results in the business—with the previous executive as his approach also addressed the risks to results that arise from people-based risks.

Business results are achieved when both the business and the project are accountable for the delivery of results. Leadership styles must be consistent with:

- The strategy that has stated;
- The project goals;
- The stated values of the leader and the organization.

If leadership is inconsistent, their walk does not match their talk. These inconsistencies and misalignments add to the challenges a project must address.

If leadership is inconsistent with the stated values of the organization, staff will begin covering their backs and will be less likely to be willing to try new things. This increases the risk of the project being rejected upon implementation.

Leadership Team Consistency

Many leadership teams are structured so that some members focus on outside issues surrounding the company (often the CEO) and others focus on inside issues (often the COO). The challenges that each of these roles faces change as the S curve changes.

For leaders introducing change into a business or for project managers, the shifting nature of the leadership challenge affects projects, business transformation, and growth.[4]

People in the organization can change more effectively when leadership displays specific consistencies in the message and values they display. This enables those who report to the C's to rely on what they say.

> *What matters in leadership is not the words hanging on the wall, it is the behavior demonstrated in the hall.*
>
> —Marshall Goldsmith

The S curve reflects two leadership challenges. Successful leadership teams and transformational project teams must display:

- Alignment to the S curve challenge—Leadership that delivers the old S curve position while demonstrating what is required for the new position. For example, a leadership team that is heavily oriented around the innovation part of the S curve will be challenged at the growth or extraction phases.
- Diversity within the team—this provides a capacity for the team to align to the diversity of business challenges driven by changes in the S curve.

A leadership team that is not aligned to the challenge of the S curve changes will struggle. Project teams that lack the diversity in leadership styles are less effective in addressing issues at hand, reducing project results.

Quality of Communicating the Goals

Vision is power, regardless of whether you are a concept/heart guy or a numbers/process gal. The power of the vision is often the motivation to deliver the results.

> *Put a man on the moon and bring him back.*
>
> —John F. Kennedy

To be successful, a large project must create a powerful vision to align people in a common direction. Most large projects cross organizational boundaries. A common vision is a powerful way to align what is otherwise a bunch of independent fiefs going their own direction.

Richard Pascale, in *Surfing on the Edge of Chaos,*[5] finds that the more fluid the organization needs to be to respond to its environment, the more necessary is the unifying vision of where the organization has been and where it is going in response to those challenges.

Goals that are clear, visceral, and appeal to a bigger picture of what is possible—like JFK's above—are more effective than those that are dull.

Strategic projects must make this link in the eyes and hearts of those who are affected by the project; else people will default back to old known safe processes and behaviors.

The most effective method to embed a vision is the learning-by-doing method. People remember and act on their own conclusions, their moment of "Ah! Hah!" far more than they respond to someone else's facts. A good learning-by-doing method brings the needs of the future back to the individual, "Ah, this is what this big picture means to me, to my place, to my company now." The typical town hall presentation leaves most of us thinking about where to find coffee and a donut.

The goals need be communicated in a way that creates an aligned individual response to get strong results.

Culture Affects Results

"It's just the way we are," someone says about culture. "It's obvious what is right."

Culture and values are strong underlying systems that frame the way we act and respond. It often sets our beliefs. Projects tend to assume what is right for us over here is right for someone else over there. Yet like individuals, projects are not all alike.

The more aligned the project is with the current company culture, the more likely it is to succeed.

Two components that affect project success are visible upfront:

1. Variations in culture and attitudes;
2. Unmentionables and politics.

Culture is like climate; it reflects the broader, underlying belief systems and values. Personal motivation reflects our own specific preferences and behaviors.

Variations in Culture and Attitudes

A fish doesn't notice water. We often don't notice the values and behaviors of our culture. It just seems normal.

Projects operate within the values and culture of the organization. Clearly a project will have a different sort of challenges to deliver sustained business results in a culture that is open to learning or positive compared to one that is cynical, angry, or doubtful.

Culture impacts business results at a second level. You may have noticed that people from other professions aren't quite "just like us." Or that people from other places seem to think differently.

For projects, this creates a challenge that few recognize. In many cases, the KISS implementation approach (Keep It a Simple Solution) assumes that everyone is the same, except for (a) job responsibility and (b) local regulations.

In practice, this assumption is not true. Even companies with as strong a business culture,[6] like IBM, have distinct cultural variations between countries and even lines of business. The variations mean that each group has its own basis for responding to a project. If a project is expected to change behaviors, understanding the variations based attitudes and behaviors is critical to designing an effective means of influencing responses to the project so that intended results occur.

Cultural variations are based on on:[7]

- Professional training;
- National cultural background (includes ethnic background).

A project leader needs to:

- Consciously work with the current culture. If the project doesn't, it will be like a fish swimming upstream—it will expend more energy to achieve its goals.
- Consciously model the future culture. Without the role-modeling from the project and the leadership groups, the organization lacks an easy reference point for what is expected.

Culture affects implementation results.

In **Project**, we evaluated the risks of a vanilla IT solution. The business context is often a mix of flavors. Any sizable company operates in multiple regions. The East Coast of the United States is different from the West Coast. North China is different from South China. The languages and cultures within Europe are different. There are different ways to interpret what is said, different ways of saying no, and a different basis on trust is developed. These are just a few factors that will affect a project's success.

If you are a multinational and your project is rolling out across several countries or even continents, local culture must be considered in your project plan.

CASE STUDY

FROM REAL LIFE

James was leading the delivery of an SAP FICO system in Thailand. There was a whole kit of "how to do it" based on what had worked in the U.S. The kit was used during the pilot and it bombed. The Thais didn't complain, they are very careful about face. But in actual fact there was no change even though the system worked.

Cultural variations go way past the basics of handling business cards or the degree of drinking expected after work.

There are specific parameters that make each culture tick.

I remember my moment of enlightenment.

When working in Thailand I read a 16-element cultural profile comparing the U.S. and Thai cultures. Not one element of culture was the same. For example, the U.S. is very individualistic, while the Thais are very team and community. Realizing this, I recognized why my initial approach had not done well. I changed my project implementation to better align with the country's particular culture.

Project success requires more than simply recognizing the diversity of cultures—or even the natural human diversity in a company. Each culture creates its own stakeholder segment. Projects that run across departmental boundaries will also run up against differences in professional cultures. The marketing department culture may be vastly different from the accounting or the processing department cultures.

The cultural stakeholder element adds complexity to the change. Its existence needs to be recognized in project planning and estimation phases, not just during training and implementation.

Unmentionables and Politics

Every organization has unmentionables: elephants in the room, pandas on the table, and emperors without clothes.

Unmentionables contribute to project failure. They create organization blind spots.

The more unmentionable elephants and pandas, the more difficult the environment will be to achieve project success.

Chris Argyris[8] calls these "undiscussables" when describing organizational defensive routines. The rest of us just call it politics or politeness or keeping our mouths shut.

Why does failure increase in these situations? It's tough to be real in these environments. A lack of reality causes failure. If a project cannot deal with the organization realities, it will fail.

Unmentionables add inordinately to the change management effort. A project must consider all that "cover your ass" energy, all the thinking and planning, conscious or not, about how to survive when the tiger gets hungry and a sacrificial lamb is required.

Failures make an important contribution to the level of cynicism and doubt in an organization. Successes contribute to a sense of belief, of "can do!" The discipline of a project delivering what it says or even challenging what is possible is powerful evidence of culture in action.

If it is unacceptable to admit that a deadline, scope, or budget is unreasonable, reality becomes muddy. Stories are created, "If we try hard, it might work" or "It is better to try than to be shot."

Facing reality takes guts and leadership.

Unmentionables complicate project decision-making and prioritization processes. Undiscussable subjects contribute to project failure.

Culture, Unmentionables, and Values

Behind culture and unmentionables lie values.

Business results[9] from IT projects can be undermined or enhanced by organizational values. Barclay's Bank in the U.K., the ANZ in Australia, and HP in the U.S. pay attention to this element and attribute it to contributing to their business performance.

Fairness and trust are big values.[10]

Ethology,[11] a Nobel Prize-winning field of psychology, has found that even our closest animal relatives operate from a sense of fairness. Fairness is hard-wired into our DNA. Where rewards are not equal, monkeys refuse to play the game. Inconsistent treatment reduces performance. Consistency is key to trust and greater performance.

It is harder to get results in businesses where fairness and consistency are not valued.

Values in the context of change projects need to be truthfully aware of the realities and consider:

- What are the real values operating in the business?
- What is the organizational history that affects current behavior?
- What is the readiness of the organization to act consistently with the values/qualities/spirit desired? Now? And in the future?

The values that underlie the business are often overlooked by IT projects.

Understanding and adjusting for these values can contribute to project success.

CASE STUDY

FROM REAL LIFE

Rick ran a major transformation program that had two executive sponsors, the COO and CIO. One was expedient, out for number one, not seen as someone who led from the front. The other was present, had clear values, and expected people to rise up to them. He listened to those around him. He made business decisions that were consistent with his values. He inspired.

One, if you gave him your sword, would spill blood. The other would coach you to be more effective the next day.

The difference between their organizations was apparent. The staff in the first group joked about who would be the last man standing. Few were willing to take on new responsibilities or try to do things they did not excel in. The visible integrity and respect that the second operated from made it easy and realistic for the staff to trust him and to follow him through turbulent times. Staff would try. Retention was excellent.

Unmentionables and culture can create a cost to the business. Stephen R. Covey calls this a "distrust tax."[12] Projects delivering in an environment with a high distrust tax pay much more for the same project to achieve the same results.

Takeaway

Business context sets the scene for project success.

Bottom line: Projects need to align with strategic systems, or the conflict between them will result in failure. The three strategic systems are:

1. External forces on the organization and the competitive business strategy;
2. Leadership and vision of the organization;
3. Culture and politics—both visible and unmentionable.

The strategic interests of stakeholders, the strategic intent of the organization, and its location on the S curve, set the big picture goals for the project. The organization's leadership style and vision provide direction. The organization's culture and values set the context for behavior and reactions.

If the three strategic systems are not aligned, it will be very hard for a project to deliver meaningful value. It might deliver technology, it might deliver great tools and capacities, but that alone is unlikely to get results. Results do not simply come from a technology or an organization chart, they come from people doing things differently to achieve a common goal, which is aligned with their personal interests and that of the company.

The business environment must be set up to move towards the goal and use the capacities that the project delivers.

CASE STUDY

FROM REAL LIFE

A global executive asked if a project had been a success. The answer was "it depends." The project had proven for the first time that IT could deliver a big, complex project rapidly (1,800 seats CRM across 8 business units and 32 roles in 6 months). The project had also demonstrated that the business could not adapt quickly enough to utilize the capacity of the new technology.

The business in this case was not ready to change.

IT projects are more likely to succeed when the gap between the organization's goals and reality is minimal. Few IT projects are equipped to address issues that affect business results arising from the strategic context.

Transformational IT projects like CRM, ERP, or ABC/value driver projects must consider the strategic context. The responsibility for closing the strategic context gaps must be assigned to business executives who are held accountable for closing those gaps. This may be formally part of the IT project; however, the business is accountable. IT can deliver a capacity, but the business owns the strategic context.

To achieve results from IT projects, the business must lead activities that bridge the gaps between strategic goals and current reality that arise from the strategic business context.

Warning Signs of Misalignment to Strategic Context

- Project is not clearly linked to a strategic or regulatory necessity.
- Project attempts to influence the current position on the S curve.
- Project outcomes require values and behaviors that are inconsistent with the current organizational culture.
- ''Undiscussable'' political elements create potential minefields.

Endnotes

1 See Wyatt Warner-Burke (2002), *Organization Change: Theory and Practice* (Sage) on organizational performance.

2 Various researchers have contributed to this including the work of Martin Seligman. From a macro perspective, consider the success of ''free'' or democratic societies over slave societies. From the perspective of social evolution, the freer people are, the greater the overall success of those societies. Not many successful slave societies in our current world.

3 Porter, M. E. and Miller, V. E. (1985), ''How Information Gives You Competitive Advantage,'' *Harvard Business Review* 63, No. 4: 149–160.

4 See David G. Thomson (2005), *Blueprint to a Billion: 7 Essentials to Achieve Exponential Growth* (Marshall Goldsmith).

5 See Richard Tanner Pascale, Mark Milleman, and Linda Gioja (2001), *Surfing the Edge of Chaos: The Laws of Nature and the New Laws of Business* (Three Rivers Press).

6 See Gert Jan Hofstede (1997), *Cultures and Organizations: Software of the Mind* (McGraw-Hill Professional).

7 See Edgar H. Schein (2004), *Organizational Culture and Leadership*, 3rd ed. (John Wiley & Sons).

8 See Chris Argyris (1985), *Strategy, Change, and Defensive Routines* (Pitman).

9 Collins, James Charles and Porras, Jerry I. (2002), *Built to Last: Successful Habits of Visionary Companies* (HarperBusiness Essentials).
10 See Richard Barrett (2006), *Building a Values-Driven Organization: A Whole System Approach to Cultural Transformation* (Butterworth-Heinemann); and Joseph Jaworski and Betty S. Flowers (1998), *Synchronicity: The Inner Path of Leadership* (Berrett-Koehler Publishers).
11 Ethology is also called the science of comparative behavior. It looks into the behaviors that seem driven from an instinctual level. Genetic or DNA if you will. Deep programming. Many of their findings are initially observed in animals, then a researcher looks at human behavior and sees if we have this behavior in common.
12 Covey, Stephen M. R. and Merrill, Rebecca R. (2006), *The Speed of Trust: The One Thing That Changes Everything* (Free Press).

Chapter 16
Fold 6, Operational Context Supports Project Intent

Operational systems keep the business going from day to day. There are checks and balances to control what is happening in detail. Operational systems affect how things change in the business. Checks and balances provide reinforcement that can help or hinder projects that try to deliver business results.

Three operational systems have significant impacts on project success.

1. IT practices that affect projects;
2. People and HR practices;
3. Financial practices.

Operational practices are often set up to support a stable business environment. Projects by their nature introduce change. When trying to introduce change smoothly and successfully, some policies and practices get in the way.

A project may need to deal with many policies and practices that reinforce stability. A project whose intent requires a different direction or new behaviors needs additional energy. This extra effort affects the risks to success and the resources the project requires.

Operational Context Reinforce

An operational system must be stable. It also needs to change continually to keep up with strategic business change and growth.

To use body temperature as an example: Our skin allows heat to dissipate. When we cool too much, our internal thermostat triggers the body to release energy to warm us. This simple thermostat allows our body to keep temperature constant. It uses the principle of feedback.

Feedback is a form of reinforcement that strengthens a function so that it stays the same.

Reinforcement can also strengthen a direction, this is called "feed-forward." This is required if a project intends to create something that does not yet exist.

The reinforcement of our goal, supported by a belief that this "can be so," fuels energy to "makes it so." It is creative and a necessary part of projects. The goal, the vision, and the belief in what is not yet real can be powerful in creating the future. It works on the principle of "what will be drives what needs to happen."

A project needs both feed-forward and feedback. Possibilities are required to create change, while control is required to keep something on track. Feed-forward possibilities must support project goals, while feedback controls avoid hindering project goals. If a feedback control is misaligned with a project goal, the project needs to invest more resources in overcoming the resulting block that the feedback creates, or it needs to change the policies and practices that define the need for that feedback.

IT Practices and Projects

IT practices affect project results.

Productivity established the necessity of effective and disciplined project management. The use of project management disciplines is taken as given. If your projects are not using them, results are highly unlikely. Enough said!

Project identified simplifying assumptions (KISSes) that lead to project failure when unverified. **Project** also identified risks that arise from how a project engages with the business.

Five IT practices reflect how IT runs its business and affect project results:

1. The project funding game.
2. Projects as an extension of the IT organization.
3. Testing is not for wimps.

4. The devil is in the data.
5. Danger of domino-style plans.

These practices must be diagnosed during project set-up to determine the impact on project results.

The Project Funding Game

There is a joke in any planning area—God laughs at a project plan, as He knows it is the one thing that is not going to happen. It's a less politically correct version of Wellington's famous "no plan survives engagement with the enemy."

A point of project failure is the pretence that the plan is certain, that all data is known, and that the future is fully predictable. It's not. People react, sponsors change, clients develop new requirements, competitors compete, and economies expand or contract.

In many organizations the only way to get project funding is to pretend everything is certain and to ignore unknowns and risks where possible. Ignoring uncertainties reduces the cost and schedule of a project, while increasing the apparent ROI.

The project plan and risk management approach must consider:

- Events—what could happen?
- Contingencies—time, resources, and budget.

A project with no built-in contingency will begin to fail as soon as something unplanned occurs. Contingency provides room to reflect, to consider options, and to deal with reality, instead of pretending "it is all okay."

The project team must have the ability to manage the trade-off of acting now to reduce a risk against letting it run.[1]

If it is easier to get project funds by pretending that everything is fine, projects will pretend. Those projects are likely to fail.

Projects as an Extension of IT

IT often is expected to deliver more, while reducing year on year budget. We hear phrases like "manage IT as a business" or ''accountability for spend'' or understand your ''total cost of ownership.'' The intent of this approach is to encourage more responsible investment of limited resources and to get better results. IT projects affect IT ongoing cost base. Projects that fail to deliver results fail simply add to the cost base.

Key IT practices which impact project success or failure are:

- Governance and accountability for IT investment including IT portfolio management.

  IT portfolio management sets up IT projects for business success or failure in the short term based on how it funds projects and how it reviews project delivery and results.
- Governance and accountability for long-term robustness and flexibility of IT.

  IT internal processes like the architecture and its alignment to longer-term business strategy along with ITIL, and CMMI are all approaches to improve the reliability of IT service delivery. All contribute to the ease or difficulty IT has in repeatedly delivering IT project results to the business.
- IT Organization Touchpoints create hand-offs and opportunities for misalignments.

  Projects require effective coordination and alignment of goals between Operations/Support, Maintenance, IT Strategy, and IT Architecture departments and other project teams. Commonly, each department optimizes for their own needs, rather than from the perspective of continuous delivery of effective improvements in the business. This is an example of the ''Beautiful Mind'' point of local optimization not leading to overall results.
- IT Project vs. the day job accountabilities.

  People on project teams have the same need as any other department: clarity of goals, internal communications, organization and role design, staff training, metrics, and rewards. The needs are often overlooked because the project team is temporary (even if the project is long term).

  Unless effectively managed, project members will focus on their ''day job''—the one that determines their pay packet and bonus at the end of the year.

Team members who feel their jobs are at risk when the project is finished will be tempted to jump ship. Smart folk often avoid projects for this reason.

Smarter organizations deal with this. Projects that are staffed by an A Team are more likely to deliver results than those staffed by the C team.

Businesses that want reliable results from their project teams address these risks.

Testing Is Not for Wimps

There are some who think that projects should simply ''go for it'' and for whom testing is an optional activity.

As Sir Humphrey used to say to the Prime Minister, ''How courageous.''

Testing takes courage. Problems will be found. But that's why it's done.

Medicine must be tested. Buildings must be inspected. IT systems must also be tested at different levels: unit, integration, systems, user functional tests are good practice. Better practices are to test processes and business operations:

- End-to-End on the business process.
- Front-to-Back from customer service to back office.

The purpose of testing is to find problems before they're in production. Once in production, fixing problems becomes really expensive.

Quality assurance takes courage. It's easy to say ''good enough'' and hand it over. But if the system doesn't do what's needed at implementation, the project will fail.

Even if the IT system works exactly to specifications, the reality is that it may not work in the business operation. Anyone who has built a house or remodeled a room knows this. Even with the best attention to detail, the reality of the built product may differ from the vision and blueprint.

Testing allows meaningful variations to be addressed prior to ''moving in.''

Since new systems can have unexpected impacts, sensible organizations have test environments that:

1. Allow IT and the business to test the functionality and stability of a new system and any updates to a system;

2. Allow IT to check that the addition of new systems into production does not cause any unexpected ripple effects in the business environment;
3. Allow the business to test operations end-to-end, front-to-back.

Ensuring this occurs in a robust, reliable manner is one of the best contributions IT can make to business continuity and stability.

Integrated IT and process test environments are critical to reducing IT implementation failures. Testing reduces the business risks to results.

CASE STUDY

FROM REAL LIFE

Bob led a project to integrate invoicing of several major suppliers—average monthly invoicing was over $75,000,000. Month 1, no invoices were produced correctly. Month 2, manual clean-up managed to produce seven clean invoices. Delays in collections followed—more testing of data and processes would clearly have been worthwhile.

The Devil Is in the Data

Many a business change relies on systems manipulating data. The formulas (algorithms in IT speak) are tested, but this is not enough.

Data that flows through the formulas also must be the right quality. Otherwise, the result is garbage in, garbage out (GIGO).

As organizations move to integrated systems, data flows from one system to another. This reduces errors from rekeying data or variations in interpretation. But if the original data quality is poor, the garbage simply moves farther faster.

As organizations move to process-based systems, data warehouses, or metrics-generating reporting systems, the quality of the data becomes critical to invoicing, billing, payment processing, and compensation calculations!

Cleaning up data means not only right quality, it also means consistent definitions for the varied uses of the data, and agreed ownership and accountability for each data field. This is time-consuming, but it is less expensive than cleaning up a data mess.

Stories abound about cost of data clean-up and the cost of wrong data found during an implementation. Even a single field, a single piece of incorrect, unchecked data entry in a data conversion, can have huge flow-on effects. Testing reduces the business risks to results.

CASE STUDY

FROM REAL LIFE

Anne reviewed problems arising from a new system. A set of monthly statements was incorrect and issued to customers. A single piece of data had not been entered correctly in the conversion. Working through the concerns these errors generated at the customer end was costly and embarrassing for customer service, marketing, and management. It still comes up years later.

Data is not sexy or glamorous, but it is critical to project success.

Checking current data quality and properly estimating the resources and effort it will take improves project results.

IT can help improve data management processes and provide tools, but ultimately the business must own the data and its quality.

Danger of Domino Plans

A project manager plans the ''critical path'' by documenting all the tasks and activities that need to be done by the project team. The project plan should include: activities, dates, resources, assigned responsibilities, and dependencies between tasks. Using a Gantt chart is very useful to see when a task begins, ends, and what follows it.

Schedule is then optimized—often to speed up delivery—and tasks are scheduled back to back. This is logical and efficient.

Compressing the project plan removes slack and lines up the project tasks like a series of dominos.

Several implicit assumptions of this approach add to project risk:

- All tasks are included.
- Estimated times are correct.
- Resources will be available as needed—and with the right skills.
- Quality will be achieved as needed—and the team will get it right in the agreed number of iterations.

None of these are true in practice. To do so would require the team to be omniscient—a rare quality.

If a project plan is built on the domino principle, whenever any of these assumptions fails, the project will be delayed, quality may be affected, and project failure follows closely.

In Chapter 3 the vital role of slack and contingency was discussed.

CASE STUDY

FROM REAL LIFE

Stephen's team approach was fast response project delivery. Every two weeks a new release of functions became available. To manage this, they assigned a function to a release based on its apparent complexity. They reviewed history and tested until they found and fixed only the average number of errors found per release. The new function was released, even if all the errors had not been fixed.

This was an unusual approach to quality, which had negative consequences for the business. Functions were released based on ease of IT development, not on business need and priority. People in the business had to adjust to new functions every two weeks. Errors were found, because testing was only to an average quantity, not a quality standard. Eventually users refused to use the system.

The cost of unexpected delays or poor quality is rarely assessed by projects, yet it is critical to the perception by the business of project success or failure.

The Power of IT Practices

IT as a department can have policies make sense for their original purpose yet have negative effects on projects. These are addressable by:

- Including risk-events and appropriate contingency management resources (time and funds) in the project plan.
- Evaluating how IT organizational practices may hinder the effective introduction of projects. IT Change Control process can be optimized with operational management practices like IT governance, CMMI and ITIL.
- Ensuring the critical path has space in it for the domino effect from the business perspective.
- Encouraging the use of full business process testing: End-to-End and Front-to-Back.
- Defining data quality and clearing up the garbage with the business.

The People Thing and Projects

People. We interact. In business speak, this is a bland way of saying people laugh, cry, position themselves, avoid things that discomfort them, or even act cynically.

People are less predictable than technology.

Where we are depends on our past. What we do is affected by our future goals. Who we are depends on how we feel now.

An IT project achieves business results when:

1. The project delivers what was expected, when it was expected, for the price expected.
2. The capacities of the project are used effectively in the business.

The human element of projects is critical to the second point. Three elements act as indicators for project success:

1. Capacity to support change in people;
2. Emotional safety to experiment and change;
3. Rewards and punishments.

When the human elements are aligned to the project goals, business results flow faster and more effectively as staff and customers find it easy to use the new capacities provided by the IT project.

When human elements are not aligned to project goals, people ignore the project capacities and stick to their current processes. Worst case, they may reject the project outright.

Project leaders that face misalignments between human dynamics and project goals need to invest additional time, energy, and resources to address the basis for the misalignment. This usually requires investment in change management or organizational development capacities.

Capacity to Support Change in People

To make business results flow from projects, people must do things differently. Some organizations are designed so that it is easy for people to change. Projects can contribute to this capacity or not. Organizations that find it hard for their people to respond, respond slower in the market.

Chapter 12 reviewed expectation and the motivation of people in the business to accept or reject the project. Three elements were considered:

1. Do people have the skills to adapt and change to new circumstances? Individuals need skills to flow with change, instead of holding onto old ways.
2. Is it rational for people to resist the proposed changes? People are unlikely to support a change that risks their jobs or reputations.
3. Do project goals align with the broad motivations of the staff?

To address differences between project goals and human motivations to change, the practicalities of the human side of the business equation must be considered.

Change Management calls this ''dealing with the three don'ts.'' If people don't, they won't.

1. **Don't** know about the change or how to change.

   Addressed by effective two-way communication and building skills in adapting.

2. **Don't** know what to do as a result of the change.
   Addressed by effective learning programs in the classroom or on the job (for projects introducing significant changes restaffing, job and role redesign may also be required).
3. **Don't** want to change.
   Addressed by understanding the basis of "resistance" and directly dealing with the underlying issues.

Safety—Dealing with Instinct

Exploration is how people learn new skills and behaviors. We can see it in children; adults show similar patterns. Some children are quite happy to go off and explore. Others want to stay with the people they feel secure with, observe, only going out and explore after they have a good sense of what is going on. This is called a safety profile in business ecology. It is thought to operate from an instinctive level.

This personality trait is stable and accessible. Our safety profile rarely changes. If you want a group to do something differently, it helps if you know how exploratory they are and where they get their sense of safety from.

If a business change is introduced in a way that runs against the safety profile of the group, the change is likely to fail.

Business ecology research provides three insights that affect how we as individuals or as groups respond to change:[2]

1. People have varying preferences to exploring new things.
2. People find safety from different sources.
3. People have different perspectives in which they view the context of change.

The first insight, exploration, focuses on how we feel about stability and about exploration.

Exploratory-oriented people are curious about the unknown, tend to be more future-focused, and explore regardless of an immediate or known benefit.

Stability-oriented people want to check that things work, are more focused on certainty, and tend to be focused on the past. Stability-focused people need more demonstrations that the change will work as promised (and need more opportunities to prove to themselves that it does).

The second insight, the source of safety focuses on "What are we attached to?" Some people are attached to data or ideas, while others are more attached to people.

A change process for a data-focused group must focus on data and ideas, while a change process for a people-focused group must focus on the human components.

Warning: we each react most strongly to challenges against that to which we are most strongly attached. Understanding group attachments helps IT project success.

The third insight focuses on individual perception of context. Some people focus how to keep things simple and about me. Others focus on interactions, what-ifs, and complexity. This affects the information and context a person needs to feel effective and capable of exploring and acting.

Project failure can often be tracked to rejections caused by overlooking these three insights during change planning and change management. Different approaches are required to introduce a change to a group that is stability-oriented (likes data and me-centric), compared to an exploratory-oriented group (likes people, needs to understand broader context).

Business results flow from IT projects if people are prepared to try something new. People must be in their safety profile. Safety profiles vary, so it is more effective to tailor the targeted approach to the actual safety needs of the group.[3] A change process that does not meet the needs of the group profile will fail.

Consistency, Consistency, Consistency

Accepting change often depends on how much you trust the party who is asking for the change in behavior. If you don't trust them, you have to overcome your reservations.

When assessing the risks to results, one must understand the consistency of the leaders delivering the requests for change. Why consistency? Because consistency breeds trust.

Trust is the intangible product which allows us to take someone's word and act on it without a large investment in:

- Ensuring it is right, if we expect something is missing or wrong.
- "Covering our ass," if we fear being misled or exposed.
- "Just in case" activities, if we fear lack of reliability.

Professor Peter Robertson points out that when a project operates in an environment of low consistency, investment and additional effort are needed to ensure that the project is seen as credible, consistent, and reliable.

Leadership consistency is critical. Inconsistent or expedient decision making in the business (and IT for that matter) adds risks to IT projects.

Recognizing these variations and adjusting the project approach accordingly works better.

Rewards and Punishments

Dostoevsky's novels have some common themes: the role of suffering, of rewards and incentives. Of what people will do to get them and the consequences.

Fundamentally, company reward systems are about psychology and affect:

- Business decision making about the project.
- Prioritization of work in the business outside of the project.

Rewards and punishments are popular methods to give feedback to people so that they will behave in a particular manner.

Decisions Are Framed by the Goal

Project reviewed the importance of clearly stating intended project goals when the risks exist due to a lack of "clarity of intent."

Stating intended goals has another impact on project decision making. Consider decisions associated with:

- Experts at NASA and the goals that led to ignoring an O ring. A spacecraft was destroyed and astronauts died.
- Shackleton's determination to bring back his Antarctic team alive. He planned accordingly, and the team returned home, while Scott failed to do so.

What is success? In war, the exit strategy is a key goal. Coming home alive is a key goal when exploring wild and dangerous places.

Before they made their conquests, Julius Caesar, Alexander, and Genghis Khan all considered how to govern the territories they conquered. A goal was stable government in the conquered territory.

Underneath it all, the goal a group sets for itself affects the quality of decision making and resources allocated to the goal.

- If the goal is to come back alive, then decisions, resourcing, and priorities when discussed will keep referring to the goal.
- If the goal is merely to be right, then discussions and decisions are different.
- Janis's work on group think[4] describes the dynamics of this self-validation.

The type of goals set also affects project results:

- Time driven: Delivery date is fixed. Quality and cost may or may not meet expectations, scope and functional completeness may be reduced, the business may not be equipped to operate effectively with the new tools.
- Cost driven: Budget is limited. Timeliness and quality may not meet requirements. Requirements (functional completeness) and business readiness may be reduced.
- Quality driven: Quality is fixed, timeliness and cost may be varied. Quality may be defined as delivery of a limited set of "perfect" functions or a broader set of "okay" functions that may or may not meet business needs. Business readiness may not be addressed.
- Profit driven: Profit target is set for this quarter; the impact of choices today on the ability to work effectively in the future may be discounted. Check if the project goal sets the right frame of reference for decision making—will the business "come back alive?"

Rewards

Many organizational reward and punishment systems reinforce and provide incentives to accept or conform to white world objectives. Even if people know it is wrong.

Reward systems are commonly set up to achieve goals set at the beginning of a project or a year.

In the absence of direct organizational rewards—the psychological power of authority and social acceptance is still at work.

This was discussed in **Project** Fold 4: ''Motivation Energized.'' These factors impact projects in two ways:

First, sponsorship. This is often the result of a coalition of senior people saying this ''will be so.'' Not all will agree. Even if a few senior people officially sponsor a project, what will occur in reality is what the most powerful sponsoring coalition wants. If the coalition does not want the success of the project, it won't succeed.

Second, most managers receive direct financial rewards if annual KPIs (key performance indicators) are achieved. These are often set at the beginning of the year.

Performing to end-of-year targets is a skill most people learn early in their careers. Most of us remember the first time we didn't— we focused on a strategic project that was not built into our targets, and even though it was well-delivered and strategic, our target was not achieved. Not only might we have been raked over the coals for failing to deliver to target, we may have had lower performance ratings or bonuses. In corporate speak, you can't take your eye off the ball—the key is knowing which balls get the rewards. Rewards usually are linked to beginning of the year targets.

In some organizations, the line job, not project team, gets the rewards.

For a project to succeed, it needs to align to KPIs that reward the business. Projects rarely do. Success may require changing selected business KPIs and targets during the year.

Expressions of shock and horror come from executives who have been working away at the original KPIs. People shout, ''My baseline is about to be changed. That is not fair.''

Priorities = KPIs (and Bonus) ≠ Project

Projects need to consider KPIs and rewards given in the business to the results of the project. If business executives do not feel the project contributes to their KPIs, they will give it short shrift—a rational dysfunction.

If there are formal or informal punishments (like the embarrassment of not meeting goals) or an increased risk of losing a job, then it is sensible for an executive to follow the safe path.

Projects often disrupt the business for a period of time, which adds a set of costs transferred to the business, which was discussed earlier in **Project**. A rational executive will think twice about doing a project, unless there is really clear alignment between the project goals and his business results.

Rewards systems reinforce goals. Social dynamics reinforce goals. If project goals are out of synchronization with current business reality, people will continue to work on goals for which they are rewarded.

KPIs may need to be adjusted mid-flight for project results.

The Swift Mover Advantage

A swift moving executive kicks off a project gets the glory of taking action, then swiftly moves on before the project delivers or results are apparent. Leaving before the chickens come home to roost ensures the project and its consequences are the next guy's problem. The next guy can deny responsibility—it wasn't his idea, or he can say leadership direction has changed and kill the project.

Like the Project Game, everyone has an interest in keeping quiet and playing—particularly in an organization where executives move around like musical chairs.

This practice sets projects up to fail. Chris Sauer[5] showed that the risk of project sponsors changing was a material risk to project success. It has almost as much effect as the risk caused by changing project managers.

Processes to manage stakeholders are an attempt to mitigate this risk. A new sponsor is an acknowledged risk to the project.

In an organization with high executive or project manager mobility, the costs of this risk and the need to handle it should be built into the project.

Games reduce if project documents include the conditions under which the project should be cancelled. In Shackleton's terms, executives must ask themselves, "At what point do we turn around, so we can return alive?"

This allows project decisions to become more about assessment of strategic fit and continued alignment than about the sponsor du jour—or about the new executive's need to put his scent on the organization.

The Power of HR and Psychology

HR practices tend to support stable business operations. Annual KPI processes and even most managerial styles operate on the basis of certainty. Things are known and thus safe. In a world of projects that introduce change into the business, HR practices and psychology need to support people in their change process. Specifically:

- Providing support (coaching and training) to equip people with change skills in the business environment.
- Commit to policies that support an adaptive workforce.
- Ensure projects are adequately resourced to deal with the three don'ts effectively.
- Identify the safety profile of each group that is affected by the project change and identify and resource appropriate change management activities to address the risks results that arise from fear and rejection.
- Monitor leadership consistency of words and actions to intended values and either provide feedback where inconsistencies are found or log a project issue and escalate.
- Evaluate if the project goal encourages decision making that is short term or "bring them back alive." It is preferable that both the project team and the organization live through the change. (On some high stress projects, I advocate the inclusion of a body count to make this point—no one wants heart attacks on their projects).
- Address the alignment of KPIs and bonuses to project outcomes particularly if the project has strategic intent.
- Monitor the pace at which the sponsor moves on from projects and escalate the risks to results if it happens more than once.

Financial Policies and Project Results

Finance policies have a large and under-recognized impact on projects' ability to deliver success.

Finance policies are usually set up to manage finance risks or to ensure that reported numbers fit approved accounting policies, like GAAP.

Five elements of risk to business results arise from common financial practices that are addressable and assessable during project set-up:

1. Tolerance of poor quality business cases;
2. Funds allocated on amount requested, not on risk profile;

3. Project funding practices: lumps vs. gates;
4. First mover disadvantage;
5. Capitalization policies.

Assessing the impact of these risks and mitigating them materially contributes to improved business results from IT projects. Two of the five elements were covered earlier.

Tolerance of Poor Business Case Quality

The quality of the business case was considered in Chapter 10: Business Case Is Robust. Twelve different cost headings summarize the necessary investment to get successful results from IT projects.

Most project sponsors know that these 12 items are required to get results, but they don't often include them in the business case.

Part of the reason is that company reward systems often make heroes of those who get funds, without holding them accountable for getting results.

Part of the reason is the result of financial practices.

Many organizations would not fund a true business case, one that fully recognizes all 12 cost headings.

In order to get funding, sensible project managers often only include the costs in the business case that are required by the finance department.

This presents a good case on the surface, but understates the real investment required.

To be fair, it takes a lot of effort to work out these costs, so most project managers will only include the costs they have to and can easily calculate. Wise executives quickly learn how to play the funding game.

This is rational for the executive, but dysfunctional for the organization, because it creates a pattern of underfunded projects which are destined to fail.

Finance sets the standards for project funding as they define how funds are allocated. They can look past a positive business case to consider if it is credible.

- Have all 12 cost headings been adequately covered?
- Have risks to results been considered adequately?

- What is the overall risk/return profile of this project? Is it adequate? Can it be improved?

Funds Allocated by Amount Requested, Not Risk Profile

The second financial practice that contributes to failed business results is the practice of funding on the assumption that all projects will succeed. Project business cases are rarely reviewed to determine the likelihood of success. The normal practice is to assume certainty.

Probability is a well-established part of economic and investment theory thanks to Keynes and Knight. It is even older in the field of insurance, which has used historical rates as a basis for assessing probability for several centuries. Projects must be reviewed using twentieth-century investment practices; they must evaluate the project's risk profile and estimate a probability of success.

The funding body can apply basic financial analysis principles: What is the project rate of return? How likely is the project to repay investment and to pay a return over that? The funding body can also establish the project risk profile it is prepared to invest in.

Funding Projects and Credit Quality

Most businesses want more than a 50 percent chance of a return on investment. Yet the IT project track record suggests a lower probability of success.

Finance can lift results by applying a credit check and allocating funds according to the likely success of the project.

Some projects managers or sponsors are more likely to deliver results than others. If the business needs real results, who would you give funds to?

1. Someone with a record of results; or
2. Someone with a poor record.

Applying insights from this book helps create project credit records.

After-action reviews allow the team and the organization to learn what worked and what did not. Then learning teams will do it better the next time.

Funding—Lumps or Gates

In many organizations, project funds are approved upfront in a Lump Sum. It's a costly practice, particularly if business needs change or the context of the project is no longer appropriate. Perhaps the initial phases of the project are not delivering the results hoped for. Or, as happens so often, costs escalate, timelines expand, and a decision review is needed.

A gated-funding approach helps projects succeed. Periodically reviewing the project status, forecasted timing and costs to deliver versus results, a business can stop sinking good money after bad.

In many cases, it is only possible to know if something makes sense after more investigation has been done.

Decisions need to be informed with data that is progressively available. Periodic reviews work, as do event-based reviews as some parts of the project will require investigation before data is reliable.

It is like house building. When we first sit down with the architect, the estimate is general. As we refine the design, how we want it to be, the materials we need . . . the cost estimate and time to build get more accurate.

Certainly, project estimation in a business case is often a "guesstimate." As the project continues, the scope gets better defined, requirements are clarified, technical feasibility is established, all of which create better estimates. Gates are useful for stopping the funds from flowing down into the money pit.

If there is only one funding opportunity, it is sensible to request as the project may conceivably need. This is particularly true if it is hard to return when estimates are better, or if it is unacceptable to say, "On mature reflection, with more data, we should not continue."

At each stage of the gated funding process, the project is evaluated, future ROI is recalculated (sunk costs may be omitted as non-recoverable), and comparing it to other options. Then fund the next project stage accordingly. Keep it or kill it.

From the financial perspective, this approach allows decision making based on future investment and returns, rather than based on sunk costs. It reduces the total sum invested and allows funds to be re-allocated to other projects that have done the groundwork to lift their probability of success.

People management is required when using a gated-funding approach. It is unsettling for a project team to have their jobs at risk every few months. A decision to shut a project down may be an investment decision, not a reflection of the team. Team performance must be evaluated independently; otherwise a team has an unconscious incentive to only admit to "yes, this project will work." Career plans and employment commitments can be defined that balance both the individual and the company needs when using a gated-funding approach.

Health warning: It takes guts to say, "We've reviewed this project. It cost us $100,000 to do a feasibility study on this project. We recommend not to proceed."

It is often easier to request for the full funds, and act as if the project will be fine, even if that is not the reality and try their darnedest to make it work.

First Mover Disadvantage and Cost Allocations

It is extremely rewarding to be the first mover in some industries. Moving first is often a disadvantage if you are delivering a large corporate project that supports many parts of the business.

If you are the P&L owner where there is project cost allocations, here are some first mover disadvantages:

1. All upfront investment is in the cost base to be allocated.
2. A common vanilla approach must be used, which may not necessarily meet the business need, because the project is so resource or time constrained to "deliver fast."
3. You subsidize other business units when they implement later.
4. There is a delay in initial benefits compared to costs, often across financial years, because it takes time to build capacity.

Challenges arise from chargeback and cost allocation practices. Project costs are usually charged out to the lines of business that use the project solution.

It can be rational for a business leader to go slow or to reject a strategic project, particularly if the there is an insufficient capacity to create incremental P&L benefits to overcome incremental project costs in his department.

There is an equivalent disadvantage to an initial cost base allocation. Those who wait for the second round only pay for the "extra." Lucky them—they get lower costs and more opportunity to meet their specific needs. Sometimes "good comes to those who wait."

These are rational dysfunctions. The standard investment question that should be considered is the timing of costs to revenues.

The business owns the revenue plan. Weakness in the business case will impact the profit picture (refer to the "benefits realization" chapter). If there is a sound plan for the project to achieve benefits, then the timing of costs to results becomes clear. It's much easier to establish a balanced basis for chargeback with this information.

Capitalization Compounds Failure

Capitalization policies are important to an executive managing his P&L and balance sheet.

In many businesses, financial practices require costs associated with human capital to be expensed and costs associated with physical assets, like hardware and software, to be capitalized. In this case, P&L management makes it smarter to invest in IT, which is capitalized and spread across the P&L for several years.

This adds to the incentive to minimize investing in the people side of a project. People costs like communications, training, and coaching costs hit the bottom line now.

If the P&L manager ignores the people costs, it encourages others to ignore them also. Yet, without adequate investment in the people side of the equation, a project is unlikely to deliver results. The accounting policy behind this practice creates a disincentive for managers (be they in the business or on the project) to fully recognize the people activities required for results.

It is nuts to use an accounting policy developed in the industrial age to justify the practice of expensing investment in people in a world based on knowledge capital.

If the organization's accounting policies fully expense investments in people, by implication this says this is a cost with no long-term benefit—yet this investment is required for results.

Capitalization policies drive executive decision making. The consequences of capitalizing the IT side of projects yet expensing the investment in the people capital side of the project doesn't favor improving the success rates of projects.

Service Levels and Third-Party Contracts

Recently two IT practices have become very common, services level and third-party contracts. They improve accountability, are seen to improve performance, and provide a structure for managing the responsibilities and expectations of multiple parties. The presence of these arrangements affects the ability of a project to deliver results.

Services level agreements define the cost bases and the basis for variations in the services provided to the business, regardless if the service provider is a shared service center or an outsourced supplier.

Depending on the terms or deal negotiated, the following issues may be found:

- Limited opportunity to review service volume (the service provider needs stability);
- Penalties for changes in volume of service (changes have costs to the service provider);
- Non-standard services are charged at a premium (particularly if the service provider had to low-ball the initial bid);
- A service provider may have different priorities and turnaround times from those of the project;
- Inability to change the terms of the contract.

It is not unusual to find service providers with unprofitable agreements (perhaps the contract was aggressively negotiated). In such a case, the service provider must attempt to make money somewhere.

If the contract has penalties for overruns, the service provider will have good reason for sticking hard to a timetable, even if it no longer makes sense to your business.

It is critical to understand how the contracts operate and what the costs are, in terms of responsiveness, quality, and charges that are carried forward from pre-existing agreements.

If new agreements are required, structure them with flexibility.

Another issue occurs when the service provider inserts another layer of outsourcing in order to deliver services cheaper and faster. For example, IT operations may be outsourced to a company with depth in managing IT operations, and these companies use third parties to manage their server farms.

This layering adds an extra level of management, complexity, and potential risk to your project, depending on the nature of your third party contract and your third party's third party contracts.

The Power of Finance

Finance policies make sense in their original business context, yet they have negative effects on projects. These are addressable by:

- Improving the robustness and completeness of the business case;
- Assessing the project's probability of success;
- Using gated funding with appropriate reviews;
- Addressing first mover disadvantages for corporate projects;
- Balancing the accounting capitalization policies so that people/technology bias is balanced;
- Consider the longer-term implications of changes in business needs on shared services and outsourced contract structures.

Takeaway

Operational context lays the ground for project success.

Bottom line: Project leaders need to identify the operational context that helps or hinders progress to project goals. Three areas most directly affect business results from IT projects:

1. IT project practices.
2. Unrecognized "people" elements at the ground level.
3. Financial practices for project funding and accountability.

The operational practices affect the capacity of the project to deliver business results. Reliable IT practices that lift the quality of project deliverables establish the initial credibility of the project. The ability to recognize and deal with the detailed people issues on the ground makes or breaks results delivery.

Financial practices contribute to accountability of project investment and results.

Results come from projects delivering capacities reliably and people doing things a new way with a common direction. Overall results come from disciplined project investment practices based on assessing the probable results and paying attention to what works, so that future investment decisions are improved.

If these three systems don't support the project, it is highly unlikely that a project will deliver meaningful value.

Warning Signs of Operational Context Misalignment

- ☠ IT project practices focus on project delivery more than project results.
- ☠ Financial policies encourage investment in tangibles (like hardware and software) over intangibles (like testing, training, or communications).
- ☠ Project goals are not formally linked to the goals of leading executives and of the business.
- ☠ Project teams have a record of burnout or turnover.

Endnotes

1 Several years ago I developed a tool with Celemi, a leading learning organization, to help project teams understand these trade-offs in order to make more informed, proactive decisions. The tool, Cayenne, exposes the consequences of these internal project decisions on the project success rates.

2 See Peter Robertson (2005), *Always Change a Winning Team: Why Reinvention and Change Are Prerequisites for Business Success* (Marshall Cavendish).

3 Profiling can be done formally using the great tools developed by Human Insight.

4 Janis, Group Think.

5 Sauer, Chris (Summer 2008), "Unreasonable Expectations, Greek Choruses and the Games Institutions Play," *Templeton Views*: 22–23.

Chapter 17
Fold 7, Flow Favors Project Intent

In physics, they call it inertia. In business studies, they call it administrative history.[1] The rest of us call it "going with the flow."

It is much easier to go with the flow, than to go against the flow.

For business results flow in the direction the business is moving. The direction is the result from all the past actions in the organization and the events surrounding the organization. It is history.

If the history of the organization supports the goals of the project, the project is more likely to succeed.

History has two components:

1. The current capacities of the organization.
2. The memory of what it took to develop that capacity.

Current organization capacities are the result of all the actions of the past. A project delivers new capacities to close the gap between the current capacity and desired capacity. The project plan, schedule, and all the components of a project focus on closing this gap.

Previous sections of this book have focused on the risks to results that arise either from the project, from the current capacities of the organization (Fold 6), or from the organization's intended goals (Fold 5). Capacities in this context are about "What do we have now?" and "What do we wish to have in the future?"

Memory plays a different role in project success.

In life, if we are successful, we expect to be successful. If we fail, we may expect future failure. This has nothing to do with physical reality. It has everything to do with our memory and the expectations it creates.

Now, some think that it is easy to deal with a bad memory. "We just need to tell people things are different!" says an enthusiastic leader.

Sadly, it is not so simple.

Twenty percent of how people are going to react depends upon what the project is doing now. Eighty percent of any reaction is from what people remember from the past.[2]

For a project to succeed, it needs to know if the reaction is likely to be in favor of the project or not.

The first step of the change management process is to address the Three Don'ts. (See previous chapter.)

The second is to understand the risks that arise from the past and to address them. This is the historical context. It keeps changing in response to ongoing events. Even so, 80 percent of it is based on the past.

The past is a fertile ground for quicksand and landmines. Projects with good detectors can approach danger carefully and diffuse it or plan a path around it.

Even well-managed businesses that run constructive and effective projects find the occasional sand pit that traps their ball.

Projects that ignore the past are often condemned to repeat it. This is not a good thing, given the benchmarked failure rate of projects (see **Productivity**).

Three areas of the past are assessable as indicators of project success:

1. Previous experiences with change in the business.
2. Quality of local or team management.
3. Reputation of the project.

Organizations that have grown organically tend to have a more common thread in their organizational memory. Those that have grown by mergers, acquisitions, and divestments find that their organizational memory is a mix of the history of each of their acquired organizations. The way each merger or divestment was handled is also part of people's memory.

Results are undermined when there is a bad memory from a negative or traumatic event. These memories can last years.

Business results from projects can be enhanced when there are good memories. Memories are held by business partners, as well as by staff.

CASE STUDY

FROM REAL LIFE

A business introduced major changes to services offered to their customers. One customer, Mr. Tanaka, shared how this business partner had been supportive of his business unit during a particularly rough period nearly 10 years ago. Mr. Tanaka was happy to support his service provider in their changes. This reduced the risks of the intended change to the business.

Previous Experiences with Change in the Business

Any project, any change of process, any merger, any divestment, any alteration of leadership or of strategic direction affects memory.

The personal lives of staff affect them, too.

A project can't do much to alter history, but they can look for memories which are likely to trigger a strong negative reaction:

- Retrenchments lead to fears of job loss.
- Major role changes lead to fears of being less competent and less able to deliver to expectations.
- Periods where staff carried extra workloads lead to fears of being overworked long-term for little compensation.

Mergers, acquisitions, and divestments are fertile business changes for creating these experiences, memories, and fears in organizations.

If a project needs staff to proactively move towards the desired goals, then the project needs to know the risks faced in this area.

Projects can also look for successes that may help. If people have recently experienced success within the business, it helps a project to remind people of that success, and to model the current project after that success.

Generational profile affects memory too! Baby boomers and to some extent Generation X people are more likely to sit out a change and try to make it work. They tend to have a memory of long service and mutual commitment to the organization. Organizations whose staff bases are high in Generation Y people or Millennials will find that turnover can increase at the hint of a change, particularly if their previous experience with change in the company was less than wonderful. They are far more likely to leave without a job.

Business results from the project may be affected by staff retention.

Quality of Local Management

The number one reason for leaving a company is the local manager.[3] The local manager also has a strong impact on the performance of his staff.

Even if staff are retrained, given new incentives, new tools, and new processes, their relationship with their manager is a leading indicator of whether they will take on the new ways of working with enthusiasm or dread.

Identifying managers who fail to inspire their staff and addressing the managerial issue is a great way to lift the performance of that team[4]—and to speed up achieving business results from the project.

Business teams led by uninspiring managers are slower to take up project capacities and to use them effectively to get results.

Reputation of the Project

This is particularly relevant for projects that are part of a transformational program or projects that take several years to deliver. Big projects get kicked off. At this stage, the only organizational "history" is the reputation of the sponsors and project managers for delivering constructive, successful change.

Remember, people can't be expected to be enthusiastic about changes that are not to their benefit.

Once the project begins, it builds a reputation: either for being open, honest, and committed to its word, or for being secret or for not telling the truth about what will happen.

CASE STUDY

FROM REAL LIFE

I was on the Executive Committee of an IT department considering outsourcing.

Nine months later: When the outsourcing transition was completed, the major player who had taken the contract said it was the smoothest they'd ever experienced. Over 50 percent of staff had transitioned, with future waves agreed to, with no operational issues, and a lot of good will. No bonus payouts either.

In the meantime: Knowing the dynamics of the organization, the program began dealing with change management questions as part of the project process. On the first day, the project was formally kicked off to 40 people on the core team from the business and IT departments. On the same day, an email was sent to over 1000 members of the IT department asking them to attend a briefing of IT's plans for the future the next day. Agenda item 3 was possible outsourcing.

No secrets: The position: open information subject to confidentiality, legal, and regulatory constraints. Commitments were made and honored. Various ongoing change readiness and support activities were included in the program, using an event-based approach to change management.

Why no secrets? There were several reasons to be transparent. The department's values included respecting people as competent adults and an appreciation that there are really no such things as secrets—the unofficial rumor mill was a reliable and effective form of communication. Honesty was the only policy consistent with the values.

Naïve? No. The people potentially affected were considered as involved from Day One. They were asked to keep it confidential. Staff respected this over the required nine-month period. External communications plans included contingency plans for any media inquiries with the Group Communications Department. We maintained and used those contingencies as required.

Net result externally:

(*continued*)

(continued)

- No negative or speculative comments in the media.
- Favorable coverage when the eventual formal agreement decision to outsource was signed.

A large complex dynamic project. More successful than most. The project deliberately built a reputation for reliable, truthful communications that the staff could trust.

Projects are set up for success when they consider the reputation required for real success—and invest in building it from Day One.

Reputations are built on history—on track records.

For IT projects with significant people change issues, creative ways to decouple and build capacities of the business people independent of the systems delivery helps bring business results forward.

Many issues that jeopardize business results from IT projects that relate to the flow of history and memory will become apparent during the course of the project. Other projects running in parallel will also affect the business. Change in economic conditions will change the optimism or pessimism of the staff. A project needs to stay current to these realities.

Takeway

Flow of history and memory affects the speed of project success.

Bottom line: Projects that need to address historical inertia have to work harder to achieve success than those that go with the flow. Results take more effort and more time when the history of the organization is less supportive of change.

Warning Signs in Flow

☠ The affect of history is overlooked in the project.
☠ The project sponsorship and management team have a poor record of success.

Endnotes

1 Bartlett, Christopher A. and Ghoshal, Sumantra (2002), *Managing Across Borders: The Transnational Solution*, 2nd ed. (Harvard Business Press).

2 Wheatley, Margaret J. (2006), *Leadership and the New Science: Discovering Order in a Chaotic World*, 3rd ed. (Berrett-Koehler Publishers).

3 Gallup research published in Marcus Buckingham and Curt Coffman (1999), *First Break All the Rules, What the World's Greatest Managers Do Differently* (Simon and Schuster Business Books).

4 Ibid.

Chapter 18
Fold 8, Balancing Dynamics to Aid Project Intent

Time does not always have a linear quality. It can have pace. It can drag. It can seem to run away. Time is needed for things to change, but sometimes not much time. Time is needed to give things a chance to mature or to recover and rest.

Projects and change often treat time as a constant. It may be constant mathematically, but in business and in projects it has moveable, dynamic qualities that affect results. With the passage of time, things age, new information comes to light, pressures build up or release.

Three elements of time affect project success most frequently:

1. Pace;
2. Tipping points or phase changes;
3. Regeneration rate.

Pace

Too often the project approach is ''do as much as possible as fast as possible.'' After all, time is of the essence.

Translate to this into music, and it's a cacophony. Instruments race to complete their parts without attention to other instruments and dynamics. Sped up, the music gets lost in the notes.

Projects in the portfolio need to be conducted. Each capacity needs to be introduced when it is most effective for the business.

At a practical level, many projects structure themselves for continuous releases. They don't allow for pace. Faster, slower, pause, faster . . . .

This is more than the domino approach to planning mentioned earlier. Pace can be the space to rest and recover. Athletes consciously include rest days into their training schedules when they realize they and their body need it to perform better.

Large projects must consider pace both for the project teams and for the people in the organization.

CASE STUDY

FROM REAL LIFE

Peter planned a major transformation and was investigating the current organizational capacities. The changes required were substantial. He realized that it was attractive to make the changes in one go, but most of the people in the organization would be lost and would not understand what they needed to do because they lacked the skills or the experience in the new ways of operating. He realized it was a change equivalent to expecting a child to go from crawling to sprinting in a few months.

The transformation program design changed to build organizational skills progressively. He communicated the end goal and why it was required. Every seven to nine months a new organizational structure was introduced with associated roles, accountabilities, and expectations. The training programs were beefed up to support all the new skills required. Partners were acquired to take on some of the burden. Within a three-year period he had a successfully operating business that had maintained services and quality to its customers, and had brought its customers along with the changes—so that they could keep up, too.

Staff eventually spotted the pattern of reorganizations. They used to joke that one must be coming soon after six months had passed. As Peter had built a reputation for regular changes that were properly supported, the possibility of a new change did not frighten them or disrupt business services.

Pace works with flow. Use pace to provide effective positive experiences with projects to improve the memory, and thus flow allows the organization to lift the pace of change.

Tipping Points

Business results can fail for reasons that have little to do with the project. This set of reasons comes down to how things interact over time.

Rain, Erosion, Landslides, and Growth

My father spoke of rain, erosion, and landslides after a trip to Madagascar. He'd met with the ministry for agriculture, whose concern was food production and the effect that it was having on erosion and waterways.

Their methods were literally washing the soil away, eroding the farm.

Erosion (slow wearing away) and landslides (sudden collapse) occur when a key structure that holds the land together is destroyed. It can happen quietly over time or rapidly due to some event.

In organizations, decisions get made, and actions are taken that have future ramifications. In some cases, the effects of these changes build up to a tipping point.

This landslide created by the tipping point becomes an unexpected hurdle in the path of project success.

Toxic Build-Up

If the past has been painful and dire, it is a fact. The project needs to recognize it and deal constructively with that reality, or else the project will fail. Change history assessments are simple and provide useful data about the current perception of the past.

Our perceptions of the past influence how we respond to the current change. When I feel good, I remember good things; when I feel rotten, everything is gray. Psychologists call this a belief filter. It is self-reinforcing.

Does this ring true to your own experience? People do this at work.

There is a build-up of memory in the organization—of what happened to other projects in the other times.

This build-up of memory can suddenly turn rotten. In school we'd add a bit more salt or sugar to a jar of water and suddenly crystals would form on the string hanging in the jar. In chemistry it's called super-saturation.

People can get super-saturated. Sometimes, they reach the point where they have had enough.

This affects projects in two ways:

1. On occasion, attitudes can turn rapidly. They can literally change state. People tip over the edge. In project parlance "it's gone pear shaped."
2. There are also high gain points that provide higher than expected positive leverage.

Successful results require understanding the movement of attitudes within groups. This requires constant polling methods and multi-directional forms of communication and information flow that are created specifically for the project. Frankly, many management lines of communication are not considered reliable and effective. They are also slow. This is why most people trust the grapevine more than they do management presentations.

A reliable means of understanding the sentiment on the ground allows the project or management to respond and head off situations that might get super-saturated.

It's like a test that gives immediate health feedback—a biofeedback mechanism or even daily insulin tests.

In many cases, if 3 percent of the people adopt a new practice, it is enough to start the snowball rolling. This can be useful if it is in the favor of the project.

A project should influence people to do things differently—or else why start the project? Knowing how to influence effectively is more than communication; it is about understanding dynamics (systems dynamics has some very useful models—tragedy of the commons, snowballs . . .) and working with them.

Ethics and integrity that leaders have has a big impact on a project's results. Their behavior affects the culture of the organization and the ultimate acceptance of the IT project. Pay attention to it.

On the positive side, this can create a virtuous cycle of growth. Values like trust and integrity exist when people see a consistent pattern of behavior over time. ''I trust you . . . my experience shows me you are trustworthy.''

''Trust until proven wrong.'' Many good negotiators recommend the principle of choosing to give the initial benefit of trust, but withdrawing it after one violation. It only takes one occurrence before trust is severely damaged.

The different versions of the story of the widows and the donkey in **Project** illustrate differing change histories and trust in the organization's capacity to support changes.

Project success requires having sensitivity to places in the organization where trust is being eroded. Or where there could be a potential avalanche. If it is ignored, the project will pay for it with slower updates and delayed benefits—or, worst case, in outright rejection and project failure.

If the causes of eroding trust are identified, then the project can develop capacity to address this contributor to failure.

Note that in a highly politicized or cynical organization, it is a more rational response on the part of the project to just keep quiet about these issues.

A better response for a project is to consider the impact of politics or cynicism and mitigate what you can.

Projects need to keep a wary eye for toxic build-up.

Regrowth Rates and Burnout

This is the third time-based dynamic in organizations. Projects affect the capacity of an organization to regenerate. This element is a cause for the pollution costs discussed in **Project**.

An illustration makes the issue more apparent. Living systems have regrowth or regeneration rates. If given adequate nutrition and environment, in time they will regrow to their previous state.

This capacity to regenerate is useful. Like seeds of hope planted, a bit of water, and voilà! It is the capacity to give a group of people the encouragement and opportunity and let them achieve what needs to be done.

This capacity can also be destroyed.

Bulldozers, Slash and Burn, and Other Ways to Destroy

The systems used to harvest value from a jungle can enhance or destroy its value over time. In a jungle, slash and burn farming methods cut down the jungle for a couple of years of harvest. After a few years, the land wears out, and a new patch of jungle must be destroyed. Bulldozers are a far more modern approach, but they too destroy the jungle as they clear it.

In organizations, there are practices that have similar effects.

Incentives that reward short-termism, and acceptance of bullying "to get things done" undermine motivation to perform or expediency in decision making, and act to destroy the long-term structures of the organization.

Short-Termism and Expediency

Short-termism assumes that resources consumed today can be replaced tomorrow at no additional cost—or at least, not at a cost that the person burning them cares about.

Putting in an IT system by mandate is expedient. But there are longer-term consequences that a growing organization may want to evaluate. Edicts reduce individual ownership of the consequences of their actions. When the next change comes along, a fear-based, protective reaction is more likely, and the next project pays the price.

Expediency has another consequence. It creates unpredictability, which leads to uncertainty and distrust. In the worst case, it leads to cynicism, ass covering, and self-serving behavior. Expedient behavior during testing (to cut corners) or implementation (to be faster or cheaper) can undermine the efforts of current and other projects.

Note: it can be tempting to ignore a part of the system . . . and let it go (or even collapse) under short-term pressures.

Frogs may not seem important in an ecosystem, but the scientists are now finding the declines and collapses in frog populations in one area are leading indicators of a broader system collapse. They now worry about frogs.

Psychologically, a lack of interest or care about something—like a job or a company—is an early indicator of disconnection. This, in turn, leads to lower attention, more protective behavior, a downward cycle of cynicism, and destructive behavior.

For project success, keeping an eye on the health of the organization may seem strange, but it can be necessary if the project is to generate business results.

Not everything that is destroyed can be replaced instantly at zero cost.

Consider the effects on the future projects in the way a current project uses tangible and intangible resources.

Burnout

Regeneration allows people and organizations to recover and avoid burnout. If an organization has several projects affecting the same business unit at any one time, that unit is likely to burn out from excessive change. People, like ecosystems, need a chance to recover and stabilize to continue growth.

Moving with Time

Time must be balanced. Time with its elements of pace, dynamics, and regeneration affects project results. If the projects fail to integrate across the time dimension in a way that works for the organization's capacity to absorb the changes, many projects will fail to achieve the intended business results.

If the projects lack sensitivity to changes in the dynamics of the organization and cannot respond or react to events that change the situation or realities, projects are more likely to fail.

Timing is crucial.

Takeaway

Balance affects the capacity to deliver results.

Bottom line: Projects implemented when a business is exhausted from other changes are unlikely to generate good business results.

Businesses that desire substantive change need to work with time-based elements to reduce the risk of burnout and to maximize the capacity of the organization to learn to lift its pace of change.

Warning Signs to Balance

- ☠ Project impacts on business per period are not considered.
- ☠ Cumulative effects of changes on a business group are not evaluated.

Chapter 19
Lifting Performance from Failure to Success

Begin by understanding the risks to the business results from your project.

This chapter provides a diagnostic summary for the basic 8-Fold Path Results Risk Management diagnostic. Use your notes. If needed, warning signs are noted at the end of each of the 8-Fold chapters and in Appendix B. This provides a check-up of the health of your projects across the eight elements that underlie project success.

Diagnostic: What Are the Risks to Business Results?

The 8-Fold Path Result Risk Management Diagnostic is a health check and determines if indicators of bad health are present.

Have a cross-section of people in your organization evaluate the project or encourage project teams to complete their own reviews. Use survey tools to facilitate this process or conduct your own interview-based survey. The perspectives can vary across the organization.

Some executives use independent parties to manage the Project Results Risk Diagnosis, because this brings a different perspective with experience outside the organization, they are neutral, and ''bad news'' can be delivered by someone whose career is not put at risk by being the messenger.

For a wider and more robust perspective on the project you've assessed, you can use the online project results risks diagnostic tools at www.successheathcheck.com to survey, assess, and deliver a private report on the likely results of a project in your organization.

Some projects require a more in-depth review because of their strategic importance or the size of the investment. As individuals, there are times that it is appropriate for us to get a full executive health check. The same is true for projects.

The Shelton Method © is a detailed diagnostic methodology to assess the heath of the project and lift project success. It has three parts:

- 8-Fold Path—Result Risk Management Diagnostic—corporate version;
- 7 Keys for Portfolio Success—Quality Assurance Review;
- 3 Phased Results Risk Management Process.

This is executive health check for Results Risk. Metaphorically speaking it includes a nutritionist, a psychologist, a financial advisor, and a personal trainer. Different expertise is appropriate depending on the health issues at hand. Experienced practitioners and organizations can be licensed to complete this diagnostic and results program.

An executive health check for a major project or for a transformation program includes:

- Assessment of over 200 specific elements within the 8-Fold Path.
- Data collection process—reviews of key project documentation and governance processes, staff surveys, and interviews of key stakeholders. Depending on the "symptoms," additional diagnostics may be required.
- Analysis of data to generate a diagnosis—considering the implications of different factors, how they affect each other, and identifying the prime risks that need attention if the project is to succeed.
- Risk prioritization and mitigation plans supported by a detailed report for each of the eight folds in the path which identifies the key risks and recommended actions to address those risks.
- Recommendations for critical action and contacts for qualified practitioners who work with the Shelton Method to deliver the stellar project success.

Table 19.1 summarizes key factors for a healthy project:

TABLE 19.1
8-Fold Path Health Check Factors

Assessment	Purpose/Outcome
Clarity of **intent.**	Clarity of the intended results of the project.
	Awareness of the intended results of the project.
Robustness of business **case.**	Completeness of investment requirements.
	Risk and mitigation for results delivery issues.
	Qualitative assessment of project plans, budget, and business case.
Reliability of results delivery process.	Maturity of a monitored process to measure results.
	Maturity of an accountable process to measure results.
	Use of simplifying assumptions that regularly undermine results.
Motivation is energized.	Project is aligned with motivation to move
	White world–Green world alignment.
Alignment to strategic position.	The pressures on the project that result from the strategic context of the business.
	The degree to which the project intent aligns with the current strategic context.
Operational controls support project intent.	The extent to which IT, people, HR, and finance practices may help or hinder project results.
	The impact of the cumulative effect of misaligned operational controls on project success.
Flow of history favors the project.	The hidden traps that come from the history of the organization that could affect project results.
	Identification of those business units most likely to be at risk.
Balance aids project success.	Evaluates the potential for sudden changes in the tolerance of change in the business.
	Identification of those business units most likely to suffer from change burnout and thus jeopardize project success.

TABLE 19.2 *Project Risks to Results Assessment*

Project Capacity for Success	Warning (2–4 Warning Signs)	Okay (1 Warning Sign)	Set Up for Success (0 Warning Signs)
Intent is clear.			
Business case is robust.			
Results delivery process is reliable.			
Motivation is energized.			

Number of warning signs circled.

Are Business Results Probable?

To pull your assessments together, count up the number of warning signs you circled for each Fold and enter this in the relevant box in Table 19.2 to reflect your assessment of your project.

Project Risks to Results Assessment

To complete the initial report using the template in Figure 19.1, fill in the circles in the left-hand quadrant based on your assessment of a current project.

> Intent: The center—Leave it white if it all is good. Shade it light gray if you have one warning sign. Shade it dark gray if you have more than one warning sign.
>
> Case, Process, and Motivation: Yellow is good; red is risky.

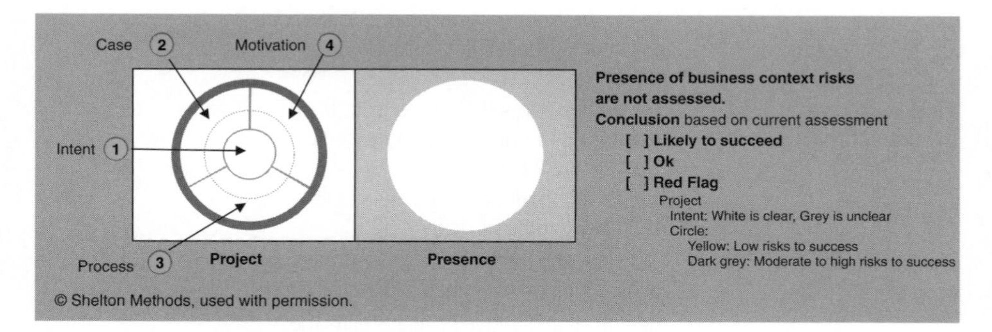

FIGURE 19.1 Presence of Business Context Risks

Color the inner segment red if a specific fold has two or more warning signs. Color the outer ring red if it is there is one warning sign for the segment. Color the remaining segments of the ring yellow.

Project: ________________ assessment.

Presence of Risks from Business Context Assessment

Fill in the right-hand quadrants using your assessment of a current project.

A quadrant is clear if the business context supports the project intent. Put color in your life and use a blue highlighter to shade a quadrant if it is set up for success. If the business context risks show a single warning sign, then the relevant quadrant is light gray. If the business context does not set the project up for success, the quadrant is dark gray (Figure 19.2).

Expected Results from the Project

The first section of the diagnostic report is a visual summary of the overall risks to results of the project like the one in Figure 19.3 along with the definition of the 8-Fold Path Health Check Factors in Table 19.1.

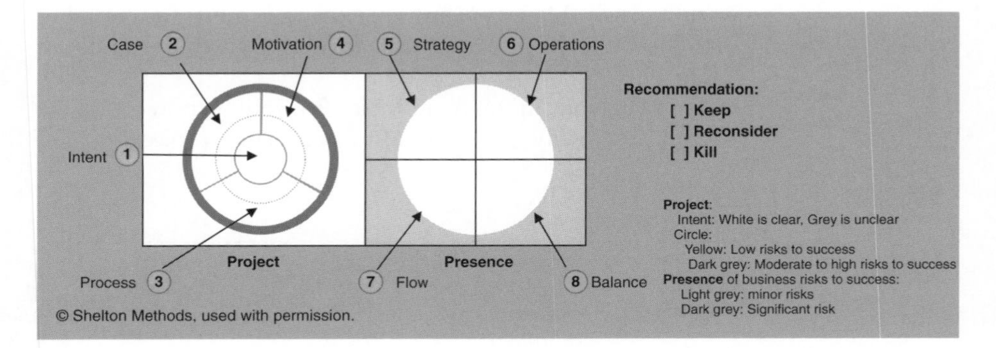

FIGURE 19.2 Recommendations

TABLE 19.3
Presence of Risks from Business Context Assessment

Business Context Shows Capacity for Success	Warning (2–4 Warning Signs)	Okay (1 Warning Sign)	Set Up for Success (0 Warning Signs)
Project aligns to strategic position			
Operational controls support project intent			
Flow of history favors the project			
Balance aids project intent			

Number of warning signs circled.

The second section of the report assesses the risks and provides a probability of success profile. Businesses managing their projects and investments proactively use this as the input for the vertical dimension of the Results Probability Map discussed in Chapter 3 Part 1, **Productivity**.

The third section focuses on prioritizing the risks to results that require action for success. Using the data you have gathered as you read the book and your summaries of those notes that you completed in Tables 19.2 and 19.3 and Figures 19.1 and 19.2, you can complete a basic diagnostic of your own project.

Visually the full diagnostic is represented in Figure 19.3.

To complete the next step of your own basic 8-Fold Path Results Risk Management Diagnostic, count the number of folds that fall into each category and enter the totals in Table 19.4.

Based on your summary in Table 19.4, you can now assess the overall probability of success of this particular project.

TABLE 19.4
The 8-Fold Path Results Risk Assessment Summary

Overall Assessment	Warning (2–4 Warning Signs)	Okay (1 Warning Sign)	Set Up for Success (0 Warning Signs)
TOTAL FOLDS			

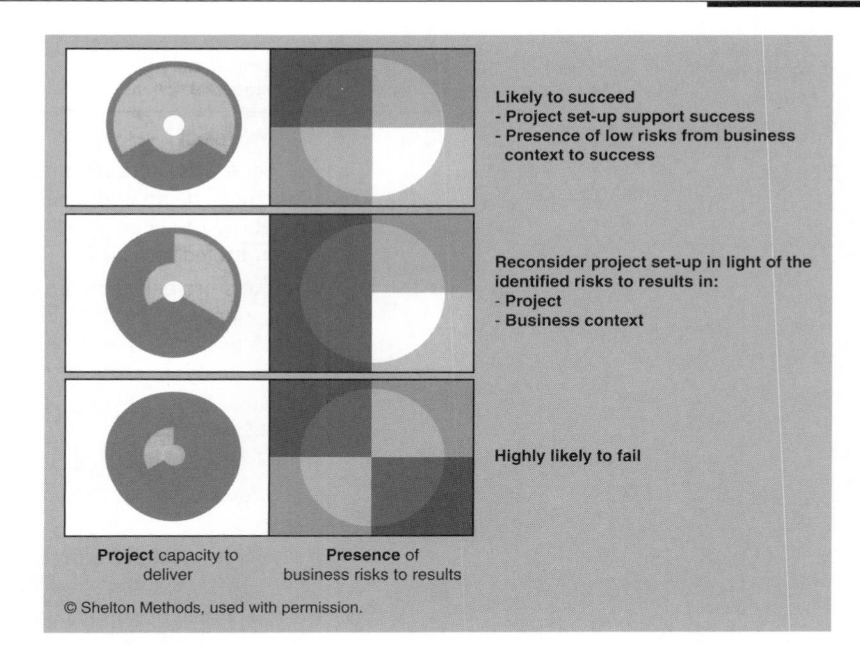

FIGURE 19.3 8-Fold Path Risk Diagnostic in Action on Three Projects

Identifying the Risks to Address

If you have taken notes as you have read, you are likely to have marked the risks to your project that stood out. If not, review Appendix C to see which ones of this short list of high impact risks stand out as the most concerning for your project results.

This is a six-step process.

1. Dimension 1: *Impact.* Identify which are likely to have the most impact on results. Classify each as either high or low impact.
2. Dimension 2: *Probability.* Identify which are the most probable. Classify as high or low probability.
3. *Complete a Project Results Risk Profile.* Map the risks based on these two dimensions onto the grid in Appendix B.
4. Prioritize *Risks.* Using Table 19.5 identify the risks that fall into each quadrant.

TABLE 19.5
8-Fold Path Results Risk Diagnostic: Success Profile

Overall Assessment	Probability of Success	Commentary and Recommended Actions
7–8 Setup for Success, remainder Okay	90%	Dream Project As success is not guaranteed (remember death and taxes), the probability of success rating for dream projects is 90%. Keep this project and consider using a project coach to lift results further and keep your eye on the goal: reducing risks to results and delivering great business results.
5–6 Setup for Success, remainder Okay	75%	High Probability of Success It is probable that the project will succeed. Keep this project. Consider refining it to get better results. Review project plans, resources and address risks to results identified by the diagnostic process to lift probable success rating higher. This can often occur without major investment of new resources. With awareness of the potential risks, project leaders can work proactively to reduce risks before they become costly. Awareness allows action. Use a project coach to improve the effectiveness of the project and to identify creative ways of reducing the risks to results.
1–4 Setup for Success, remainder Okay	50%	Moderate Probability of Success The project has a moderate or 50% probability of success. Most projects fall in this category. Chris Sauer reported that 60% of projects deliver a little less, a little late for a little more. This may be "average,"

TABLE 19.5
(Continued)

Overall Assessment	Probability of Success	Commentary and Recommended Actions
		but you may not want to be. Refine this project to lift its success rating. The project must address the risks to results and receive adequate adjustments to resources, schedule, and funds if it is to materially lift the probability of success. Get a project coach and reformulate the project.
1–4 Warning	30%	Low Probability of Success The probability of success rating for projects in this category is 30%. Consider Killing this project. If it is necessary, Refine it so that it is more likely to succeed. The project should be re-evaluated and the risks associated with each of the eight indicators strongly addressed. The leaders behind the original proposal may require more understanding of what it will take to deliver results. Significant changes to schedule, resourcing, and funding are likely to be required. Once these are established, the business case should be re-evaluated. If this is a license-to-operate project, employ expert help.
5–8 Warnings	10%	Very Low Probability of Success Kill this project. Don't waste further resources. The probability of success is 10%.

5. Address risks to results. Address risks in order of priority, identifying mitigating actions, ways of monitoring for the risks, required resources, and accountable parties.
6. Manage the risks to results. Add the results risks to the project risk management plan and manage them.

Address the warning signs based on the assigned priority.

Note: Step 5: If resources are limited (as they usually are), invest resources on high-impact risks first.

Adjust the ROI of the project based on the investment required to address the risks identified. Update the Project Risk Matrix in Figure 19.4 to reflect the results risk assessment and the revised ROI:

The next governance step for each project is clear.

1. **Keep** the project with a revised budget and risk management plan.

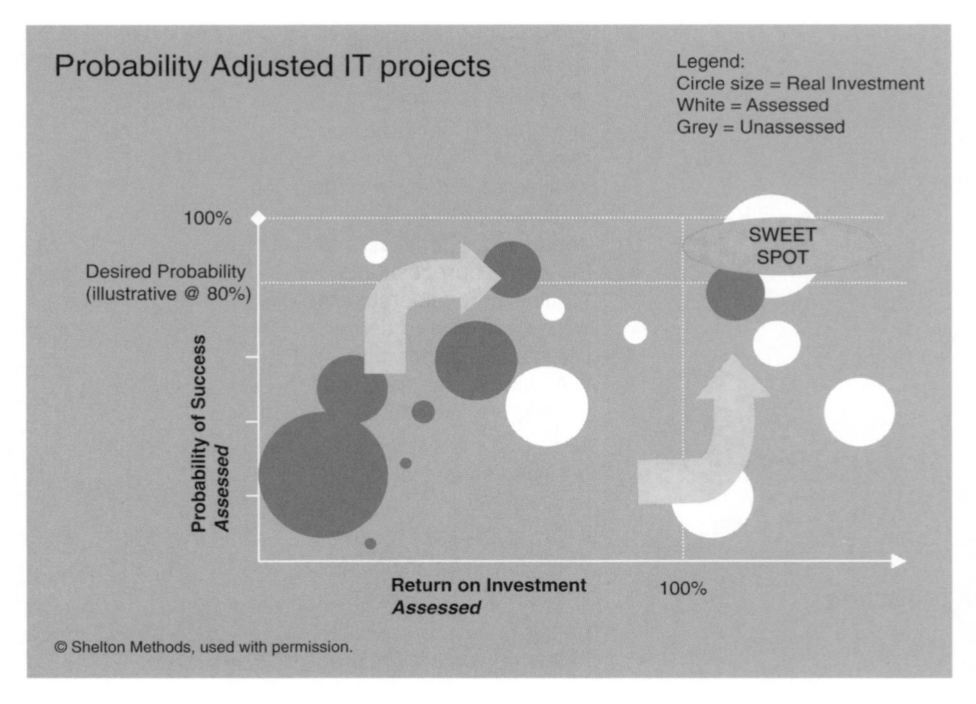

FIGURE 19.4 Where Is Your Project?

2. **Reconsider** the project. Evaluate requirements to lift the success rate. Given the expected return of the project, consider whether the investment in time and resources is appropriate.
3. **Kill** the project. Reallocate resources (people's energy and company capital) to projects that are likely to succeed.

CIO Moment: Credibility Check

Check to see if your data is consistent from another angle. If it is not consistent, then simply ask, "Why am I getting two stories?"

In Part 1: **Productivity**, a series of questions was asked about the productivity health of your projects. Refer to your notes and consider your organization's history of using:

- Project management reliably and effectively.
- Change management reliably and effectively.
- Results risk management reliably and effectively.

Is your project data consistent with your organization's history?

If not, verify that your project is actively doing things differently. Verify that the project has aimed for success and that there is substance in the assessment, not only hopeful optimism.

If you are using your historical methods and are hoping for a better result . . . some call this the definition of optimism.

Take Action to Improve Business Results from IT Projects

The whole aim of productivity growth in businesses is that more projects succeed than fail. The more that succeed, the faster productivity and results will grow.

One great leap forward from a breakthrough innovation can be eaten away by creeping underdelivery elsewhere.

TABLE 19.6
Project Results Risk Profile

High Probability	Priority 3	Priority 1
Low Probability	Priority 4	Priority 2
	Low Impact	High Impact

Projects that are not set up for success directly affect overall productivity and business results as measured by the functional yield. Depending on where risks to results issues are, the impact affects different parts of the functional yield. Some issues affect time, others quality or cost.

The risks in each fold affect a different component of the Functional Yield equation as summarized in Table 19.6.

Organizations that explicitly choose to monitor and measure the functional yield will take action formally.

Once the project has been reformulated, re-assess the probability of success and the project business case to decide if the project should be retained or not.

Project team continuity contributes to project results. Teams that are uncertain about their roles are likely to look for other opportunities either on other projects or elsewhere (Table 19.7).

TABLE 19.7
Impact on Functional Yield

8-Fold Path Factor	Component of Functional Yield Most Effected When Not Set Up for Success	Action Required
Intent is clear	Functional yield and perceived value	Clarify intent and sources of value
Business case is robust	Inadequate Budget	Review the business case, then: Increase the investment OR Adjust the intended scope (Fold 1)
Results delivery process is reliable	Time with some budget impact	Review the project plans Make appropriate additions and alterations so that reliability of results is improved. Incorporate necessary budget adjustments into

TABLE 19.7
(Continued)

8 Fold Path Factor	Component of Functional Yield most Effected When Not Set Up for Success	Action Required
Intent is clear		the business case (Fold 2)
Motivation is energized	Perceived value	Review the stated intent (Fold 1) Update the Business Case and Budget (Fold 2) Improve the results delivery plan (Fold 3) to address the issues that undermine the business results from project
Alignment to strategy	Long-term results that show up in: Perceived Value Underperforming Functions Inadequate Budget	Align project goals (Fold 1) to current strategic context AND Adjust the plan and funds (Fold 2) to address gaps between current situation and desired strategic position (Fold 5)
Operational controls support project intent	Long-term results that show up in: Perceived value Underperforming Functions Inadequate Time	Adjust the project plan and funds (Fold 2) to address risks to acceptance (Fold 4)
Flow of history favors the project	Inadequate Budget and time	Adjust the project plan and funds (Fold 2) to address risks to acceptance (Fold 4)
Balance aids project intent	Time	Adjust the project plan so that implementation does not create burnout

Address the likely reaction of project team members to any uncertainty.

The diagnostic process identifies risks that need high-priority attention as project leaders consider what needs to be done to lift probability of success.

Any risks identified should be noted on the project risk log. The project plan should include mitigating actions, describe how the risk will be monitored, and include necessary resources to address the risks to success.

Take action. Address the risks to success.

Monitor and mitigate them.

Succeed.

Part 5

Performance

Lifting performance:

1. Expect results from projects.
2. Take action to address the risk to results.
3. Create accountability for PAR.

And . . . recognize reality: people react. Projects succeed when they respond effectively to that reality.

Chapter 20
Where to? Success Is a Journey, Not a Destination

Success, like life, is a journey not a station.

—Inspired by Ralph Waldo Emerson

This book was written to help business executives address an expensive source of frustration—projects that consume resources and don't generate business results. Assessments and questions are provided to help you assess your organization's project success and failure rates—to help you build a picture of where real project stresses exist.

As a business executive, selecting projects likely to succeed will lift your success.

As a project manager, knowing how to set up projects for success makes your work life simpler.

Would you like success or failure?

Leadership Implications

Projects are an investment. Costs are significant: direct costs, implementation costs, and pollution costs. The results of IT investment are poor: only 7 percent deliver what was wanted, when it was wanted, for the price agreed. This suggests systemic organizational failure:

- Of productivity lost.
- Of opportunity missed.

There is a major opportunity for executives to add value simply by reducing the number of failed projects in their organizations.

CASE STUDY

FROM REAL LIFE

Nick reflected on his organization and projects. Years of working out what makes a star performer had led the organization to conclude that it was career and promotionally enhancing to initiate a big glamorous project. The key event for promotional success was to kick off the project and deliver a successful pilot or proof of concept. Delivery of results from the overall project was secondary.

Comment: As a C-level executive, this is an expensive game to have operating in the business.

Assess Risks, Take Action

A project is successful when:

- The project delivers the expected capacity, when it is expected, at the expected price.
- The business uses these capacities effectively.

Better still is when the project delivers capacities that allow the business to exceed expectations. With less than 1 in 10 projects managing to meet or exceed expectations, projects like this are the stuff of dreams.

All of this requires proactive Results Risk Management.

It is far easier to succeed when a project starts set up for success. When a project is underway and fears failure, it first has to recover, and then pull ahead to succeed.

It is like running a race. If a runner is ill-prepared or faces additional hurdles, she is less likely to run a successful race than another runner who is prepared to clear the hurdles.

A runner who wants to succeed gets a coach. The coach helps identify what may hinder success and what helps success. In sports, this may be a combination of fitness, of health, or of mindset. A coach helps the runner stay on track and push through to the result. A great coach also considers the fitness and capacities the runner needs for the next race.

A project is bigger than a simple race. Marco Polo's caravan to Kashgar was a large project with a clear, intended goal, arriving in Kashgar, healthy, with trade goods intact. The caravan leader, Marco Polo, had a reputation for knowing his business. He consulted experts along the way.

As sponsor or leader of an equivalent project journey, there are many things you need to know before you set out:

- What will the daily journey be like? Will you arrive fit and healthy, able to do what you intended to upon reaching Kashgar?
- What will the journey cost? Funding needs will depend on the challenges that the journey will face—mountain passes, deserts, brigands, distractions of oasis and hospitality on the way . . . .
- What is the safety record of the caravan train and the route?
- Will you be accepted when you arrive? What reception and accommodation is expected? Accepted? Will you do your business effectively in Kashgar?

Answers to each of these questions give you an indicator of the likely success of your project, in this case, a trip to Kashgar.

Successful businesses should focus their scarce resources on projects that are likely to deliver a return, rather than on those that aren't. This is the first and most practical way of improving success: If something is doomed to failure, don't do it.

If it must be done, find a way to do it so it will succeed. This often comes down to the capacity of the organization to invest and the commitment it makes to achieve that result.

Are the financials required to achieve the results REAL? Capital always needs to be well managed. If the financials are not robust, if results are highly risky, consider whether this is a journey that should be undertaken.

If you don't have the funds to get to Kashgar with Marco Polo, you wouldn't join his caravan.

In Chapter 3 of Part 1, **Productivity**, predictability is defined as a key element of PAR—achieving Predictable, Accountable Results from projects. This chapter identifies four critical business and projects practices for business results from projects.

Project performance was benchmarked so that the real results of investment in projects would be apparent in Chapter 4. A Portfolio Health Check diagnoses the historical health of project results in Chapter 5.

Setting projects up for success goes beyond the neutrality of "not failing." Eight indicators of success can be used to diagnose the likely success level of a specific project.

Productivity also introduced the concept of rational dysfunctions where what makes sense at one level in the organization, affects the capacity of the whole organization and projects to succeed. These "hurdles" reduce the capacity for business results from projects. The hurdles add risk if they are ignored.

Part 2, **Probability** introduced the 8-Fold Path to Project Success and the role of a reliable results delivery process.

In Part 3 **Project**, the focus is to assess four indicators of risks to successful results that arise from the project:

1. Clarity of intended goals of the project. If the goal is not stated, it is highly unlikely for it to appear.
2. Quality of the business case goals, plans, and resourcing. The financials in the business case often negatively impact a project.
3. Quality of the process that delivers results. This depends on the relationships between the project and the business—and symptoms that show up when they don't function together well. This gauges where the processes around business results delivery could be hindering project success.
4. How motivation to accept a project impacts the willingness of people in organizations to change their behaviors and thus generate new business outcomes.

While in Part 4, **Presence**, the focus is to assess the risks to successful results that arise from the business context:

- How aligned the project is with the current strategic context of the business. The bigger the gap between the current context and the project, the greater the number of hurdles it faces.

- How operational practices can help or hinder project goals. These are often mini-hurdles and bumps that slow down project success.
- The degree to which flow of the organization's history was in the direction of the project or not. If the project is "rowing" against the tide, it has more work to do than if it is going with the flow.
- The capacity of the business to absorb this and other changes. The pace and balance that are needed to continue business operations as changes are introduced. In turbulent times, the capacity to lift the pace becomes important, so that change can take place at a faster rhythm.

Risk assessment allows proactive action.

Chapter 19 provides an overall diagnostic process for the probability of project success based on the basic 8-Fold Path Results Risk Management Diagnostic.

Performance Reflects Proficiency

Performance is about this race and the next race.

In golf, many courses will only grant a handicap after players have played 10 games—to demonstrate their proficiency. The proficiency card is the record of their reliability of playing a round of golf in a particular number of strokes—that is their productivity. Low handicap, high productivity.

Just like golf, an organization needs a regular practice of delivering results to get a handicap and say it is playing at PAR.

For projects this means delivering predictable, accountable results. PAR. An unhealthy project can't deliver results into the healthiest of organizations. A healthy project can't deliver results into an unhealthy organization.

The **Probability** diagnostics in **Project** and **Presence** provide the insights to identify where a specific project is unhealthy, and where an organization may lack the health to change effectively.

Experience Is More than Headlines

Reading about something is not the same as actually doing it. Knowing how to achieve project success is the first step. There is an image of what it takes. Now for action.

The process move from words to action is:

Step 1: Use the diagnostics in this book to assess the risks to your project. Begin with the project business case and its stated intent.

Use the diagnostic available online at www.successhealthcheck.com to generate easy-to-use reports on the risks to success for your project. Use the online diagnostic to collect the viewpoints of other key stakeholders.

Step 2: Identify the risks to success.

Step 3: Develop a plan to reduce or address those risks.

Step 4: Secure additional funds required to achieve success and get approval for any changes to scope or schedule needed to lift the project success rate.

Step 5: Get started! With confidence that you are on the right track.

Observe what really goes on as you deliver the project. When a project is started, additional risks become visible. After 10 percent duration, assess the early warning signs. Add risks to your checklist based on what changes in your organization and in your business environment.

Where Are You Now?

Businesses aim to lift the value they deliver. Projects aim to do the same.

In Part 1 **Productivity**, we studied actual performance of the IT industry and measured productivity using the Functional Yield as the benchmark. Results were poor: 93 percent of projects fail at some level.

How do projects in your organization perform?

When projects are evaluated as a portfolio, the cost of under-delivery hits home. Data shows that benchmark IT portfolios generally do not deliver expected results:

- Portfolios results are –27 percent or more based on benchmarks.
- Even projects with experienced project managers deliver 20 percent less than expected.

What did you find when you evaluated your portfolio's performance in Chapter 5?

Not all projects will succeed. Not failing is simply neutral. Real results are more likely if the project is set up for success.

Identifying projects that are doomed to fail and cancelling them improves overall portfolio performance.

Identifying projects that are likely to succeed and increasing their likelihood of success improves overall portfolio performance. The 8-Fold Path diagnostic for Results Risk Management provides indicators of success. These can be evaluated before a project starts and reassessed during the course of the project.

What is your assessment of the probable success of your project from Chapter 19?

Where Do You Want to Be?

A journey of 1,000 miles begins with a single step.

—Confucius

And a direction.

—J. A. Flinn

It begins with the intent. Do you wish for your projects to succeed? Predictably and reliably? Or through unusual feats of heroism? In IT terms, what maturity level are you aiming for?

Perfection comes from intent and practice. Do you want your projects to succeed predictably or reliably? How will you move from intent into action? A golf champion must practice hard to reach PAR.

Begin with Accountability for Results

Results require accountability at two levels.

1. Productivity is results delivered by the projects in the IT project portfolio.

   Determine who owns responsibility for lifting productivity of internal investments. Is it a C-level issue or an issue for the entire organization?

   How will the business address issues that repeatedly contribute to project failure?
2. Business results from the project are the result of project delivery.

   Identify who owns the project's results. Are they addressing the risks identified in your assessment?

   How will they be held accountable for results from the project investment?

Recommendation: Establish a basis for assessment, funding, and accountability that rewards project leaders who address risks to successful results, rather than those who ignore risks.

Refine Predictability at the Project Level

Develop a program plan using what you have learned from this book.

Involve others in your project or organization—have them complete an assessment to add depth to your program.

Address the people issues. People can walk; they can check out mentally or walk out physically. Two decades of research have consistently found that lack of attention to the people is the fundamental cause of projects failing to deliver results in the business.[1]

Track Risk and Results

Set serious business ROI goals for your projects and deal with the business governance issues of projects delivering results.

Monitor them. Use Credit Checks. Use after-action reviews. Use gated funding.

Perseverance

All skills are honed with practice and learning. Only the Fairy Godmother can wave a wand and transform a pumpkin into something magical.

An individual's fitness and health are the result of training, nutrition, and discipline.

A farmer's rice paddy productivity is a result of understanding his farm, learning, adjusting inter-dependent systems, discipline, and patience.

A project leader's results come from addressing physical delivery issues, people issues, and risks from the organization. Stellar success occurs—instead of a 93 percent chance of failure.

For a C-level executive, a board member, or an entrepreneur, productivity growth will outperform the competition when projects deliver Predictable, Accountable Results.

The Leadership Challenge

Triage

Remember the scenes from TV shows *M*A*S*H* and *ER* when the wounded come into the Emergency Room? The doctors and nurses used triage methods to evaluate which patients could be saved or not.

A project or portfolio needs triage if scarce resources are to be applied where they can do the most good. Resources like time, money, and motivation are too precious to waste.

Use Result Risk Management diagnostics like the 8-Fold Path to Success to assess projects then use the data gathered to triage projects.

1. **Keep** performing projects.
2. **Kill** non-performing projects in a way that respects the various people contributing to the project. Morale is important.
3. **Reconsider** and strengthen mediocre projects.
4. Realistically consider the resources at hand and what it will take for a healthy project delivery. In tight conditions, resources need to be husbanded especially carefully. Work is a rat race, and smart rats leave sinking ships.

Triage is a powerful part of a portfolio value management process.

It *Is* Personal

People follow people. More people will accept and follow a change if they trust the leader. Few people will accept and follow a leader with little credibility because of the logical arguments for the change.

As a leader, it's personal—do they trust you? Trust is earned from reliability and consistency of what you say and do, particularly under stress.

Begin with the End in Mind

Be clear about the goal of your project—the technology, the delivery, and the business outcomes. At a minimum—explicitly state that the business goal of your project is to achieve PAR.

Predictable. The more reliable project estimates, costs, resourcing, delivery, impact, risk management . . . the more predictable the project outcome. You may choose to take on risky projects—that's informed decision making. A portfolio with unpredictable projects is usually operating from ignorance.

Accountable: Project goals must be aligned with business strategy and intent. Project teams and team members need to know where they are and what they need to do.

Results: You got what you asked for!

What is owned gets cared for, what gets measured gets done.
—attributed to Peter Drucker

Success and Courage

It is too easy to focus on failure. Each team member, project manager, and business sponsor needs to be an expert in success. A success denied or ignored is not a success. It is insignificant.

It takes courage to take decisions that lead to success. The Keep, Kill, or Reconsider decision takes courage. Acknowledging the reality of your data or of a deteriorating situation takes courage. Evaluating the health of your project, portfolio, and organization takes courage. Recognize, celebrate,[2] and encourage both leadership of results and courage.

Endnotes

1 PwC-MORI in the 1990s confirmed by my research into complex global projects in the first decade of the millennium. These issues go back to the early days of management research: read about the Hawthorne experiments. See John Kotter (1995), ''Leading Change, Why Transformations Fail,'' *Harvard Business Review* (April): 59–67.

2 I am aware that to some this sounds hokey. However, if your teams and people in the organization don't know what success looks like, how are they to model it?

In many high performance teams, success is celebrated—watch the guys on the soccer field. It builds confidence, it raises energy, it motivates people to keep trying. As Nike would say ''Just do it!''

Appendix A
Calculating the Functional Yield

The initial basis for calculating the yield of a project requires:

- The project business case (quality assured to reflect the risks to results in the 8-Fold Path diagnosis).
- The organization's track record for project delivery.
  This allows us to assess the expected variations from the business case.

This is what is expected based on the business case.

Once a project has delivered and results are assessed, then a real yield can be calculated.

The functional yield[1] can be calculated in a three-step process.

1. What's the cost of the likely overrun?
   Expected Cost Overrun = Budget × average project cost variance (percent).
2. What's the cost of late delivery to the business?
   Time Cost = [Budget + Expected Cost Overrun] × average time variance of IT projects (percent) × 0.25
   The 0.25 is a weighting factor to reflect the cost of time delays.
   The **notional cost of the project** = Budget + Cost Overrun + Time cost.
3. Functional Yield
   FY = Budgeted cost of project/Notional cost of project
   * % functions delivered
   * Perceived Value (%) –1

The Perceived Value can be estimated based on project uptake and the feedback of sponsors and business executives. It is the customer's perception of how successful the project is. Let's assume that the project's interaction with the business is acceptable, that what is delivered is used effectively, and that it operates as expected so the PV = 1.

We subtract 1 so that if we get what we expect the Functional Yield is neutral as 1 – 1 = 0. If the Functional Yield is negative, we got less than we expected. If the Functional Yield is positive, we got more than expected.

That is, if the budget is $100, and projects usually overrun by 100 percent and are delayed by 100 percent, then the notional cost of the project based on the track record is $250. If the business gets 60 percent of the functions it expects and is satisfied (PV = 1), then the functional yield is:

$$FY = 100/250 \times 0.6 \times 1 = 0.24 - 1$$

$$FY = -76\%.$$

Endnote

1 Developed from financial yield calculations used in Financial Management. Weighting factors developed are used to factor in the cost of delay.

Appendix B
CIO Moment—Results Track Record

If you are a CIO or considering the impact of your project investment in your business, you may want to take this a step further and consider the distribution of results of all your projects. This looks at the results of the portfolio, not a single project.

This process provides a cross-check to PAR—just how predictable, accountable, and results-oriented are IT projects in your organization overall?

This is a two-step process.

Step 1: Consider the distribution of success levels

Evaluate how your projects are distributed in terms of their actual results delivered (completed projects) or their capacity to deliver results (those in progress or planned).

If you have high quality business cases (see Fold 2 in **Project**), compare the results delivered to those intended in the business case (Table B.1).

To provide a comparison, recent research by the *Economist* shows that 55 percent of CIOs in Asia, 31 percent of CIOs in

TABLE B.1
Results Rating

Rating	1	2	3	4	5
Description	Fail Completely (Written Off)	Get Part of the Results, but Not the *Real* Results	Just Deliver or Break Even	Get Business Results without Too Much Pain	Do Very Well in the Eyes of the Business
% of projects (by # or value)					

Keep this at the "back of the envelope" level. Get a sense of what the returns on your projects are.

Then consider the value of improving on project results.

Use your gut reaction for now. You can get solid data to verify this later.

Europe, and 41 percent of CIOs in the Americas think that less than half of their projects deliver the intended business results. That's an honest self-reported level of failure. It suggests that many projects fall into Categories 1–3.

This says it is likely that a problem exists.

This assessment can be taken further, into the actual financial impact of the projects.

Step 2: Assess the actual delivery of the project portfolio (Table B.2).

This analysis requires project budget data from the business case and project results metrics from a results or benefits management process.

The results are usually interesting. These figures give a handle on the probability of achieving business tangible results. If the past was not a success . . .

To put these assessments into practical terms:

What value does a 10 percent improvement have for your business?

1 & 2 decrease by 10 percent (this is a reduction in write-off)	_______
3 & 4 improve by 10 percent (this is an improvement in results)	_______

What would it mean to your business if one key project converted into a success instead becoming a failure?

TABLE B.2 *Portfolio Value as ROI*

Rating	1	2	3	4	5
Description	**Fail Completely (Written Off)**	**Get Part of the Results, but Not the *Real* Results**	**Just Deliver or Break Even**	**Get Business Results without Too Much Pain**	**Do Very Well in the Eyes of the Business**
$ value invested (a)					
$ value achieved (b)					
Basic ROI (a/b)					

Between us: As you read this book, note the actions you can take to improve your success rates. The margins are wide deliberately. When you get ideas or see actions that can improve your results, write them down. Recommend this book to three people you respect, ones who also want their projects to succeed and their businesses to be more productive.

Assessment 4 provides the CIO with an evaluation of the likelihood of a project succeeding. If most projects fail, then it is likely that this one will too. If most succeed, then it is likely that the next one will too. The quality of the game is unlikely to change without deliberate effort, attention and a new approach.

This is a cross-check to the other assessments.

If the project track record is poor, then expecting this project to differ is optimistic, *unless*, you and the teams are doing things materially differently and are planning and managing for success.

Appendix C
The Basic Health Check: Warning Signs

Circle the warning signs that apply to your project. See **Performance** for the debrief of the risk assessment.

Fold 1: Warning Signs for Intent

- They are not clearly documented.
- They are not commonly known.
- **Test:** Can peers who are not close to the project tell you the gist of what the project is for?
- They are dull, uninspirational, or hard to understand.

Fold 2: Warning Signs for Business Case

- Costs are not recognized.
- Estimation factors are not credible.
- Dependencies are undocumented.
- Sponsors have track record for not attending meetings.

Fold 3: Warning Signs for Results Delivery Process

- Business's main role is to accept delivery and sit on the Steering Committee.
- The plan is to be completed later.
- Risks and Contingency are "not applicable."
- Implementation is out of scope. It is "someone else's problem."

Fold 4: Warning Signs in Motivation

- ☠ People in the organization have a reputation for resistance.
- ☠ Privately the view is that other parts of the organization are cynical or ineffective.
- ☠ People are expected to conform to corporate or project direction.
- ☠ Project does not pay attention to motivation in the organization.

Fold 5: Warning Signs of Misalignment to Strategic Context

- ☠ The project attempts to influence the current position on the S curve.
- ☠ The project outcomes require values and behavior that are not consistent with the current organizational culture.
- ☠ Undiscussable political elements are create potential minefields.

Fold 6: Warning Signs of Misalignment with Operational Context

- ☠ IT project delivery practices focus on project delivery over project implementation.
- ☠ Financial policies encourage investment in tangibles (like hardware and software) over intangibles (like testing, training, or communications).
- ☠ The project goals are not formally linked to the goals of leading executives.
- ☠ Project teams have a record of burnout or turnover.

Fold 7: Warning Signs in Flow

- ☠ The organization's history is overlooked in the project.
- ☠ The project sponsorship and management team have a poor record of success.

Fold 8: Warning signs to Balance

- ☠ Project impacts on business per period are not considered.
- ☠ Cumulative effects of changes on a business group are not evaluated.

Take Action and Identify the Risks to Address

Review the items you have circled.

1. Identify which are likely to have the most impact on results. Classify as high or low impact.
2. Identify which are the most probable. Classify as high or low probability.
3. Map them onto the grid below:

High Probability	Priority 3	Priority 1
Low Probability	Priority 4	Priority 2
	Low Impact	**High Impact**

Address the warning signs based on the priority given. If resources are limited (as they usually are), preference is for investing those that are usually given to events that will affect results greatly over low-impact risks to results.

Appendix D
The Cost of Lightweight Business Cases

If a business case and project plan are lightweight, the business will find that the traditional results of cost overruns, schedule overruns, and quality and scope shortfalls will continue.

A short summary of the implications of the impact of the warning signs in terms of these three measures of project results:

High risk of cost overruns if:

1. Relevant costs are not recognized.
2. Estimation factors and processes are not credible.
3. Risks to results are not identified and the relevant mitigation activity or contingency is unfunded.

High risk of schedule overruns if:

1. Risks to results are not identified, if they are not mitigated or if the contingency is not funded within an approved budget.
2. Plans and resources to address and bridge the issues between people, processes/policy, data, and systems are ignored.
3. Dependencies and milestones are not identified with the project and between the project and external projects.

High risk of functional short-fall or reduced perceived value if:

1. Gaps between desired results and current state are not addressed by plan and resources.
2. The business sponsors have a poor record of following through and contributing to project Steering Committee meetings.

Appendix E
Requirements Are Not Always Words

Many systems are defined in terms of requirements—pages of the written work. Effective communications of requirements may require diagrams (visuals), interactive mock-ups (prototypes) or even demonstration (role-play).

In Intent is Clear, an illustrative exercise asked you to instruct someone to fold a piece of paper in half, and then draw three circles on the outside in the middle. On the inside on the opposite side, two circles, with a smaller one underneath them then a curved line.

If you actually did ask several people to do this, you are likely to have had several quite different interpretations of what appears to be simple instructions.

One option (the one I had in my mind when I described it) is below.

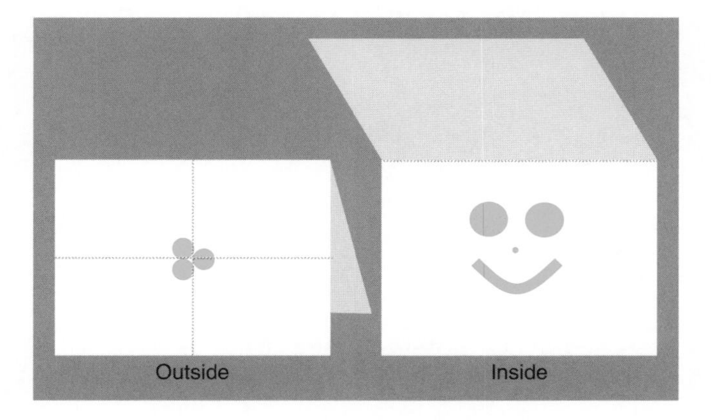

Words in this case, are not the best tool to describe what's required.

Bibliography

Albrecht, Karl (2006), *Social Intelligence, The New Science of Success, Beyond IQ, Beyond EQ, Applying Multiple Intelligence Theory to Human Interaction* (San Francisco: Jossey-Bass).

Agility Forum (1996), *Agile Enterprise Reference Model and Case Study.*

Argyris, Chris (2007), *Immaturity/Maturity Motivation Theory,* Accel.

Argyris, Chris (1985), *Strategy, Change, and Defensive Routines* Boston: Pitman Publishing.

Argyris, Chris (1991), ''Teaching Smart People How to Learn,'' *Harvard Business Review Reflections 4* (Boston: Harvard Business School Press), No. 2: 4–15.

Barrett, Richard (2006), *Building a Values-Driven Organization: A Whole System Approach to Cultural Transformation* (Woburn: Butterworth-Heinemann).

Barrett, Richard (1998), *Liberating the Corporate Soul, Building a Visionary Organization* (Woburn: Butterworth Heinemann).

Bartlett, Christopher A., and Ghoshal, Sumantra (2002), *Managing Across Borders: The Transnational Solution,* 2nd ed. (Boston: Harvard Business Press).

Berkun, Scott. ''How to Detect Bullshit.'' http://www.scottberkun.com/essays/53-how-to-detect-bullshit/.

Brooks, Michael (2008), ''The Power of Belief,'' *New Scientist,* August 23.

Bryan, Lowell and Joyce, Claudia (2005), ''The 21st Century Organization,'' *McKinsey Quarterly,* No. 3.

Bourne, Vanson (July 2008), "Getting Smarter about IT Risks." http://mitsloan.mit.edu/cisr/pdf/EIU_GettingSmarterAboutIT Risks.pdf.

Buckingham, Marcus and Coffman, Curt (1999), *First Break All the Rules, What the World's Greatest Managers Do Differently* (New York: Simon & Schuster Business Books).

Buckingham, Marcus (2006), *The One Thing You Need to Know . . . About Great Managing, Great Leading and Sustained Individual Success* (New York: Pocket Books).

Buede, Dennis, Forsberg, Kevin, Mooz, Hal, Plowman, Catherine, and Tufts, Bob, "Systems Engineering Processes," *A Guide to the Systems Engineering Body of Knowledge (SEBoK).* http://www.paper-review.com/g2sebok/seboksection2.htm.

"Capturing Talent," *The Economist,* August 18, 2007, 56.

Cardin, Lewis, Cullen, Alex, Cecere, Marc and DeGennaro, Tim (2007), *The Forrester Wave™: Project Portfolio Management Tools*. Q4 2007 Forrester Research Inc.

Calculating Property Rental Yield, http://www.investinproperty.com.

Cialdini, Robert B (2001), *Influence, Science and Practice,* 4th ed. (Needham Heights: Allyn & Bacon).

"Clinical Depression, Something in the Way He Moves," *The Economist,* September 29, 2007, 81.

Collins, James Charles and Porras, Jerry I. (2002), *Built to Last: Successful Habits of Visionary Companies* (New York: Harper Business Essentials).

Collins, James Charles (2001), *Good to Great: Why Some Companies Make the Leap—and Others Don't* (New York: HarperBusiness).

"Common Sense, Economist Focus," *The Economist,* August 2, 2008, 73.

Covey, Stephen M. R. and Merrill, Rebecca R. (2006), *The Speed of Trust: The One Thing That Changes Everything* (New York: Free Press).

Eccles, Robert G., Herz, Robert H., Keegan, E. Mary, and David M. H. Phillips (2001), *The Value Revolution, Moving Beyond the Earnings Game,* (New Jersey: John Wiley & Sons).

Ellis, Keith (2008), *Impact of Business Requirements on the Success of Technology Projects,* Information Architecture Group Consulting. http://www.scribd.com/doc/12597574/the-impact-of-business-requirements-on-the-success-of-technology-projects.

"Evolution, Patience, Fairness and the Human Condition," *The Economist*, October 6, 2007, 87.

Fisher, David (2004), "The Business Process Maturity Model, A Practical Approach to Identifying Opportunities for Optimization," BP Trends, September, 1–7.

"For Your Brain, It Is as Good as Being There," *New Scientist*, August 16, 2008.

Frei, Brent and Mader, Mark (2008), "Explaining the Productivity Paradox," ZDNet, January 31. http://resources.zdnet.co.uk/articles/comment/0,1000002985,39292540,00.htm.

Gemino, A., Reich, B., and Sauer, C. (2007), "A Temporal Model of Information Technology Project Performance," *J. Manage. Inf. Syst.* 24, No. 3: 9–44. DOI= http://dx.doi.org/10.2753/MIS0742-1222240301.

Giles, Jim (2008), "Our Psychology Helps Politicians Bend the Truth," *New Scientist*, October 10: 9.

Goleman, Daniel and Senge, Peter (2007), *Working with Presence, a Conversation with Peter Senge* (Audio Renaissance).

Grayling, A. C. (2008), "7 Reasons Why People Hate Reason," *New Scientist*, July 26.

Hammer, Michael and Champy, James (1993), *Reengineering the Corporation: A Manifesto for Business Revolution* (New York: HarperBusiness).

Hofstede, Gert Jan (1997), *Cultures and Organizations: Software of the Mind* (New York: McGraw-Hill Professional).

Howard, Sue and Welbourne, David (2004), *The Spirit at Work Phenomenon* (London: Azure).

"How to Work and Play a Little Better," *The Economist*, September 8, 2007, 81–82

IBM CEO Survey 2008, IBM.

"In the Blood, Attitudes Towards Re-Distribution Have a Strong Cultural Component," *The Economist*, June 6, 2009, 72.

"Innovation Maturity Model," Think for a Change.com (2007).

International Labor Organization, *Key Indicators of the Labor Markets,* 5th ed.

Iyengar, Sheena S. (2007), "How to Make Better Choices," *New Scientist*, May 5, 35–43.

Janis, I. L. and Mann, L. (1977), *Decision Making: A Psychological Analysis of Conflict, Choice, and Commitment* (New York: Free Press).

Jaworski, Joseph and Flowers, Betty S. (1988), *Synchronicity: The Inner Path of Leadership* (San Francisco: Berrett-Koehler Publishers).

Johnson, Jim, Interview. Standish Group. http://www.infoq.com/articles/Interview-Johnson-Standish-CHAOS.

Johnson, Jim,"Why Were Project Failures Up and Cost Overruns Down in 1998?", Standish Group. http://www.infoq.com/articles/chaos-1998-failure-stats.

Jones, Capers (2009), "Return on Investment in Software Project Management Tools and Software Quality Controls," Software Productivity Research. http://www.itmpi.org/assets/base/images/itmpi/privaterooms/capersjones/Capers_PrMgtROI2009.pdf.

Kaplan, Robert S. and Norton, David P. (2001), *The Strategy-Focused Organization: How Balanced Scorecard Companies Thrive* (Boston: Harvard Business Press).

Kaplan, Robert S. and Norton, David P. (1996), *The Balanced Scorecard: Translating Strategy into Action* (Boston: Harvard Business Press).

Keil, M., Cule, P. E., Lyytinen, K., and Schmidt, R. C. (1998), "A Framework for Identifying Software Project Risks," *Communication of the ACM* 41, No. 11: 76–83. doi: http://doi.acm.org/10.1145/287831.287843.

Khan, Habibullah, and Islam, M. Shahidul, "Outsourcing, Migration and Brain Drain in Global Economy," U21Gobal Working Papers No. 004/2006. http://www.u21global.edu.sg/PartnerAdmin/ViewContent?module=DOCUMENTLIBRARY&oid=157296.

Kotter, John (1995), "Leading Change, Why Transformations Fail,"*Harvard Business Review* (Boston: Harvard Business Press), April: 59–67.

Krigsman, Michael,"New IT Project Failure Matrics: Is Standish Wrong?" ZDNet. Dec. 7, 2007. http://blogs.zdnet.com/projectfailures/?p=513,

Lackoff, George (2008), *Visceral Politics*. Letter to *New Scientist,* July 5, 20.

Land, George and Jarman, Beth (1993), *Breaking Point and Beyond* (New York: HarperBusiness).

"Latest Standish Group CHAOS Report Shows Project Success Rates Have Improved by 50%." *BusinessWire,* March 25, 2003. http://findarticles.com/p/articles/mi_m0EIN/is_2003_March_25/ai_99169967/.

Kappelman, Leon A., McKeeman, Robert and Zhang Lixuan (2006), ''Early Warning Signs of IT Project Failure: The Dominant Dozen,'' *Information Systems Management*, Fall: 31–36.

Levinson, Meridith (2009), ''Recession Causes Rising IT Project Failure Rates,'' June 18. http://www.infoworld.com/t/deployment-and-management/recession-causes-rising-it-project-fail ure-rates-189.

Levinson, Meridith (2008), ''Project Management: The 14 Most Common Mistakes IT Departments Make,'' *CIO*, July 23. http://www.cio.com/article/438930/Project_Management_The_14_Most_Common_Mistakes_IT_Departments_Make.

Matta, Nadim F. and Ashkenas, Ronald N. (2003), ''Why Good Projects Fail Anyway,'' *Harvard Business Review*, September: 109–114. http://www.willer.ca/steve/articles/why-good-projects-fail/.

Morgan, Gareth (1997), *Images of the Organization* (Thousand Oaks: Sage).

Murray, Peter (2003), ''So What's New About Complexity?'' *Systems Research* 20: 409–417.

Parker, Sharon (2004), ''From Puny to Powerhouse: Transforming Organizations through People,'' *Australian Graduate School of Management*.

Pascale, Richard Tanner, Milleman, Mark, and Gioja, Linda (2001), *Surfing the Edge of Chaos: The Laws of Nature and the New Laws of Business*, New York: Three Rivers Press.

Petouhoff, Natalie L., Chandler, Tamra, and Montag-Schultz, Beth (2006), ''The Business Impact of Change Management, What is the Common Denominator for High Project ROI's?'' *Graziiado Business Report* (Los Angeles: Pepperdine University. http://gbr.pepperdine.edu/063/change.html).

Pich, Michael T., Loch, Christoph H., and De Meyer, Arnoud (2002), ''On uncertainty, Ambiguity, and Complexity in Project Management,'' *Management Science* 48, No. 8: 1008–1023.

''Private Life of the Brain,'' *New Scientist*, November 8, 2008, 28–31

Prosci (2004), ''Prosci's Change Management Maturity Model,'' http://www.change-management.com/Prosci-CM-Maturity-Model-writeup.pdf.

''Public Order, the Kindness of Crowds,'' *The Economist*, February 8, 2009, 76–77

Reed, April (2007), ''Critical Risk Factors in Virtual Software Projects,'' Interim Report, De Paul University.

Reich, B. H., Sauer, C., and Wee, S. Y. (2008), "Innovative Practices for IT Projects," *Inf. Sys. Manag.* 25, No. 3: 266–272. doi: http://dx.doi.org/10.1080/10580530802151210.

Porter, M. E. and Miller, V. E. (1985),"How Information Gives You Competitive Advantage,"*Harvard Business Review* 63, No. 4: 149–160.

Project Management Competencies for Complex Projects. DCEO Speech to ProMAC2006, 21st IPMA World Congress on Project Management.

Puryear, Rudy, Berez, Steve, and Shah, Schin (2008), "Is Your Company Caught in an IT Alignment Trap?" *Financial Times* (ft.com), December 6. http://www.bain.com/bainweb/publications/publications_detail.asp?id=26465&menu_url=publications_results.asp.

Robertson, Peter (2005), *Always Change a Winning Team: Why Reinvention and Change Are Prerequisites for Business Success* (Singapore: Marshall Cavendish).

Rock, David and Schwartz, Jeffrey (2006), "The Neuroscience of Leadership," *Strategy + Business*. http://www.strategy-business.com/press/freearticle/06207

Rubinstein, David,"Standish Group Report: There is Less Development Chaos Today," *SD Times on the Web*, March 1, 2007. http://www.sdtimes.com/content/article.aspx?ArticleID=30247.

Sauer, Chris (2008), "Unreasonable Expectations, Greek Choruses and the Games Institutions Play," *Templeton Views*, Summer: 22–23.

Sauer, C., Gemino, A., and Reich, B. H. (2007), "The Impact of Size and Volatility on IT Project Performance," *Communications of the ACM*50, No. 11: 79–84. http://Doi.Acm.Org/10.1145/1297797.1297801.

Schein, Edgar H. (2004), *Organizational Culture and Leadership*, 3rd ed. (New Jersey: John Wiley & Sons).

Senge, Peter, Scharmer, C. Otto, Jaworski, Joseph, and Flowers, Betty Sue (2005), *Presence, Exploring Profound Change in People, Organization and Society* (New York: Nicholas Brealey Publishing).

Slater, Lauren (2005), *Opening Skinner's Box, Great Psychological Experiments of the 20th Century* (New York: Bloomsbury).

"Social Networks, Primates on Facebook," *The Economist*, February 8, 2009, 77.

Standish Group Report *Chaos* (1995). http://net.educause.edu/ir/library/pdf/NCP08083B.pdf.

Stang, Daniel B. and Hanford, Michael, Magic Quadrant for IT Project and Portfolio Management, Gartner Research, June, 132008. http://mediaproducts.gartner.com/reprints/oracle/article75/article75.html.

Stern, Joel M. and Shiely, John S. (2003), *The EVA Challenge: Implementing Value-Added Change in an Organization* (New York: John Wiley & Sons).

Tesch, Debbie, Kloppenborg, Timothy J., and Frolick, Mark, ''IT Project Risk Factors: The Project Management Professionals Perspective,'' *Journal of Computer Information Systems*, July 1, 2007.

Thomson, David G. (2005), *Blueprint to a Billion: 7 Essentials to Achieve Exponential Growth* (New Jersey: John Wiley & Sons).

''Top Five Reasons Why Organizations Fail at Project Management,'' *Tech Republic*, August 20,2008. http://blogs.techrepublic.com.com/tech-manager/?p=580.

U.S. Bureau of Labor Statistics (2003), Non-farm U.S. Productivity Growth, 46.

Wallace, L. and Keil, M. (April 2004), ''Software Project Risks and Their Effect on Outcomes,'' *Communication of the ACM47*, No. 4: 68–73. http://Doi.Acm.Org/10.1145/975817.975819.

Warner-Burke, Wyatt (2002), *Organization Change: Theory and Practice* (Thousand Oaks: Sage).

Wheatley, Margaret J. (2006), *Leadership and the New Science: Discovering Order in a Chaotic World* 3rd ed. (San Francisco: Berrett-Koehler Publishers).

''Words of Wisdom, Positive Thinking's Negative Traits,'' *The Economist*, June 13, 2009, 80.

Young, S. David and O'Bryne, Stephen F. (2002), *EVA and Value-Based Management: A Practical Guide to Implementation* (New York: McGraw Hill).

Zohar, Dahan and Marshal, Ian (2004), *Spiritual Capital, Wealth We Can Live By* (San Francisco: Berrett-Koehler Publishers Inc.).

Index

C

D

E

Q

R